VIRTUE BOMBS

HOW HOLLYWOOD GOT WOKE
AND LOST ITS SOUL

CHRISTIAN TOTO

BOMBARDIER
BOOKS

BOMBARDIER BOOKS

An Imprint of Post Hill Press

ISBN: 978-1-63758-099-8

ISBN (eBook): 978-1-63758-100-1

Virtue Bombs:

How Hollywood Got Woke and Lost Its Soul

© 2022 by Christian Toto

All Rights Reserved

Cover Design by Matt Margolis

Post Hill Press

New York • Nashville

posthillpress.com

Published in the United States of America

1 2 3 4 5 6 7 8 9 10

This book is dedicated to Abbott, Costello, and my Father, all of whom made me fall in love with movies in the first place.

TABLE OF CONTENTS

FOREWORD
WHY I LOVE THE BLACKLIST—AND CHRISTIAN TOTO

By
Andrew Klavan

"WRITING IS A LONELY JOB," said almost every writer ever. You can Google the sentence and you'll see how many names come up. But if being a writer is lonely in general, being a Conservative screenwriter in Hollywood is a quantum leap into infinite solitude.

When you understand that, you will understand the importance of Christian Toto and his remarkable website, *Hollywood in Toto*. For a Conservative screenwriter to know there's a prominent critic out there who does not despise him, to know that someone who understands the structures of film also understands the politics of freedom, to feel that someone with the critical intelligence to assess his work also has the moral intelligence to understand his worldview can make all the difference.

If that was true over the last few decades when Hollywood was merely insanely left wing, it is even more true now when the film business is suffering from a particularly ugly form of left-wing insanity called *wokeism*. To paraphrase the one-sheet to an old Sylvester Stallone action flick: If wokeism is a disease, Christian Toto is clearly going to be part of the cure.

Let me tell you how my Hollywood career ended and you will see what I mean.

I had never wanted to be a screenwriter, but my thriller novels had attracted the movie crowd, so every now and then, over the years, I took on some film work for fun and profit. Then, when I was in my forties, a couple of my novels were made into major films. I decided to seize the moment, move to Los Angeles, and really put some effort into the profession before I aged out entirely.

Providentially, the excellent spook show *The Ring* was released around the same time. Suddenly, PG-13 ghost stories became a hot item. I am a ghost story aficionado. I love eerie tales of the uncanny, long on fear and short on gore. I began turning out scripts in the genre and was soon making an excellent living.

Then one day, I was invited to pitch my version of a major studio remake of a 1950s science fiction horror film. I went "in the room," as they say out west, and described to the producer-in-charge how I'd write the screenplay.

It was the best pitch I ever did. I was about five minutes in when I realized I was outlining a masterpiece. It was beautiful. Scary, original, and deep, with a powerful tragic love story at the center. Like any good writer, I already knew I was incredibly brilliant, but this was another level. Even I was impressed.

I reached the shattering conclusion of my tale and leaned back on the sectional, smugly waiting for the producer to up-end a bucket of gold in my lap. Instead, he said to me, "Do you think we could make the villains the American military?"

I hesitated, slack-jawed. The story had nothing to do with the military, but that wasn't what stumped me. It was this. Not long before, a group of Islamist terrorists had murdered 3,000 people in New York City's World Trade Center. The president had ordered our troops into Afghanistan and Iraq to wreak vengeance on what he called "the evildoers." Right at that moment, as we spoke, American soldiers were being shot at and killed by medieval lowlifes serving what the poet John Keats might have called a "fierce miscreed."

I told the producer, "I don't think American audiences want to see our military depicted as villains right now." At least, that's what I was planning to say, but somewhere between "right" and "now," I found myself out in the parking lot.

Over the next few years, things got steadily worse. Expressing hatred for the American military and its commander-in-chief became a kind of shibboleth for entry into the Hollywood job market. You could be up for a Smurf cartoon, but if you weren't willing to curse out the president and our troops, you weren't going to get hired.

Personally, I thought that knocking off Islamists was a fine way for American youngsters to spend their idle hours. However you felt about the war effort, it was clearly despicable to make movies attacking the mission while our troops were in harm's way. And yet that's what Hollywood proceeded to do. As the wars went on, the industry turned out film after film depicting our soldiers as rapists, murderers, lunatics, and fools. Any movie with even a hint of sympathy for the war or the warriors was excoriated by the press as jingoistic.

Again, have any opinion about the Terror Wars you like. That's fine. But you don't make propaganda for your nation's enemies while your soldiers are facing death for your sake. I said as much in articles and speeches and sometimes even "in the room."

And my phone stopped ringing. The jobs dried up. In short order, my income went from the mesosphere to six feet under. I didn't care. American kids were having their legs blown off by squirrely dirtbags far from home. I wasn't going to curse them out in L.A. meetings so I could get work in Hollywood.

I can't prove it, but I know it's so. I was blacklisted—and by the same perfidious toads who'd just spent fifty years whining about the last blacklist.

But here's the punchline. The guys who toed the line, who kept their heads down and their mouths shut, who traded whatever teaspoon of decency a screenwriter has in order to keep their Teslas charged—they're all out of work today. Because the blacklisters, encouraged, have come to run the town.

In Hollywood right now, it's not enough to disrespect your mother country onscreen. You have to despise it. You have to depict it as a cesspit of racism and cruelty. Your hero has to be a victim. Your victim has to be a minority. Preferably female. Preferably with a penis. This is the twisted, unpatriotic, small-minded, racist, and wicked philosophy called wokeism, which has come to dominate not just Hollywood storytelling but Hollywood hiring as well. Heterosexual white males need not apply.

And yet this particular heterosexual white male is pulling down more film work than ever before. Why? Because patriotic American Liberals, now called Conservatives, have finally gotten wise to the need to create a culture with sane and generous Western values. These folks need me—and guys and girls like me—to tell good stories about true things, which, by definition, no woke person will ever be able to do.

If screenwriters continue to act alone, the counter-revolution will get nowhere. If my sad tale proves anything, it proves we need more than just stories. We need people who love stories, who understand stories. We need an infrastructure of cultural appreciation: review outlets and award ceremonies and interviews and publicity—all the things that make writers less lonely and thus help popular culture thrive.

Which is why we need Christian Toto and Hollywood in Toto more than ever. And why we need books like this one, *Virtue Bombs*, to help explain how American culture has been hijacked and polluted, and how we might begin to get it back.

Wokeism is not just bad for storytelling. It's a form of moral darkness.

Christian Toto shines a light.

CHAPTER 1:
Hollywoke or Bust

PITY THE POOR SCREENWRITER trying to make a go of it in the Age of Woke.

He opens his laptop, eager to tell a story to grab every demographic possible. His notepad is brimming with killer anecdotes. His last three scripts paid off his mortgage, boat, and that nagging timeshare he thought would haunt his great-grandchildren.

A Thermos full of Joe sits on his desk for mental rocket fuel, and a good four-hour time block awaits with nary a distraction in sight. His fingers practically shake in anticipation.

And then he hits the mental brakes. Hard.

Will the story be diverse enough? Could the characters or plots offend a special interest group? Are there enough women in the narrative and will the script pass the Bechtel Test? (You mean you don't even know what that test is?)

A tiny seed of doubt begins to grow.

Who is this privileged white male from Arkansas to bring an Asian character to life in the third act—even if she's vital to the plot and unabashedly heroic?

It's enough to make him gently close the laptop and wonder if film school was the right idea after all.

That's a fictional scenario, but one shot through with the reality of our new woke world.

Today's woke culture is everywhere, infesting boardrooms, media out-lets, public schools, social media, and virtually every professional sport.

We'll assume Curling hasn't waved the woke flag…yet.

~~Grease was the word when John Travolta wooed a shy Aussie in the~~ classic movie musical (a film now considered "rapey"). Today, that word is "woke," and you dare not disagree. And it's consumed Hollywood with a speed that would make the Flash envious.

In just a few short years, Tinseltown surrendered to the Woke Police, with only a few brave souls standing up to its cultural enforcers.

Movies like *Moxie, Booksmart,* and 2021's *Cinderella* luxuriate in woke impulses. Hulu trotted out a sitcom literally dubbed *Woke.* Other shows and films dabble in woke, making sure you're unable to get a break from it while Netflixing and Chilling.

The biggest stars in Hollywood bow to the woke mob, from late night hosts to Oscar winners.

Sure, an ex-MMA fighter stood tall as woke Disney robbed her of her breakout role—Cara Dune in *The Mandalorian.* Yet Scarlett Johans-son, arguably Hollywood's most powerful actress, couldn't muster an inch of Gina Carano's guts when the mob came knocking on her door. She let them in as they tracked Social Justice mud all over her eggshell white carpet.

Even woke TV shows can't escape the tractor beam of do-gooder fury. An egregious example came when the key player behind CBS's *All Rise,* a show dedicated to storylines decrying our racist culture, got the heave ho.[1] Executive producer Greg Spottiswood failed to follow up on com-plaints of "racial insensitivity."

"We had to do so much behind the scenes to keep these scripts from being racist and offensive," writer Shernold Edwards told *The New York Times.*[2]

Just about everything is "racist and offensive" to the woke mob, though. Here's a short list of things that are now irredeemably racist.

- Dr. Seuss

- Beyoncé lyrics

- Dunkirk

- Grammar

- Aunt Jemima

- University rocks

- Master bedrooms

- Infrastructure

- Soap dispensers

- Fonts

- Cheese

- Sheet music

- Hoop earrings

- Filibusters

- Anyone who voted for President Trump or landed on Tucker Carlson's Fox News show without immediately channel surfing away

No one in Hollywood wants to be labeled a racist, arguably the swiftest way for a career to come to a screeching halt. Today's stars are understandably frightened of what could happen to them next.

Then again, Tinseltown has always been driven by fear, in one shape or another.

Fear of getting older…of losing a gig to the Flavor of the Month…of missing an open table at that trendy L.A. eatery…of losing your creative mojo…of angering the wrong director at the wrong time on the wrong project.

Even the biggest stars in Hollywood worry their next film could be their last. There's always someone younger, prettier, and more talented lurking over one's shoulder. The busiest stars are one bust away from having their careers come to a crashing halt.

One A-list demotion means the scripts coming your way suddenly aren't as fresh, as vital, as those you read just a few weeks ago. What happens after that?

Dancing with the Stars. If you're lucky.

It's enough to make even the most jaded Hollywood reporter have sympathy for those entering the business, let alone calling it home for decades.

It's an industry built on fear from the ground up. Always has been, always will be.

The newest fear, though, may trump them all.

Celebrities fear being "canceled" for past or present sins (or just the appearance of committing them). They worry about saying the wrong thing (or the right thing without enough enthusiasm), or not leaning too hard into the cause *du jour*.

Others are frowned upon for their skin color and genitalia.

Am I virtue signaling enough? Or will doing it better, harder, faster, put a target on my back?

An actor who takes the role of a lifetime is suddenly on the defensive after being "educated" on how they should have given the role up to a disadvantaged group member.

Faith-friendly artists Chuck Konzelman and Cary Solomon once plied their trade in Hollywood, Inc., but they couldn't process what they called the industry's moral content decline.

"We've reached a point of fundamental disagreement of what the 'good' is," says Konzelman, who co-created *God's Not Dead* and *Unplanned*, among other projects. "No one agrees what the happy ending is anymore. We can't agree as a society that's the goal of a romantic comedy."

Solomon has a similar disconnect with the industry's woke revolution, which he calls the antithesis to creativity. "It's the total opposite. It's not 'woke.' It's 'sleeping.'" Solomon says. "The stories that the woke people want to tell are for only one point of view and one perspective… [T]hey don't want our virtues. They don't want our vision of what's right and wrong. They don't believe in families, in traditions."

"The goal should be to tell a good story or great story. You can't put other restrictions on that. You can't start with a theme of diversity and create great work," Konzelman says.

John Nolte, Editor at Large at *Breitbart News* (and a former colleague of this author) doesn't mince words about the current state of Hollywood.

"It's no better than the McCarthy era when it comes to blacklisting and destroying careers over the ideas that people hold, and it's worse in a number of ways," Nolte says. "First off, there is no way back. Apologies and penances are not accepted. You can't even name names."

McCarthy-era artists like Dalton Trumbo often worked under pseudonyms or found other creative workarounds to keep on writing. That isn't the case in the woke era, Nolte says.

"Any ideas that in any way question the Woke Gestapo are forbidden. Just suggesting such a thing could ruin your career," says Nolte, who dubs the modern age of Hollywood an "anti-human-nature phase of storytelling."

"We're in a terrible place where busybodies, snitches, and pious scolds—the very people Hollywood taught us to laugh at for a hundred years—are portrayed as virtuous," he says.

Only in Woke Hollywood could a brilliant auteur like documentary filmmaker Ken Burns come under fire for his "white privilege." Burns's liberal bona fides are beyond reproach, but that didn't stop a fellow director from assailing him for no reason other than his skin color.[3]

Two things happened after that op-ed.

A gaggle of fellow wokies agreed, wondering why PBS was lavishing so much attention—and cash—on one of the most respected documentary filmmakers of the modern era who just so happened to be a straight white male.

To quote climate change activist Greta Thunberg: "How *dare* you?"

Nearly 140 non-fiction film-makers signed a letter criticizing PBS for a lack of diversity and asking for transparency about the public broadcaster's programming, spending, and staffing practices.

The new letter, released by a group led by BIPOC filmmakers and known collectively as Beyond Inclusion, also questions PBS's relationship with Burns, saying: "Public television supporting this level of uninvestigated privilege is troubling not just for us as film-makers but as tax-paying Americans."[4]

"How many other 'independent' film-makers have a decades-long exclusive relationship with a publicly-funded entity?" the letter asks.

PBS fought back, to a degree, citing statistics and facts—like how the company aired "58 hours of programming from Burns and 74 hours from [Henry Louis] Gates [Jr.]," who is black, over the previous five years.

Kudos to the liberal news outlet for not bowing immediately, but it's worth noting the woke mob doesn't care about facts or context. That's like shooting a pellet gun at Godzilla's big green toe.

PBS did eventually buckle, agreeing to create a new Senior Vice President of Diversity, Equity, and Inclusion along with initiatives to "promote diverse voices."[5]

And, of course, Burns himself went into backpedal mode. He demanded PBS start doing something, and fast, about the platform's lack of diversity. Just don't start with *him*, of course.

That's the implied message from many of these apologists. *Yes, I'm luxuriating in my White Privilege…but I can still keep my gigs, right? I've got three ex-wives and alimony payments as far as the eye can see.* Most woke celebrities want the buck to stop over there, not at their feet.

So, what does "woke" even mean?

Merriam-Webster takes a crack at it, suggesting the word is culturally appropriated from Black culture.

> If you frequent social media, you may well have seen posts or tweets about current events that are tagged

#staywoke. Woke is a slang term that is easing into the mainstream from some varieties of a dialect called African American Vernacular English (sometimes called AAVE).[6] In AAVE, awake is often rendered as woke, as in, "I was sleeping, but now I'm woke."

Dictionary.com takes a more direct stab at it:

having or marked by an active awareness of systemic injustices and prejudices, especially those related to civil and human rights:[7]

Meanwhile, *The Guardian* worried in 2020 that the "Right" had "weaponized" the term. Or exposed it for all to see, to be more accurate.[8]

Anyone who grew up loving movies and TV shows may be in for a rude awakening by today's content. This scribe spent a large chunk of his childhood watching majority black shows like *The Jeffersons*, *Good Times*, *Sanford and Son*, *What's Happening!!*, and *Diff'rent Strokes*.

No woke finger wagging, just funny stories with funny characters doing funny things.

That's a thing of the past.

Woke sensibilities are flooding screens large and small now, cutting across shows no matter their demographic breakdown. Broadcast TV regularly churns out propaganda disguised as police procedurals, medical dramas, and yuk-a-minute sitcoms.

And if you think it's an accident, just know there are several groups dedicated to nudging screenwriters to stick to the script. *Their* script.

Think: Everytown for Gun Safety, Define American, and likely other groups we haven't heard about. They don't care about the award-winning stories or films that stand the test of time. They want content that changes hearts and minds, and they'll badger screenwriters until they take their "tips" to heart. Though, to be fair, there's precious little arm-twisting needed these days. Storytellers seem all too eager to weaponize their work for the "right" causes.

"This is long-term work," says Jose Antonio Vargas, Define American's founder. "This is not like, 'How do we pass a bill next month?' This is, 'How do we create a culture in which we see immigrants as people deserving of dignity?' These policies don't make sense if we don't see immigrants as people."[9]

Andrew Breitbart famously warned his fellow conservatives that "politics is downstream from culture." They didn't listen. What we're seeing today is a direct byproduct of failing to heed Breitbart's warning.

A year after Black Lives Matter stormed the country in the wake of George Floyd's death following a police altercation, TV shows began pumping out woke, pro-BLM storylines. Here's just one example:[10]

The March 26, 2021 episode of *MacGyver* found our hero (Lucas Till) confessing to black co-star Tristan Mays's character, Riley, that he joined a BLM protest in the weeks following George Floyd's death. His shame? He didn't do so earlier.

> *Riley:* You were at the Black Lives Matter protests? How has this not come up before?
>
> *MacGyver:* I was honestly embarrassed that it took me this long to join the cause.
>
> *Riley:* Better late than never, I guess. I'm curious, though. What made you go?
>
> *MacGyver:* After we defeated Codex, I had a lot of time to think about the world I wanted to be saving. And that world didn't prop up institutional racism and treat you and Bozer worse than me because I'm white and you're Black.
>
> *Riley:* Honestly, I...I never really thought you saw my skin color.
>
> *MacGyver:* What? Of course, I do. I see you.

That's not how real people talk. It's the way screenwriters who traffic in propaganda do, though. You can spot the woke moments a mile away because the story typically stops cold to give the lecture the spotlight.

(Is it worth adding *MacGyver* got canceled mere weeks after that show aired?)

Sundance-friendly films, always eager to promote progressive causes, turned up the ideological heat in recent years by cranking out movies championing threesomes, abortion, and eeeeee-vil I.C.E. agents tearing mothers from their children.

The famous, and famously misattributed, Hollywood maxim—"If you have a message, send it by Western Union"—no longer applies.

And show *business* be damned.

Iconic characters find themselves attracted to the same sex out of the blue, simply to check off boxes on an Identity Politics scorecard. It's what happened to Hikaru Sulu, the intrepid *Star Trek* character who suddenly became gay in the under-performing 2016 sequel *Star Trek Beyond*.

Canon, schmanon.

Over at the other "Star" franchise, the rascally Lando Calrissian came back to life via actor Donald Glover in the 2018 film *Solo: A Star Wars Story*. Suddenly, the smooth-talking pilot was "pansexual," flirting with a robot in between blaster battles.

Did anyone bother to tell Billy Dee Williams, the man who originated the character? Would he dare object? Even the coolest cat in the galaxy knows he's one news cycle away from being digitally tarred and feathered by the woke mob.

Who knows what they'll do to poor R2-D2 next?

Of course, *Star Wars* is yet another woke hotbed, from what we see on screen to the franchise's social media mavens.

To celebrate 2021's "Transgender Day of Visibility," the official *Star Wars* Facebook account shared a book tease about trans non-binary Jedi knights.[11]

Do *Star Wars* fans overwhelmingly approve? Who knows? Who cares? Team Disney, which gobbled up the saga for a cool $4 billion, just assumes so. All the while watching the *Star Wars* film grosses sink with each new "Episode."

Over at Marvel Comics, chasing countless readers away with its superwoke stories is the New Normal. It's why the male character Iceman started romancing men in the comic book pages.[12]

That's on top of Iron Man becoming Iron Woman; Chris Hemsworth handing over Mjolnir to Natalie Portman in *Thor: Love and Thunder* in the Marvel Cinematic Universe (MCU in geek speak); and other woke switcheroos.

And let's not forget the new Marvel superheroes taking the culture by storm: Snowflake and Safespace. Here's how Marvel described the new characters:[13]

> Safespace is a big, burly, sort of stereotypical jock. He can create forcefields, but he can only trigger them if he's protecting somebody else. Snowflake is non-binary and goes by they/them, and has the power to generate individual crystalized snowflake-shaped shurikens. The connotations of the word "snowflake" in our culture right now are something fragile, and this is a character who is turning it into something sharp.
>
> Snowflake is the person who has the more offensive power, and Safespace is the person who has the more defensive power. The idea is that they would mirror each other and complement each other.

If you've never heard of either character, it's because they didn't cause so much as a ripple in the pop culture waters. Is there a Snowflake MCU movie coming soon?

Naturally, some woke comic book fans found fault with the patronizing effort.

Woke bomb after woke bomb fell upon an unsuspecting public in recent years, from a disastrous *Charlie's Angels* reboot to a new *Party of Five* pushing open border policies.

If there's one lesson to be gleaned from this tome, it's simple: *You can never, ever be woke enough.* It's a point that teeters on satire, but it's one of the few rules associated with this progressive movement.

Does the public at large embrace these woke changes? Not necessarily. In fact, the answer far more often is a big, fat "no."

Studios seem unaware of the cold, hard truth. Audiences would rather not get lectured, thank you. Many can sense a progressive finger wagging a mile away, and they act accordingly.

The Hollywood studios either ignore those results or they just don't care. Hollywood reporters are eager to hide the inconvenient truths from industry folks.

Meanwhile, the stars are running scared from the Woke Police.

It's vital to understand the role reporters play in Hollywood's extreme woke makeover. They love it. They embrace it. They cheer it on in every conceivable way. They shame those who don't agree with their strong-arm tactics.

The Wrap, one of the more influential entertainment news sites, ran a four-part series on Cancel Culture in 2021 that all but waved pom-poms to promote the cultural scourge.

For example, the "new" Lando sparked this think piece over at CNET. com from some pleased, gender-fluid writer:

> Star Wars character Lando Calrissian is pansexual, and
> I couldn't be happier
>
> *Commentary: When it comes to representation in a galaxy*
> *far, far away, it's good to know Lando sees beyond gender*
> *to fall in love the way I do.*[14]

Reporters will pounce on any star who doesn't toe the woke line. Those who do are treated with the utmost love and respect. Any star who believes he or she is a victim is rewarded with sympathy, even awe. That's because Victimhood is the ultimate currency in the woke hierarchy. Even Meghan Markle, with all the wealth and royal trappings, posed as the ultimate victim in 2021 via her Oprah Winfrey sitdown.

Disagree? You might lose your gig. Just ask Piers Morgan or Sharon Osbourne, who both got canned for sharing the wrong thoughts on divisive issues. Those who speak real truth to power, or merely flirt with that notion, can expect to be battered and bruised by the next news cycle.

Part of the woke revolution is supposed to be about empowering women in Hollywood—a noble pursuit, on paper. So, the media and the

Social Justice types cheer when women take their rightful turn behind the camera. Just make sure you tell the story Woke, Inc. wants you to tell, or else.

Pop songstress Sia probably thought she was woking up the joint with *Music*, her directorial debut. The film features a woman (Kate Hudson) getting to know her mentally challenged sibling.

What Sia didn't see coming was the blowback for hiring a non-autistic performer (Maddie Ziegler) to play the sibling in question. Plus, a scene from the film shows that character being physically restrained, which some medical experts say can be harmful to people with autism.

Except it's a *movie*, not an instructional film screened for impressionable med students. That didn't stop Sia from apologizing and deleting her Twitter account amidst the social media frenzy.[15]

Maybe the richest "you can never be woke enough" saga involves Lena Dunham. The *Girls* actress is the near perfect amalgam of today's progressive celebrity. She's aggressively feminist, eager to inject woke talking points into her projects, and always ready to define herself as a victim. She's defiantly overweight, too, which doesn't stop her from over-sharing her curves on social media.

She's also a raging capitalist, God love her. Dunham launched a new clothing line for plus-sized women in 2021.

"11 Honoré x Lena Dunham" offers women size 12 to 26 the chance to be fashionable without breaking the bank. Items cost between $98 and $298, hardly at the Gwyneth Paltrow Goop level of commerce, but not Walmart approved.

The Daily Beast called the line "size inclusive" in announcing it before savaging Dunham's venture a mere four days later: "Lena Dunham's Plus-Size Fashion Line Is Another Missed Opportunity."[16]

NBC News pounced, too, weaponizing Dunham's skin color and wealth along the way.[17]

The line stops at size 26, which is the first problem. Other brands go up to size 40, so, right away, Dunham's inclusivity credentials short-circuited:

> Studies show that plus-size people consistently earn less money than their straight-size counterparts. Because of this, plus-size consumers are, generally speak-

ing, more mindful about where they choose to spend their money. This collection's prices range from $98 to $298, which may be affordable to some but will make the clothing largely inaccessible to many. (Obviously plenty of fashion is inaccessible, especially in the luxury market, but it's still important to remember the way structural inequality impacts fashion consumers.)[18]

Dunham herself is problematic because she can be critical of her own body, like the time she worried about sporting a "triple chin."

That oh, so relatable comment proved "problematic."

"That is definitively not a body-neutral viewpoint," NBC News noted with alarm, adding that the star is considered "small fat" in plus-sized circles.

Here comes the NBC haymaker:

> Dunham is also a wealthy white woman, and here it's important to recognize the way privilege—and its lack thereof—is intersectional. Women of color, especially Black women, have worked tremendously hard to empower and publicize the body positive movement.[19] Women like Gwendolyn DeVoe[20] and Toccara Jones were pioneers in the plus-size fashion industry.[21]

HuffPo hits Dunham on similar ground, as well as her body's natural state:

> Dunham says in the *Times* interview that her body has settled around a 14/16. Considering the average American woman is typically stated to be a size 16, Dunham's size is, well, just that—average. Plus-size, but just barely.[22]

The collection also over-emphasizes neutral colors, another apparent no-no.

At some point, celebrities like Dunham are going to have "red pill" moments after these digital thrashings, where they wonder not just about the woke insanity but the Left's undeniable ties to the movement. For

Durham, that moment has yet to arrive. Her fellow stars may not have clothing lines to call their own, and be attacked mercilessly, but they must walk a very fine line in taking roles outside of their own experiences—or, as it used to be called, "acting."

It wasn't always this way.

Daniel Day-Lewis earned an Oscar for playing a physically challenged character in *My Left Foot*. Eddie Redmayne, right on the cusp of the woke revolution, earned his Best Actor honor for portraying Stephen Hawking, a super scientist suffering from motor neurone disease, in 2015's *The Theory of Everything*.

Maddie Ziegler's casting as an autistic woman was the worst thing possible. Yet straight actor Stanley Tucci portrayed a gay man in *Supernova*, a sensitive 2021 release about an older gay couple, without much fallout. The versatile actor must have known the press would weaponize his heterosexuality against him, but he was ready for the challenge:

> I think that acting is all about not being yourself. If we were to use that as a template, then we would only ever play ourselves. I think what we need to do, we need to give more gay actors opportunities.[23]

Tucci survived both the interview and defying the woke mob...for now. There's always a chance his comments could "resurface" and he'll be forced to recant that position.

It doesn't help that his on-screen lover is Colin Firth, another straight white male.

Why did Tucci and Firth escape the woke mob, yet Ziegler didn't? Your guess is as good as mine. Better, likely. The woke rules are always changing, along with the English language.[24]

This brave new woke world is a fusion of Identity Politics, Cancel Culture, and straight up Progressive 101, shaken and stirred for maximum power.

Woke is all about power, control, shaming others, and in many cases, cold hard cash. Some people are getting fabulously rich off Woke, Inc.

Patrick Courrielche got a personal glimpse at Hollywood's future woke reign while taking his young daughter to a private school alongside several industry players.

Think Jason Bateman, Steve Carell, and Melissa McCarthy, along with some studio big shots.

The Courrielches shared their experiences in their *Red Pilled America* podcast, including the time they caught a fellow parent literally in bed with a child. They attempted to report the incident, doing so with the brief support of fellow parents. When the latter group learned the Courrielches were conservative, that support vanished like that meme of Homer Simpson disappearing into the bushes.

That's how the right is viewed in Hollywood, he says. It's also how the unwoke are treated in an industry dripping with progressive righteousness.

The Courrielches learned from experience how woke culture would evolve. The rules protecting people from nasty attacks suddenly disappear if the people targeted weren't from an approved group or, heaven forbid, conservative.

Comedians like Sacha Baron Cohen and Jim Jefferies sexualized First Lady Melania Trump, for example, and not a single women's group complained about the matter. Nor did anyone else in Hollywood.

Flip the party, though, and you can be assured the outrage meter would hit red and those comics would be forced to apologize over and again. TBS's angry late-night comedienne, Samantha Bee, might require sedation if someone sexualized Dr. Jill Biden or former First Lady Michelle Obama.

The woke revolution might never have happened if not for social media. It's the perfect vehicle for the movement, a way to bully complete strangers while holding them to often-unattainable standards.

Once upon a time—say, a few years ago—people flocked to social media to share baby pictures and opine on the latest news headlines. Today, we do so more cautiously if our views don't align perfectly with the woke groupthink. Those Facebook jails sure fill up in a hurry.

Meanwhile, Social Justice Warriors are working the web and social platforms, waiting for an "enemy" to say the wrong thing.

The examples are legion, but here's one from the creative class. One comedian told *Virtue Bombs* about a colleague who was warned his social media feed "was becoming a liability" to the company, and he should consider cleaning it up.

"So much of his work was about pushing the envelope," the anonymous comedian told this author. "Now, he's told, you might end up f***ing a deal up. That's the world we're living in."

Artists who aren't yet household names are even more frightened about the new woke world order. Climbing the Hollywood ladder is as tough as cracking the New York Yankees's lineup. It takes talent, skill, impeccable timing, and a great network of peers to score the gig that will make your star shine.

Now, add the ability to ruin all of the above by a single unsavory tweet, and imagine the trepidation of being on social media today. Cue the *Psycho* shree-shree-shree sound effect.

You'd assume older, more established stars would have far less to fear. They're fabulously wealthy, have massive fan bases, and enough critical adoration to stand up to any woke attacks. They made it to the top of the mountain. Surely, they're immune to these random rules that stop others in their professional tracks.

And you'd be wrong.

Stephen King tweeted in January 2020 that he would "never consider diversity in matters of art. Only quality. It seems to me that to do otherwise would be wrong." It's a sound opinion.

So naturally, the corrupt and biased press weaponized Twitter users against King, rationalizing their venom as being part of a major movement against him. Fellow artist and hard-left activist Ava DuVernay was among the higher-profile accounts savaging King for making total sense.

Did the reaction constitute a massive blowback or just a few thousand Twitter trolls? Just remember Twitter isn't real life.

Yet King did more than a customary backpedal. He rushed to the pages of *The Washington Post*, where Journalism Dies in Bias. King's op-ed said he "stepped over" the line with his tweet, along with the oh-so-woke declaration that "The Oscars are still rigged in favor of white people."[25] King's comments paint Hollywood as being full-on racist. What would have happened if he had stood his ground and said, "I cheer a Hollywood that accepts all voices, but my critics haven't changed my mind. Art matters more than checking off a given Identity Politics box."

More outrage, of course. And then? Would any of King's bazillion dollars suddenly vanish? Would any publisher dare cut ties with a prolific money maker? Would anyone save the most deranged reporter suggest the tweet dinged his creative legacy?

He caved anyway. And he's far from alone.

Author Dav Pilkey created a juvenile empire with his *Captain Underpants* books. His personal web page boasts his *Captain Underpants* and *Dog Man* graphic novels "have sold millions of copies worldwide and have been translated into many languages."

Who knows how many children caught the reading bug thanks to Pilkey's signature creation shouting, "tra la LA!" (If that reference landed with a thud, you, dear reader, likely don't have children.)

Pilkey's cultural legacy didn't stop the woke mob from targeting his off-shoot title, *The Adventures of Ook and Gluk: Kung Fu Cavemen from the Future*. An online petition sparked the book's cancellation as well as blocking any future "Ook and Gluk" stories from hitting store shelves.

The first book in a proposed series featured "passive racism," and both Pilkey and his publisher agreed in perfect harmony to digitally burn the book—a.k.a., it's no longer available to delight young minds.

Melissa Chen savaged the move in the pages of *The New York Post*:

> In a world that values cultural pluralism and inclusivity, "The Adventures of Ook and Gluk: Kung-Fu Cavemen from the Future" should be widely celebrated and beloved. Indeed, the 2010 children's graphic novel spent 33 weeks on *The New York Times* Best Seller List...
>
> Master Wong is a prime example of a positive portrayal of an Asian character in literature, and just like Mr. Miyagi in *The Karate Kid*, he comes across as endearing and full of wisdom, wisdom that he communicates via "stereotypical Chinese proverbs." What could be more representative of Chinese culture than Chinese proverbs?

Wong teaches Ook and Gluk that "the wisest warrior wins without a battle," and advises them "to walk the path of peace."

How can this be interpreted as a bad representation of Chinese philosophy? Or be seen as encouraging passive racism?[26]

"How" isn't important, of course. The woke mob lusts for power and control, a message you'll see repeated here sans apology. It's not about making society a better, more humane place. Just the opposite, actually.

Other entertainment giants also buckled when their product didn't align with the new world order.

Matt Groening offered a dollop of hope before he and his most famous creation caved to the mob. Groening is the mind behind multiple projects, but his long-running *The Simpsons* series stands as his crowning achievement.

Writer/star Hari Kondabolu offered a feature-length attack on Apu Nahasapeemapetilon, the Indian immigrant who runs the Quik-E-Mart on the animated smash.

The Problem with Apu documentary suggests the character offers a negative stereotype that causes real-world harm. Plus, the actor who voices Apu, versatile performer Hank Azaria, isn't an Indian.

It didn't matter that few people complained about Apu prior to the documentary, or that the character over the years grew richer, and stronger, becoming a full-bodied soul in a cartoon teeming with silly caricatures. Think the fornicating Mayor with the Kennedy-esque accent, or Groundskeeper Willie.

Groening initially defended Apu in 2018:

I go, maybe he's a problem, but who's better? Who's a better Indian animated character in the last 30 years? I've been to India twice and talked about *The Simpsons* in front of audiences. That's why this took me by surprise. I know Indians are not the same as Indian-Americans....

As many people have pointed out, it's all stereotypes on our show. That's the nature of cartooning. And you try not to do reprehensible stereotypes.

Groening even had little Lisa Simpson, as progressive as Bernie Sanders wolfing down a Ben & Jerry's cone, defend the character.

Something that started decades ago and was applauded and inoffensive is now politically incorrect. What can you do?[27]

You can fold, that's what.

The woke mob was not happy. So, Azaria quit playing the character and offered up a series of apologies for giving joy to countless viewers:

"Once I realised that that was the way this character was thought of, I just didn't want to participate in it anymore. It just didn't feel right," he told the *New York Times*.[28,29]

More recently, Azaria said he wanted to personally apologize to every Indian-American, if possible. John Cleese, a rare foot soldier against the woke mob, mocked Azaria's mea culpa with this precious retort:

"Not wishing to be left behind by Hank Azaria, I would like to apologise on behalf on Monty Python for all the many sketches we did making fun of white English people," Cleese joked. "We're sorry for any distress we may have caused."[30,31]

Comedian Lou Perez penned a powerful piece defending both Apu and a comedian's right to find the funny wherever it may lead.

I wasn't born an activist. But I had no choice but to become one after I watched Kondabolu's documentary. It assured me that it is okay for a grown man to be angry at a cartoon.[32]

Like Apu, my dad has a "funny" accent. Think of The Most Interesting Man in the World from those Dos Equis commercials, but gruffer and with a more limited English vocabulary. I exploit that accent whenever I can—in stand-up routines, comedy sketches, on dates. Not only is it funny, but it is a reminder of my roots. And I like hearing others put on my dad's accent, too.

But even now that Apu is no more, Kondabolu is still upset. He lamented the news of his departure on Twitter, saying that "there are so many ways to make Apu work without getting rid of him…this sucks."[33]

You can't make a documentary in which you liken *The Simpsons* to a "racist grandfather," accuse the white guy voicing a character you dislike of committing "cultural appropriation" at best or doing a minstrel show at worst, and then act shocked when the show's producers decide to kill off the character.

Kondabolu doesn't seem entirely sure what the solution to the Apu problem would entail, suggesting that Apu should simply become wealthier:

The idea that Apu is still working at the Kwik-E-Mart versus owning these places seems weird. Make him a mogul. Make him wealthy. Make him somebody who's actually had things work out for them—an immigrant who's successful.[34]

Actually, Apu *is* a successful immigrant with a large family and a seemingly happy marriage. Besides, that scenario doesn't sound remotely funny for a comedy series. Also, did Kondabolu realize that it's a… *cartoon*, one featuring characters who haven't aged a day in thirty years?

And—spoiler alert—the controversy essentially erased Apu from the show, leaving TV with one less Indian-American character.

Hollywood's woke makeover is likely to stick around for some time. So why should the average consumer care?

What happens in Hollywood doesn't stay in Hollywood, for starters.

In 2019 Adam Carolla and Dennis Prager made a little docudrama called *No Safe Spaces*. The movie warned about how free speech was under assault on college campuses nationwide, and those students would soon enter the work force and insist their new rules be applied there.

It may be the most prescient documentary ever filmed. In just a few short months, much of what Carolla and Prager warned us about came to pass in both Hollywood and the culture at large.

What happens in Hollywood now is an extension of what plays out across America. An actor may lose a key part in a film for having said something "problematic" a decade ago. The next day your plumber could get kicked off Twitter for sharing the wrong political meme. And then his business's website hosting service suddenly calls about canceling the account.

Carolla famously said the Cancel Culture movement is "progressive," a statement with two distinct meanings. It's certainly fueled by progressives—well-meaning souls who get a blast of dopamine when they form a cancellation mob on their own.

It's also progressive because it's always growing, evolving from one form to the next. The woke virus is all around us, enforced by social justice warriors and their enablers in the press.

And they are legion.

Courrielche shared some deeply personal stories on his *Red Pilled America* podcast, including tales of his family getting to know Hollywood elites at an elite school where they enrolled their daughter years ago.

He recalls back in 2012 he started seeing parents claiming their kindergarten-aged children were trans. This was several years before the trans movement exploded across the country.

"Many on the Right who aren't associated with Hollywood don't understand…these narratives we see in culture almost uniformly start in Hollywood," Courrielche says, be it Critical Race Theory, the trans movement, or other progressive issues. "These people end up creating the content that defines what American culture is."

Several years later, he notes, former athlete Bruce Jenner became Caitlyn Jenner, adding that the narrative on the trans lifestyle "had been building in Hollywood for quite some time," including shows like *Orange Is the New Black*, featuring trans performer Laverne Cox. "A very small group of people start the narrative" but it doesn't stay in their circle.

"A lot of other kids started coming out as trans" [at the school], he notes. "It was celebrated at the school. People have a hard time understanding how much control Hollywood has over the narrative. They create the content everyone is watching."

This author isn't casting a judgment on trans Americans, but the cultural trend-making is worth noting.

Just ask Joe Biden.

The nation's forty-sixth president summed up the impact shows like *Will & Grace* had on both popular culture and the culture at large when it came to accepting gay marriage in a relatively short amount of time.

> "When things really began to change is when the social culture changes," Biden told *Meet the Press* host David Gregory in 2012. "I think *Will & Grace* probably did more to educate the American public than almost anybody's ever done so far. People fear that which is different. Now they're beginning to understand."[35]

It might be the smartest thing Biden ever said, a small but notable accomplishment.

What's the most frightening aspect of Hollywood's woke revolution? We've seen this movie before, and it most assuredly doesn't end well.

The Chinese Communist Party's "Struggle Sessions" of the 1960s, a key element of Mao's Cultural Revolution, sound as frightening now as they did during the era for those who lived through it.

"Lived" being the operative word.

Author Peggy Noonan sets the scene, since most media outlets likely aren't too keen on sharing this part of twentieth century history.

> [Chairman Mao Zedong] unleashed university and high school students to weed out enemies and hold them to account. The students became the paramili-

tary Red Guards. They were instructed by the party to "clear away the evil habits of the old society" and extinguish what came to be known as "the four olds"— old ideas and customs, old habits and culture. "Sweep Away All Monsters and Demons," the state newspaper instructed them.

With a vengeance they did.

In the struggle sessions the accused, often teachers suspected of lacking proletarian feeling, were paraded through streets and campuses, sometimes stadiums. It was important always to have a jeering crowd; it was important that the electric feeling that comes with the possibility of murder be present. Dunce caps, sometimes wastebaskets, were placed on the victims' heads, and placards stipulating their crimes hung from their necks. The victims were accused, berated, assaulted. Many falsely confessed in the vain hope of mercy.

Were any "guilty"? It hardly mattered. Fear and terror were the point. A destroyed society is more easily dominated.[36]

Dean Cheng and Mike Gonzalez of The Heritage Foundation share more about these sessions and the modern-day parallels. Cheng notes one of the more chilling aspects of this chapter in history, one with a direct correlation to what's happening with the woke groundswell today.

"The rules were constantly changing.... What was okay on Monday would next be counter-revolutionary thoughts," says Cheng, a Senior Research Fellow at the group's Asian Studies Center. "In Maoist China, whatever Chairman Mao says is right, is right. Even if that changed overnight."

Cancel Culture, in turn, is about "being able to manipulate others to accepting whatever I say is true, is true," Cheng adds, noting how comedian Bill Burr got attacked for being, allegedly, a white supremacist even though his wife is black. Those attacking Burr, even some white liberals, responded by saying she was likely a sex slave, and it doesn't mean he doesn't hold white supremacist views.

"There is no way to defend yourself," he says.

One of the many chilling aspects of this historical nightmare? Chinese factory workers and friends alike would turn on each other, with one of the more insidious practices being a clapping ritual where people were afraid to be the first one to stop.

"They were literally clapping until their hands were bloody," Cheng says.

Gonzalez says Critical Race Theory, another cog in the woke structure, aligns with these practices on an elemental level. He compares it to instilling a "revolutionary fervor" in minority populations while getting the white working class to renounce their race and privilege.

"Accept that you have white privilege, tell workers you're racist, and admit to all your wrongdoing," says Gonzalez. "You finally get revolution…economic Marxism that works through the culture. I see Cancel Culture as nothing more than a censoring instrument to make sure there's no dissent from what's being done."

Cancel Culture, Cheng argues, is rooted in post-modernism. "If there's no real truth, there's no inconsistency…. At the end of the day, it all melds into a miasma," Cheng says.

"Truth," adds Gonzalez, a Senior Fellow at Heritage's Douglas and Sarah Allison Center for Foreign Policy, "is just a narrative to be replaced by a counter-narrative."

The Cultural Revolution did end, of course, but as Cheng notes, those moments don't wrap quickly.

"In the meantime, the number of impacted lives, shattered careers and relationships, are legion," Cheng says. "China, to this day, is still suffering from the impact of that decade-long descent into insanity."

Part of this "insanity" involves Identity Politics, an obsession with a person's race, religion, sexual identity, or other traits that have nothing to do with their character. Naturally, Hollywood is all in with this disturbing trend, and its impact will be felt for some time.

Like many elements of the woke agenda, Identity Politics flows from a kernel of good intentions. In Hollywood's case, it means providing more opportunities to women and people of color, two major groups given the shaft for too long within the industry.

The straight definition for Identity Politics describes people of various groups getting together to protect their overall interests. Here's the generic Dictionary.com rendition: "political activity or movements based on or catering to the cultural, ethnic, gender, racial, religious, or social interests that characterize a group identity."[37]

That doesn't sound awful, in the abstract. In fact, we've seen variations of this for some time in the culture. Think of the Anti-Defamation League, the National Organization for Women, and the NAACP (we won't spell out that last one for obvious reasons).

In Hollywood, though, Identity Politics leads to actions that actively hurt the creative process. In short, artists are now less able to tell stories outside of their specific life experiences.

For blockbusters, that means a female director must be put in charge of female superhero films. Think:

- *Captain Marvel*—Anna Boden, Ryan Fleck

- *Black Widow*—Cate Shortland

- *Wonder Woman, Wonder Woman 1984*—Patty Jenkins

Black-cast stories are now mostly directed by black talent. When that isn't the case, like with *Coming 2 America*, the white director must fend off a volley of questions on the subject. Even if, as in the case of director Craig Brewer, he boasts an extensive resumé showing his sensitivities in capturing a variety of cultures on screen.

More broadly, this often requires a gay character must be played by a gay actor, a disabled character should be brought to life by an actor with a similar disability, and so on.

Saturday Night Live, a progressive comedy showcase that mostly avoids mocking woke culture, did just that with a 2019 game show skit. The contest, featuring a trio of actors, featured a self-explanatory name: "Can I Play That?"

The contemporary version of *SNL* is the equivalent of a stopped clock. It nails the cultural zeitgeist, but only by accident.

Anyone seeking a smart rebuttal to Identity Politics can rent or stream *How Jack Became Black* by director Eli Steele. The multi-racial filmmaker weaves his personal story into a sound examination of why this thinking is so corrosive.

There's another, less obvious, reason to fear Hollywood's woke upheaval. It directly affects the kind of stories flowing into our flat panel TVs, smartphones, or whatever gadget we'll soon be unable to live without.

We need Hollywood to provide us with an escape, a way to duck the pressures of day-to-day living. Bumper-to-bumper traffic. Surly restaurant servers. Nosy neighbors. Inconsiderate bosses. Pandemics.

Hollywood routinely gave us just that, along with memories we passed down from generation to generation. Tinseltown tales did something else, too. They reminded us of our common humanity and what it meant to be an American.

Classic films like *We Were Soldiers*, *Mr. Smith Goes to Washington*, and many, many others speak to the uniquely American experience.

That matters.

The woke revolution threatens all of the above.

So much divides us today. Politics. Religion. Ethnicity. Cats versus dogs. Social media. Pineapple on pizzas. (It ain't pizza with this topping. Settled!)

A great movie or TV show can rally us all together, if only for a spell. Did anyone fight about abortion or gun control while talking about the latest episode of *Game of Thrones*?

Losing that means losing something valuable in our shared cultural experience.

Need proof?

Walt Disney Television chairman of entertainment Dana Walden said ABC prevented several TV projects from joining the broadcast network's lineup.

"I will tell you for the first time we received some incredibly well-written scripts that did not satisfy our standards in terms of inclusion, and we passed on them," Walden said during an April 9, 2021 panel discussion.[38]

One show focused on a white family, with the assumption that supporting characters might add some diversity to the show. Not good enough, Walden proudly said.

> That's not going to get on the air anymore because that's not what our audience wants. That's not a reflection of our audience, and I feel good about the direction we're moving.

Walden failed to share any polls indicating the public no longer has an interest in white families on television. Given that logic, one of TV's most celebrated shows wouldn't get made today—ABC's own *Modern Family*.

That series earned eighty-five Emmy nominations, endless critical love, and became arguably the best sitcom of its era. Under the new woke rules, it wouldn't even make it on air.

***

Hollywood's woke transformation has hit this reporter particularly hard.

I became a movie critic because I loved film dearly. My late father indoctrinated me in the glory of Hollywood, first via Abbott and Costello movies on Sunday mornings via New York's Channel 11 and, later, classics like *Jaws*, *Alien*, and the 1953 Western, *Shane*.

Try watching the last few minutes of that sublime Western without tearing up at the end. I dare you.

I remember walking into my first VHS rental store in the early 1980s, agog at the shelves of movies waiting for me to rent them.

"Wait. You mean I can watch *Abbott & Costello Meet Frankenstein* any time I want? Really?"

Nirvana.

A few years later, I worked at the local Mom and Pop video store, sharing my movie passions with the customers. I took pride in knowing which customers might like which movies, offering my personalized tips in between filling up popcorn boxes flavored by a butter-like substance. (Just remember: Be Kind, Rewind!)

Every Saturday night at 7:30 p.m., sharp, I popped the VHS cassette of *Raising Arizona* into our store's VCR and punched "Play." Saturday nights were crazy busy, and having that film's yodel-heavy soundtrack, and the greatest diaper theft in screen history, as the store's backdrop seemed…perfect.

By the way, for some reason I never forgot the numbers affixed to the story's two copies of the film: 2690, 2691.

I studied art in college, but the closest I ever came to using my art professionally was when I drew recreations of the latest movie posters for the video store's walls. I left them all behind when I moved out of New York, saving only my acrylic take on *Child's Play*. It hangs in my movie room all these years later. It's my friend to the end!

All of this explains why I elbowed my way first into journalism and, later, entertainment reportage. I wanted to review movies so badly I took on any task at the *Pittsburgh Tribune-Review*, large or microscopically small, to curry favor with the entertainment editor.

They hired me as a local reporter, and I eventually switched over to the Features Desk. That wasn't enough. I wanted to be Pittsburgh's answer to Siskel and/or Ebert.

They don't just hand you that gig, though.

I worked overtime to get closer to the job, became the paper's de facto opera critic without knowing the first thing about the art form, and said "yes" dozens of times whenever my editors asked me about a potential assignment.

So, when the newspaper's movie critic went on vacation, I saw my chance. I asked my editor if could fill in for him in his absence. My first published movie review, of Jeff Bridges's *Wild Bill*, went live December 1, 1995. I still have the yellowed clipping.

I made it…at least until the critic returned from vacation.

I pulled a similar stunt when I moved to the nation's capital and began working for *The Washington Times*. I gently elbowed my way onto the newspaper's entertainment desk there, too, and my persistence paid off. Again.

I've been reviewing films professionally ever since.

Through the years, I've interviewed some of the biggest stars in Hollywood (Kevin Spacey treated me…perfectly well), visited movie sets (underwhelming), and did the whole "film junket" experience (surreal).

Along the way I leaned into my budding conservative values and realized something about my fellow film critics. They were overwhelmingly liberal, and it showed in their work.

So, I came out as a conservative film critic, giving voice to the half of the country often ignored by my peers.

Today, I'm conflicted about the job I worked tirelessly to make a reality.

I look around at the Hollywood I once adored and see a vastly different landscape. The movies are too often woke and wobbly. TV shows peddle disinformation and political beliefs that starkly contrast with my own deeply held views.

And then there's the stars themselves. These actors, alternately cowardly and cruel in their barbed rhetoric, refuse to stand up for free speech. Instead, they follow their woke marching orders to the letter.

Those unhappy with this cultural transformation, and I suspect this group makes up the bulk of the industry, are too afraid to speak up, with rare expectations.

I get it, but at the same time I'm also deeply disappointed.

Is it too much to ask Steven Spielberg, Martin Scorsese, Denzel Washington, or Julia Roberts to take a stand for free expression? Can somebody, anybody, decry the conservative blacklist that keeps right-leaning talent afraid of the industry learning their voting habits?

Who will stand up for movies being canceled and stars silenced for sharing the "wrong" messaging?

No one, apparently.

This book exists, in part, because I'm rebelling against the woke revolution. I've never considered myself a rebel, though. I'm not a red-meat type, and when I'm driving, I get antsy if I drive more than five miles above the speed limit.

I might have been the only teenager who never questioned his parents' wisdom.

Nerd alert: In my perfect world, I'd hunker down, watch movie after movie, and file my reviews in the hope of guiding readers to the best content around.

But that's no longer enough for me. Woke Hollywood made me an accidental culture warrior, someone obsessed with defending creative freedom.

Hollywoke is hurting my country, my culture, and the movies I hold so dear. The industry that gave me so much joy for so very long has lost its mojo, if not its fractured soul.

Let's hope it's not too late to save it.

CHAPTER 2:
Virtue Signaling on Parade

FOR ALL THE CONSERVATIVE CRITIQUES of Hollywood, including those in this book, one thing is clear. Some of Hollywood's heavyweights get things done.

Matt Damon co-founded Water.org, a group that has helped more than thirty million people gain access to clean drinking water in Africa, Southeast Asia, and Latin America.[39]

Back to the Future standout Michael J. Fox turned his personal fight with Parkinson's disease into the world's largest nonprofit research arm.[40]

Dolly Parton alternately spreads her joyous music and gives to one worthy cause after the next. Gary Sinise's relentless work on behalf of the troops deserves a book, and a biopic, all its own.

Heck, just having A-listers like Chris Evans and Chris Pratt visit children's hospitals in their superhero regalia represents an undeniable "good."

But then there's the other side of Hollywood in the woke era. These celebrities think they're healing the world one profound statement at a time. It's virtue signaling on steroids, and it deserves far more mockery than praise.

Their comments cover a wide swath of cultural territory, from apologies for past thought crimes to proactive attempts to appear noble and pure. In their defense, it often sparks headlines, but it simultaneously makes fair-minded types shake their heads in mild disgust.

The ultimate storytelling maxim is show, don't tell. For do-gooders, it should be act—don't pretend your precious tweet will change the world.

The most laughable part of virtue signaling is how often it blows back in the celebrity's face.

Mark Wahlberg is that rare star with a self-awareness gene. He made headlines in 2013 when he mocked his fellow stars for comparing their work load, and travel, to those who serve in the U.S. military.

> "For actors to sit there and talk about 'Oh I went to SEAL training'? I don't give a f*** what you did." He said angrily during an audience question and answer session in Los Angeles.

> "You don't do what these guys did. For somebody to sit there and say my job was as difficult as being in the military? How f***ing dare you, while you sit in a make-up chair for two hours.

> "I don't give a s**t if you get your a** busted. You get to go home at the end of the day. You get to go to your hotel room. You get to order your f***ing chicken or steak."[41]

More recently, Wahlberg tried piggybacking on the Black Lives Matter movement shortly after it exploded in 2020. The *Boogie Nights* star shared an innocuous message featuring a snapshot of the late George Floyd, the black man who died after a Minneapolis police officer held him down by his neck for an extended period:

> The murder of George Floyd is heartbreaking. We must all work together to fix this problem. I'm praying for all of us. God bless.

Who could find fault with such a gentle, generic message? Social Justice Warriors, that's who.

Some SJWs either knew about Wahlberg's checkered past or learned about it via Google. Either way, social media erupted at an actor who, as a much younger man, co-starred in three racially-charged assaults.[42]

Wahlberg had long since apologized for the incidents, moving past them to build an impressive life as an actor, husband, and dad.

No matter. The woke mob wanted blood, and they might have had it if Wahlberg took the bait and apologized anew. Here's betting his agent had a "hostage"-style mea culpa teed up and waiting for Wahlberg's approval.

Except the star ignored the outcry as if it never occurred. Guess what happened next? The mob moved on.

> *Truth Trailer*: Podcaster Adam Carolla's "no apologies" approach to the woke mob matters. So do his insights into mob activity. "You retreat, they encroach," the comic said on his podcast. Truer words...you know the rest.

The Wahlberg imbroglio represented a chilling look at how even someone doing the "right" thing isn't immune from Cancel Culture-style attacks. After all, aren't stars supposed to genuflect toward the BLM movement?

Confused? Don't be. The rules are purposefully meant to be confusing.

Imagine how Emma Watson felt after she, too, tried to co-opt the BLM message. The *Harry Potter* actress posted three black squares on her 57.2-million-strong Instagram account at the peak of BLM's rise. She tweaked the images to include a white border that matched her existing design.

That's Social Media 101, but it caused an outcry all the same.[43]

Unlike Wahlberg, Watson doubled, tripled, and quadrupled down on her virtue signaling to keep the mob at bay. Here's part of her mewling apology.

> There is so much racism, both in our past and present, that is not acknowledged nor accounted for....
>
> White supremacy is one of the systems of hierarchy and dominance, of exploitation and oppression, that is tightly stitched into society. As a white person, I have benefited from this....

Make. It. Stop. No, it's not over yet:

> I'm still learning about the many ways I unconsciously
> support and uphold a system that is structurally racist.

So, did Watson turn her house over to a family of color, letting them luxuriate in the spoils of her structurally racist life? Perhaps she relinquished her next three film roles so that women of color, perhaps differently abled, could take them instead. We're waiting…

> I see your anger, sadness and pain. I cannot know what
> this feels like for you but it doesn't mean I won't try to.

Yes, the fury around her white border aesthetic wasn't easily subdued, but with daily counseling there's still hope.

How much joy would a star like Watson bring if she uncorked a gargantuan "Bleep you" when the mob called her out for absurdities like this?

After all, it's not a literal mob. It's dozens, maybe hundreds, of woke foot soldiers who think their passions are reflected by millions of fellow Americans. They're not, but the culture treats them as if they were.

Other stars prompt eyebrow raises with unforced woke platitudes.

Actress Keira Knightley idly declared that she would no longer allow male directors to film her in lovemaking scenes.

A nation mourns.

"I don't have an absolute ban, but I kind of do with men," the actress told the podcast Chanel Connects.

> "It's partly vanity and also it's the male gaze…. I feel
> very uncomfortable now trying to portray the male gaze.
> Saying that, there's times where I go, 'Yeah, I complete-
> ly see where this sex would be really good in this film,
> and you basically just need somebody to look hot.'"

The *New York Post* noted she previously sang the praises of male director Joe Wright in their 2007 collaboration on *Atonement*.

The director "choreographed the scene within an inch of its life," Knightley told *Vulture* in 2019. "It was absolutely, 'Foot goes up there, hand goes up there.' So, both me and James [McAvoy] felt utterly comfortable and not exposed, and like we could deal with it. It's never gonna be fun, but we could deal with it."[44]

Going woke means never having to explain yourself, let alone make sense. Bully on *The New York Post* for doing a quick web search to shred her hypocrisy. Here's betting they were the only mainstream outlet to do just that.[45]

Reporters love virtue signaling. It's their brand of woke, and it's an easy story to write.

Ewan McGregor is one of Hollywood's busiest actors, yet he's never been called up to the Pitt-Denzel-Streep leagues. Perhaps he had that sentiment in mind when he gave *The Tonight Show* host Jimmy Fallon an earful on why his mediocre movie, *Birds of Prey*, could crush the Patriarchy™ once and for all.

> It's about time that we've got this female made, female driven, superhero movie. It's a really powerful film. It was just exciting to be part of. A film that covers some of the misogynist nonsense that you ladies have to deal with on a daily basis.

Like leaving your wife of twenty-two years for a younger woman, eh, Ewan?

> I was honored to be the chief misogyner in the movie. I'm not a very nice character in it. I was proud to be part of it and start to get that message out there.[46]

What a way to rally fans to the film. *Birds of Prey* went on to earn a disappointing $84 million domestically, a paltry sum for a modern-day superhero film, let alone one opening outside the competitive summer months.

The film opened so poorly the studio swiftly retooled the movie's name from *Birds of Prey (and the Fantabulous Emancipation of One Harley Quinn)* to *Harley Quinn: Birds of Prey*.

> *Truth Trailer*: The media ran cover for *Birds of Prey* like they did with the lady *Ghostbusters*. Case in point:

TheVerge.com blamed the film's poor box opening on "marketing issues." "Adding Harley Quinn's name to the beginning of the title also gives moviegoers a better understanding of what *Birds of Prey* is about, an issue the movie has faced in recent weeks." Spoiler alert: The name change didn't reverse the film's fortunes.

For years, actresses clamored to work with Woody Allen, arguably the most distinct comedy director of the modern era. Allen wrote complex female characters, netting his stars two Best Actress Oscars (Diane Keaton, *Annie Hall*; Cate Blanchett, *Blue Jasmine*) and four Best Supporting Actress honors (Mira Sorvino, *Mighty Aphrodite*; Dianne Wiest, *Bullets Over Broadway* and *Hannah and Her Sisters*; Penelope Cruz, *Vicky Cristina Barcelona*).

Actors essentially shrugged after learning of dueling Allen controversies. They kept flocking to his movie sets after he wooed, and later married, his then-girlfriend Mia Farrow's adopted daughter Soon-Yi Previn. They did the same after Allen's adopted daughter, Dylan Farrow, accused the filmmaker in 1992 of sexually molesting her.

"Wait? Woody called? Tell him I'll take the part! Scandal-schmandal… it's Woody!"

The toxic headlines didn't slow Allen down, nor did his work or reputation suffer in any serious way. "Hollywood has the best moral compass," as Harvey Weinstein famously said.[47]

When the #MeToo movement rose up following Weinstein's sexual assault history, the industry looked at Allen's reputation with new, not-so-rose-colored glasses. Suddenly stars who just worked under Allen's direction recoiled at their choices.

A Rainy Day in New York stars Rebecca Hall and Timothée Chalamet both said they'd donate their Allen-based salaries to help fight sexual assault. Other Allen cohorts, including Greta Gerwig, Colin Firth, Hayley Atwell, Griffin Newman, Mira Sorvino, and Elliot Page, shared shockingly similar excuses.

> "I did a Woody Allen movie and it is the biggest regret of my career. I am ashamed I did this," Page wrote. "I

had yet to find my voice and was not who I am now and felt pressured, because 'of course you have to say yes to this Woody Allen film.' Ultimately, however, it is my choice what films I decide to do and I made the wrong choice. I made an awful mistake."[48]

Kelly Marie Tran's biggest claim to fame was playing Rose Tico in *The Last Jedi*. It's a bland character in a movie that turned many *Star Wars* fans against the franchise, no easy feat. Naturally, she became a victim in the eyes of the press after moviegoers decided her character was a dud.

It's not totally her fault. It's a poorly written character meant to connect with woke audiences—not the real kind.

Tran clearly realized her victim status worked on her behalf. She also proved a quick study on how to earn woke points. So, when she provided a voice for a Disney animated film, *Raya and the Last Dragon*, she knew exactly what to do.

My character is a lesbian!

> Tran told *Vanity Fair* that when she was recording her voice for the role of Raya, she decided there were "some romantic feelings going on there" between main character, Raya, and Princess Namaari.

The scene itself is perfectly innocuous, but Tran knows where her woke bread is buttered.[49]

Natalie Portman may get a woke book all her own one day, given her extreme woke-ocity. For now, she's content to write a few herself. The actress spent part of 2020 trumpeting the "Defund the Police" movement from the comfort of her (can we just assume) palatial home, but later refused to comment on how the movement directly, or indirectly, led to higher crime rates.[50]

The actress rewrote fairy tale classics like *The Three Little Pigs* and *The Tortoise and the Hare* to be "gender neutral."

Why? That way young readers can "defy gender stereotypes."

> "I found myself changing the pronouns in many of their books because so many of them had over-

whelmingly male characters, disproportionate to reality," the *Thor* star said. "Boys need to see that wom-
en have a multitude of opportunities open to them,
to consider what they think and feel, and how they
experience the world."

Another woke trend in Hollywood is apologizing for movies that
weren't sufficiently woke—even projects shot well before the term went,
well, Hollywood.

Call it Time Travel Wokeism.

Several stars of the Oscar-winning film *The Help* later disparaged the
film and wished they never set foot on the movie's set.

The film starred Emma Stone as a white woman interviewing the
black maids in her life. The problem? The story focused more on the
white characters than the black ones. Viola Davis told *The New York
Times* that she regretted playing Aibileen Clark in the 2011 film:[51]

> I just felt that at the end of the day that it wasn't the
> voices of the maids that were heard. I know Aibileen.
> I know Minny [Octavia Spencer won a Best Support-
> ing Actress Oscar for the role]. They're my grandma.
> They're my mom. And I know that if you do a movie
> where the whole premise is, I want to know what it
> feels like to work for white people and to bring up
> children in 1963, I want to hear how you really feel
> about it. I never heard that in the course of the movie.

Bryce Dallas Howard's career took a huge leap from the film, which
earned an astonishing $169 million, the kind of coin action blockbusters
make. Yet Howard similarly rejected *The Help* when it made a second
splash on Netflix. Audiences may have fallen in love with the film anew
thanks to the streaming giant, but they don't know any better.

> "I've heard that *The Help* is the most viewed film on
> Netflix right now," [actress Bryce Dallas] Howard wrote
> in a post. "I'm so grateful for the exquisite friendships
> that came from that film—our bond is something I

treasure deeply and will last a lifetime. This being said, *The Help* is a fictional story told through the perspective of a white character and was created by predominantly white storytellers. We can all go further."[52]

Count Jonah Hill as another star who looked back in shame at a film that helped supercharge his career. The comic actor's *Superbad* gave him a massive comedy hit, one that also helped co-star Emma Stone reach the A-list. The film may be best remembered for the wackiest name in modern screen history.

McLovin.

No matter. Hill isn't too proud of the film's toxic masculinity,[53] a trait you can connect to the film's co-screenwriter—uber-liberal Seth Rogen.

> "I love those films, but I also think that if you look back at those films, a lot of what they're showing is major bro comedy, and bro masculinity," he said.

> "But at the same time I'm learning I've got to unlearn a lot of stuff, and maybe some of the people that liked *Superbad* will come with me on that journey."

Rogen also swung into Apology Mode, likely knowing his far-left reputation will protect him from any Cancel Culture attacks.

> "There are probably some jokes in *Superbad* that are bordering on blatantly homophobic at times," Rogen continued. "They're all in the voice of high school kids, who do speak like that, but I think we'd also be silly not to acknowledge that we also were, to some degree, glamorizing that type of language in a lot of ways."[54]

I used to share Tweets commenting on the relative woke-ness of today's stars.

I'd see a celebrity quote, note the social justice sloganeering, and give it a "woke meter" rating. Yes, it's a subtle ode to *This Is Spinal Tap*, although these meter ratings sailed far past 11.

Case in point—courtesy of Conan O'Brien:

> "I'm ready for the all-female reboot of America." (Nov. 11, 2017)

The tweets made me and, I hope, a few of my right-leaning followers, chuckle. I stopped doing them after Twitter revealed itself to be an anti-conservative, anti-free-speech platform that helped sway a presidential election.

I think every conservative should use social media to embarrass the corrupt press, praise strong conservative leaders, and encourage right-leaning artists to keep on going.

End of sermon.

I don't share these woke ratings as much these days. There's too much to rank, for starters.

When would I eat? Walk the dog? Brush my teeth?

Another reason I curtailed these Tweets? The cultural stakes are far higher today. What was once funny is now freedom-snuffingly serious. The joke is still funny, but not the "ha ha" variety, like it once was.

Still, it's worth highlighting some of Hollywood's woke declarations to show just how far celebrities will sink to appease the woke mob—or to keep it from knocking on their trailer door.

Colin Trevorrow, the director behind *Jurassic World* and the 2022 release *Jurassic World: Dominion*, shared a snap from the set of the latter to build anticipation for the project. That kind of social media share is how movie marketing is done these days, and it makes perfect sense. Drip, drip drip…and keep future audiences thinking about your project.

The image featured the franchise's iconic logo slapped on a director's chair, a classic staple of film sets. Only the chair didn't have his name on it, nor the names of franchise stars like Chris Pratt, Bryce Dallas Howard, Jeff Goldblum, or Blue, the adorable velociraptor!

Why?

"We took the names off the chairs. Everyone matters the most," the director said on social media.

Isn't Trevorrow in charge? After all, the director calls the shots, not the lead actress, gaffer, or best boy. If "everyone" matters the most, how does his salary compare to the extras lining the set? What about the intern stocking the fridge with bottled water (who still has nightmares from working 6.2 days on a Scott Rudin set)?

Do they matter most...or nah?

It's pure virtue signaling, but it does come with a blockbuster-sized asterisk.

Team Jurassic might be feeling a tad defensive after HighHeelGate.

The woke crowd freaked out over Trevorrow's *Jurassic World* back in 2015. The blockbuster featured a stick-in-the-mud heroine, played by Howard, running from the prehistoric baddies in high-heeled shoes.

USA Today leaned into the shoe "controversy" (imagine going to J-school and getting *that* Pulitzer-level assignment), dredging up all those who were offended by her sartorial selection.

> Back in 2015, publications such as *The Atlantic* called the shoe choice "ridiculous" in the jungle action adventure—especially alongside the properly attired male hero, Owen Grady (Chris Pratt).[55]

> Howard still stands behind the creative choice as the franchise's next chapter, *Fallen Kingdom*, arrives in theaters Thursday night, with Claire in heels once again (at least initially).[56]

> She maintains that Claire's shoes and pristine white business suit, quickly destroyed in the first *Jurassic World*, were indispensable aspects of her dinosaur park operations manager being unexpectedly pulled from the floor of her power job to the jungle.

Of course. It's called creating a character. It requires a script, a performer's full attention, and, yes, some costume decisions to cap it all off.

When Howard laughed off her critics, though, *USA Today*'s crack reporter framed her current wardrobe choice this way:

> The *Jurassic World: Fallen Kingdom* star smiles while teetering slightly atop floral Sophia Webster heels as

she makes her way across a plush-carpeted suite at the Palihouse West Hollywood Hotel.[57]

Teetering? What is she, sixteen, and wearing Mommy's heels for the first time?

Remember, journalists are just as woke as most celebrities, except they're true believers.[58]

Forgive the segue, but this is the same McNewspaper that printed an entire column on *Jurassic World* being "another aggressively sexist blockbuster."[59] That piece quotes *The Daily Beast*'s Marlowe Stern, one of the web's most hard-left entertainment scribes, describing *Jurassic World* this way:

> *Jurassic World* is inherently a movie "about a woman's 'evolution' from an icy-cold, selfish corporate shill into a considerate wife and mother."[60]

Who knew?

Social media is the ultimate place for celebrities to embrace their inner woke. Take celebrated author Joyce Carol Oates, whose stock in many eyes continues to decline due to her insipid posts. Here's a classic example.

> 2017 the year it became embarrassing to be "white"…
> especially if from a "white, rural" region of US.[61]

It's plain, ol' bigotry, but it's coming from the Left so no one batted an eye. Then again, this is the same author who complained about a hunter posing before a dead animal on Twitter:

"So barbaric that this should still be allowed," Oates wrote. "No conservation laws in effect wherever this is?"

Fellow Twitter users called out her outrage, revealing the "hunter" in the photograph was Steven Spielberg and the animal was a large dinosaur prop.[62]

She claimed her initial tweet was in jest.

Major corporations jumped aboard the woke train in recent years, giving little thought to its economic impact. Being woke means never saying, "Our business lost *how* much?"

That's turned the annual Super Bowl commercial barrage into a progressive lecture-fest. Imagine spending millions to wag a finger at potential customers.

For a major entertainment player like Netflix, going woke is a twofer. You scratch the progressive corporate itch while appeasing Hollywood's woke word police. Case in point, this tweet from the company:

> Quick PSA: Can we stop calling films "chick flicks" unless the films are literally about small baby chickens? Here's why this phrase should absolutely be retired (thread).[63]

Dear Netflix: We'll keep Netflixing and chilling if you'll stop haranguing us about a term that's been acceptable, and benign, for decades. Thanks!

Yes, Netflix is the same company that not only uncorked a garish film called *Cuties* upon an unsuspecting public in 2020—a film with gyrating ten-year-olds strutting like they're auditioning for *Coyote Ugly*—but that created a promotional poster so morally wrong they quickly pulled it after a sharp outcry.

Quick PSA: Let's learn how it got approved in the first place!

Award shows are the perfect place to virtue signal. The Oscars, Emmys, and SAG Awards virtue signaling could fill up a tome of its own, but let's use this one to capture the sentiment.

Actress Thandie Newton used her podium time at the 2018 Emmy awards presentation to mock people of faith…twice!

> "I don't even believe in God, but I'm going to thank her tonight."

One of the sadder states of affairs today is how comedians are often at the top of the woke pecking order. For every Adam Carolla, John Cleese, or Ricky Gervais there's a Judd Apatow trying to virtue signal so hard they're popping blood vessels in the process.

Here's Paul F. Tompkins of *Best Week Ever* weighing in on films that should ignore reality…if it saves just one life.

If no characters smoked cigarettes in movies and TV made today you wouldn't miss it. You wouldn't be like "Hey shouldn't that cop be smoking?" Even in a period piece it'd be a while before you noticed it if at all. It would also eliminate a continuity distraction on set.[64]

Yes, he spends many a sleepless night worried about set continuity. As do we all.

Comic maestro Judd Apatow, the genius behind *Knocked Up* and *The 40-Year-Old Virgin*, isn't as funny as he used to be. Blame his Trump Derangement Syndrome. He spent the Trump years raging against all things GOP and making movies without the heady laughter of his early days.

When Louis C.K. attempted a comeback following his cancellation over sexually aggressive acts, the stand-up poked fun at the Parkland students for being dubbed instant gun control experts. It's a very tricky move to craft humor around students who survived a mass shooting, but sometimes comedy demands that kind of approach. C.K.'s point is important and valid.

We often christen people as experts far too fast. Some, like Michael J. Fox, do significant research after a tragedy strikes close to home. Yet we rush to praise Parkland activists without seeing them do the necessary research to become experts on gun violence. And C.K. really goes there.

"They testify in front of Congress, these kids? What are they doing?" he says. "Because you went to a high school where kids got shot? Why does that mean I have to listen to you?...You didn't get shot, you pushed some fat kid in the way, and now I've gotta listen to you talking?"

Apatow dubbed the comic "hacky," adding he was "all fear and bitterness now." This scribe wonders if Apatow's newly woke turn is cover for something else.

Apatow spent years dealing up comedies with primarily white casts. His bros told plenty of raw, off-color jokes along the way. Consider his "Do you know how I know you're gay?" riff from *The 40-Year-Old Virgin*. Talk about problematic!

Celebrities are always looking for press, presumably the good kind. Alec Baldwin doesn't do a happy dance whenever his pugilistic tendencies draw a throng of reporters. Still, they want the attention, and understandably so. It's a brutally competitive business, so the more ink (cyber or real) you generate, the better.

That has led stars to embrace positions that seem, well, absurd or fanciful.

Take Charlize Theron. She hijacked a few news cycles early in 2021 by saying she wanted to headline a *Die Hard*-style franchise. Now, an actor north of forty knows that getting gigs will soon become harder (because Hollywood is inherently sexist, doncha know?). So, any actress saying she wants an action franchise is obviously in an attempt at career life support.

Theron went one step further. She wants to be a lesbian John McClane! Here's *People* magazine fawning over her not-so-secret wish:

> Charlize Theron Really Does Want to Remake Die Hard with a Lesbian Twist: It's 'Kind of Brilliant'

> "Yeah, I mean, it's a great idea. That's why I replied on Twitter. Because I just thought that was kind of brilliant," she said. "I was like, 'This person needs to start pitching. That's a great idea.' And the fact that it would be two women, I was like, 'Yeah, sign me on.'"[65]

What's brilliant about it beyond the overt virtue signaling? There's literally nothing fresh or novel about an action hero having a gay partner. Nothing.

Unless…the movie stops cold to lecture us about gay romance, and wouldn't that slow a *Die Hard*-style actioner down to a crawl?

Of course, if she said she wanted to star in her own action franchise, that wouldn't get nearly as many stories or clicks.

In fact, she did star in her own wannabe franchise starter, *Atomic Blonde*. And it was good…but it didn't sell enough tickets to spark a franchise ($51 million stateside). So, she virtue signaled to get some easy press.

Embracing the LGBTQ agenda is an instant way to snag fawning press coverage. Just ask Tom Holland, the British star of the latest *Spider-Man* features. He signed on to a gay Spider-Man in a *Sunday Times* interview:

> Holland said he'd be open to his Marvel superhero coming out as gay and agreed with the overwhelming sentiment that the Marvel Cinematic Universe needs to start getting more inclusive on the LGBTQ front as soon as possible.

> "Yeah, of course," Holland answered when asked if he'd be okay with Spider-Man/Peter Parker being gay. "I can't talk about the future of the character because honestly I don't know and it's out of my hands. But I do know a lot about the future of Marvel, and they are going to be representing lots of different people in the next few years."

> Holland added, "The world isn't as simple as a straight white guy. It doesn't end there, and these films need to represent more than one type of person."[66]

Okay, Tommy Boy. Quit. Man up and demand a black, differently abled trans actor play the ol' web slinger. No? That sweet, sweet MCU cash feels too good? Okay, then, we know you're not really serious.

Breitbart News's John Nolte, unrivalled in sniffing out a buried lede in mainstream reporting, found this humdinger in the middle of a *Hollywood Reporter* story. The feature in question concerned Gina Carano, the independent-minded actress who got canned by Disney for sharing a perfectly reasonable message about demonizing our friends and neighbors. (More on her saga shortly.) The story snuck in this tidbit several paragraphs below the start of the article:

> A Hollywood public relations representative admitted this week if you work in the entertainment business, "anything that's going to offend the left is a problem."[67]

She added this extraordinary statement: "I have clients who are making an extraordinary effort to post what the social left wants to see."[68]

That amazing admission matters for two distinct reasons. One, it confirms a McCarthy-like attempt to silence performers on the Right. Can you interpret that admission any other way?

The more interesting reveal? Some—many?—stars simply regurgitate woke platitudes to curry favor with their peers and, potentially, stave off future Cancel Culture attacks.

How?

The woke mob is more reticent to bring someone down if they're a force for the progressive Left. It's that simple.

It's why Howard Stern's decades of deeply "problematic" content get ignored. He waged a radio war against President Donald Trump during the 2020 election cycle, and that earned him endless goodwill (for the moment). It's also why Jimmy Kimmel, whose background includes girls jumping on trampolines, sketches many would deem misogynistic today, and repeated blackface appearances, has yet to suffer any professional repercussions for his actions.

Staying woke is what modern actors do to keep gainfully employed. Keep fit. Chase those wrinkles and crow's feet away. Ignore the wave upon wave of younger, prettier stars about to flood the industry. And, just to be safe, share woke platitudes on social media for career preservation.

Let's end on the silliest note possible.

Colombian singer Karol G apologized in 2020 for a "tone deaf" message, according to the liberal *Entertainment Weekly*. Her thought crime? She shared a snap of her dog, complete with black and white fur, as "The perfect example that Black and White TOGETHER look beautiful," plus #BlackLivesMatter, following the "mostly peaceful" protests after George Floyd's death in Minneapolis.

> "I was wrong and I apologize. I want to make clear that my intentions were right in the photo I posted earlier. I meant to say that racism is terrible and that I cannot begin to understand it," she wrote. "These past few

days have been hard and its extremely painful to see it
continue to happen. IT NEEDS TO STOP. There is
only one race and that is the human race. I recognize
that the way I expressed myself was not right."[69]

She naturally praised BLM, because an apology without such praise
wouldn't be humanly possible.

"I am still learning and taking active steps to help, aid and evoke
change and I continue educating myself to understand the experience,"
the singer wrote.

Even that "struggle session" wasn't enough, *EW* rushed to point out.
Some people took issue with the message "there is only one race" in Karol
G's apology, and just the day before, she caught flak for a tweet claiming
race didn't exist.

One fan criticized the Latin artist in Spanish, responding that ignoring race "invalidates minorities' historic fight for their rights."[70] Another,
in English (sort of), said, "My people are losing there life BECAUSE of
the color of their skin. You might not see color but racist do."[71]

Karol G also got hit, and hard, for sharing a photo of herself luxuriating on a boat with this message, "It's all about living it. Today I'm happy."

The days after? Not so much, thanks to the social media mob.

The lesson learned? Virtue signal at your own risk, celebrities!

CHAPTER 3:
The Hostage Apology

SCARLETT JOHANSSON IS the closest thing we have to Hollywood royalty.

The Oscar nominee is as stunning as any starlet, past or present. She's a key cog in the Marvel Cinematic Universe who finds spare time to snag award-worthy roles between defeating purple aliens.

In 2019 she earned not one but two well-deserved Oscar nominations—for her work in *Jojo Rabbit* and *Marriage Story*.

Men want to date her. Women want to be her…or at least share her bank account for a weekend.

The superstar still bowed down to the woke mob in near-record time after accepting the role of a trans character in the film project *Rub and Tug*.

The proposed feature followed transgender gangster Dante "Tex" Gill, sentenced to thirteen years in prison but who only served three. Gill oversaw a "criminal empire of brothels," according to *The Daily Mail*. So, it's not like Johansson was ready to play the Mother Teresa of the trans movement.

No matter. News of the gig rocked the Hollywood news cycle. The blowback was swift and severe from both the LGBTQ community and the press.

A cisgendered woman—feel free to look up the term, we'll wait—cannot play a trans character. Period. Who cares how beautiful, talented, or marketable Johansson is?

The industry's most powerful woman not only quit the gig but served up a cringing apology for taking it in the first place.

It wasn't her first response, though.[72]

> "You know, as an actor I should be allowed to play any person, or any tree, or any animal because that is my job and the requirements of my job," she said in the interview obtained by *Daily Mail*. "I feel like it's a trend in my business and it needs to happen for various social reasons, yet there are times it does get uncomfortable when it affects the art because I feel art should be free of restrictions."[73]

She's right.

Hollywood's Black Widow then sent what she imagined would be the rhetorical kill shot via her rep:

> "Tell them that they can be directed to Jeffrey Tambor, Jared Leto, and Felicity Huffman's reps for comment."

Tambor earned late-career accolades for his work on Amazon's *Transparent* until a former assistant and series co-star accused him of sexual harassment. Leto won an Oscar for playing a trans character in *Dallas Buyer's Club*. Huffman scored an Oscar nomination for her own trans character portrayal in 2005's *Transamerica*.

Game, set, match…Johansson. Except in the twenty-first century the old rules no longer apply. The woke mob pounced, and she backpedaled faster than Wile E. Coyote hopped up on Red Bull.

> "I recognize that in reality, there is a widespread discrepancy amongst my industry that favors Caucasian, cis gendered actors and that not every actor has been given the same opportunities that I have been privileged to," she said. "I continue to support, and always have, diversity in every industry and will continue to fight for projects where everyone is included."

Translation: Make it stop. Except she wasn't done with her Apology Tour™. Months later, the press brought up the imbroglio and she groveled anew.[74]

> "In hindsight, I mishandled that situation," the *Marriage Story* star said in a cover story for *Vanity Fair*. "I was not sensitive, my initial reaction to it."

> "I wasn't aware of that conversation—I was uneducated," she added. "So I learned a lot through that process. I misjudged that.... It was a hard time. It was like a whirlwind. I felt terribly about it. To feel like you're kind of tone-deaf to something is not a good feeling."[75]

Who knows how many more apologies she'll make after this book goes to print?

And she isn't alone.

Oscar-winner Halle Berry performed her own hostage-like apology after she flirted with playing a trans character. The key phrase? Berry now "vows to be an ally."

It's not enough to avoid woke land mines. One now must be an "ally" to the cause. No independent thinking here, mind you. And make sure you do your "ally-ing" on our terms, or we'll be back.[76]

> "As a cisgender woman, I now understand that I should not have considered this role, and that the transgender community should undeniably have the opportunity to tell their own stories," she wrote.

> Berry added: "I am grateful for the guidance and critical conversation over the past few days and I will continue to listen, educate and learn from this mistake. I vow to be an ally in using my voice to promote better representation on-screen, both in front of and behind the camera."

And let's not forget the media's culpability in this cultural fecal storm.

The *USA Today* scribe, after dutifully reporting on Berry's backpedal, wasn't convinced she's paid enough dues: "*USA TODAY* has reached out to Berry's rep for further comment."

What's left to say? More apologies? More arm twisting? Maybe force a sizable contribution to the "right" cause or community? Hasn't she suffered enough for daring to consider playing a role outside of her life experiences?

USA Today isn't sure, but it hopes to squeeze a little extra out of this black superstar. Racist?

Berry's apology was swift and mostly complete, and the mob had no other reason to keep punishing her, so it moved on to other targets.

And there are always other targets.

What's missing in both examples is…show business. Without Johansson attached to the project, it withered on the proverbial vine until it became a TV series pitch powered by trans creatives on both sides of the screen.

Will it thrive? Who knows? Chances are a movie starring Johansson has a far better chance at success, though.

We'll never know.

The same holds true for the Berry project. Her star value would have drawn plenty of attention to it. Plus, she *is* an Oscar winner, which in theory would help the project reached its creative potential.

That's no longer a critical part of the decision-making process.

> *Truth Trailer*: Ever wonder why we don't have one right-leaning late night talk show from a traditional, mainstream platform? Such a project could be a massive money maker given the right talent and writing team signed up. So why doesn't such a show happen? Hollywood suits would rather push potential money away than allow right-leaning observations on their network. Show *business*? Not so fast. Fox News attempted to fill that void with *Gutfeld!* The panel show stands tall against corporate-run talk shows, and mid-2021 the program topped *The Late Show* in the ratings

wars. Who saw that coming? Well, everyone outside the show biz bubble.

Other celebrity apologies proved short and far from sweet. You could practically feel the press representative combing over every word, every inflection, to make sure the client didn't violate the first rule of holes.

Stop digging.

It doesn't matter if said client made perfect sense or inflamed a micro fragment of the Twitter community. Apologies must be made, and swiftly, to stem any serious career damage.

Consider the following celebrity apologies for veering away from the woke plantation. Here's what Mario Lopez said after the unforgiveable sin of questioning a three-year-old's right to determine his or her gender.

> "I have been and always will be an ardent supporter of the LGBTQ community, and I am going to use this opportunity to better educate myself," Lopez told NBC. "Moving forward I will be more informed and thoughtful."[77]

Is there a PR firm that types out all these apologies? Is that why they all sound the same?

Actress Florence Pugh of *Black Widow* retreated after committing the unforgivable sin of cultural appropriation.

How?

She got henna tattoos and flirted with a corn row hairstyle briefly. The apology went on for three pages. Three, not one or two. Here's a sample.

> The world is trying to make change and I'm learning a tidal wave of information that frankly, was always there but I was unaware of. I've tried my best to post, learn, pass what I've learnt on to others and of course, echo the voices of those who don't have a platform to share their wisdom.[78]

Here's more:

> And here's the problem: I actually wasn't being respectful in how I was using it. I wore this culture on my terms only, to parties, at dinner. I too was disrespecting the beauty of the religion that had been taught to me those years ago.
>
> I cannot dismiss the actions I bought into years ago, but I believe that we who were blind to such things must acknowledge them and recognize them as our faults, our ignorance and our white privilege and I apologize profusely that it took this long.

Compare her crimes to those of Alec Baldwin, who enjoys a thriving career despite:

- Using racial slurs

- Using homophobic slurs

- Attacking photographers

- Bullying women

- Hoping a female reporter would "choke to death"

- Harassing airline crew members after he refused to follow basic protocols.

He's yet to offer a groveling, "don't cancel me" apology quite like these.

Or consider Oscar-winner Anne Hathaway, who changed her appearance for a role in the HBO Max feature *The Witches*. The beauty transformed her hands into three-fingered claws to approximate a character featured in Roald Dahl's classic text.

The resulting image looked like the effects of ectrodactyly, a disease which leaves the recipient with fewer than five fingers per hand or foot.

That sparked a social media uprising. Hathaway apologized instantly.

> I have recently learned that many people with limb differences, especially children, are in pain because of the portrayal of the Grand High Witch in *The Witches*.

> Let me begin by saying I do my best to be sensitive to the feelings and experiences of others not out of some scrambling PC fear, but because not hurting others seems like a basic level of decency, we should all be striving for.[79]

Note: Hathaway previously mocked President Donald Trump and his supporters for "gassing children" at the border, a bizarre spin on the harsh reality facing border enforcement officials.

> For those that still believe in voting for the man who recommended using lethal force on families fleeing violence and persecution: this is the policy you like?

Back to Hathaway's groveling apology.

> As someone who really believes in inclusivity and really, really detests cruelty, I owe you all an apology for the pain caused. I am sorry. I did not connect limb difference with the GHW when the look of the character was brought to me; if I had, I assure you this never would have happened.

Give Ryan Reynolds and Blake Lively a modicum of credit.

The Hollywood couple not only got ahead of the apology curve before a woke mob formed, but they injected a dash of personality into the groveling apology.

What was their sin?

The couple tied the knot at a former South Carolina plantation called Boone Hall. Note the word "former." Should all former plantations be burned to the ground and never used again?

The power couple clearly sensed what might happen if a Black Lives Matter activist or wannabe wokester "uncovered" their "crime."

> "But shame works in weird ways," he said. "A giant f***ing mistake like that can either cause you to shut down or it can reframe things and move you into action."[80]

By action, Reynolds meant creating a new group to invest in communities Hollywood too often ignores. Safe to say conservatives and Christians won't be part of the group's annual holiday party?

> Representation and diversity need to be completely immersive.... Like, it needs to be embedded at the root of storytelling, and that's in both marketing and Hollywood.

Cultural critic Kyle Smith's snark over that apology, shared via the *New York Post*, deserves repeating:

> Barack Obama used to live in a house—a large, white one—that was originally built with slave labor. Did he apologize, or marvel at how things have changed for the better?[81]

Anyone caught using the n-word today is destined for a global Apology Tour, and deploying the word given the full brunt of its hurtful history deserves that fate.

That wasn't the case with young country superstar Morgan Wallen. He got caught dropping the dreaded word during a private moment caught on video; but it wasn't aimed at any black person, nor was it used with cruel intentions.

Wallen used the term in a friendly way with a chum, akin to how it's occasionally deployed in rap videos, for example. That innocent context didn't spare Wallen, though.

> "The video you saw was me on hour 72 of 72 of a bender, and that's not something I'm proud of," he

says. "I accepted some invitations from some amazing Black organizations, some executives and leaders, to engage in some very real and honest conversations." Admitting he was nervous to accept the invitations because of his hurtful behavior, he added, "They had every right to step on my neck…to not show me any grace, but they did the exact opposite. They offered me grace and also paired that with an offer to learn and grow…. That kindness really inspired me to dig deeper on how to do something about this."[82]

Naturally, the apology was accepted/not accepted. One organization used the incident to smear an entire music genre and, by default, its fans.

The Black Music Action Coalition issued a statement praising the moves, but added, "we know that there are deep rooted racist practices and beliefs within the country music sphere, and the incident with Morgan Wallen is only one small example. There is much more to be done to continue to raise anti-racist awareness, to demolish racism wherever it is encountered, to achieve racial equality, and to support Black country music artists and Black country music executives."

Oh.

The Billboard Music Awards later nixed Wallen from its showcase because, you know, forgiveness.

Sometimes a revealing documentary will spark a brief but blubbering Apology Tour. It's what happened to superstar Justin Timberlake, who came off poorly in the 2021 Hulu documentary *Framing Britney Spears*.

The two were once an item, and apparently Timberlake could have been a better boyfriend. Imagine all the mea culpas that would be unleashed if we all had documentary crews chronicling our love lives.[83]

"I am deeply sorry for the times in my life where my actions contributed to the problem, where I spoke out of turn, or did not speak up for what was right," Timberlake wrote in a statement posted on Instagram.

"I specifically want to apologize to Britney Spears and Janet Jackson both individually, because I care for and respect these women and I know I failed."[84]

Here comes the woke:

"The industry is flawed. It sets men, especially white men, up for success. As a man in a privileged position, I have to be vocal about this. Because of my ignorance, I didn't recognize it for all that it was while it was happening in my own life but I do not want to ever benefit from others being pulled down again."

One of the few stars to avoid apologies altogether? Hip hop star Lil' Nas, who introduced a line of Satan sneakers complete with a drop of human blood.

No apologies here! Instead, he cooked up a faux apology via YouTube:

"Okay guys, I see everybody's been talking about this shoe and I just want to come forward and say—" At this point the apology cuts to the lap dance scene from the Montero music video.[85]

The aforementioned apologies all have a similar tone and groveling nature, no? They sound more like hostages trying to appease their captors than genuinely remorseful souls.

It's vital to note that these mea culpas aren't from B-listers or aspiring stars eager for early career damage control.

Johansson. Reynolds. Berry. Hathaway. It's the Hollywood elite apologizing for micro aggressions suddenly deemed beyond the pale. Who knows what benign actions today will merit similar apologies tomorrow?

Meanwhile, Hollywood spent four long years inciting violence on a sitting president, labeling half the country racist, and cheering on racially charged mob violence. We're still waiting for the first apology from that troupe. Don't hold your breath.

Like Jerry Seinfeld and Jim Gaffigan, Jay Leno toiled for years as one of the industry's cleanest comics. His *Tonight Show* run was mocked by the hipster crowd for being square and inoffensive. Leno's political bromides feel like something heard decades ago, jokes meant to tickle a rib or two, nothing more. You never saw "Leno Destroys Mitch McConnell" or similarly scorching headlines.

Yet the woke mob inspired Leno to hop into the Wayback Machine in 2021 to apologize for jokes based in actual fact.

The media narrative at the time obsessed over an uptick in anti-Asian hate crimes. The details weren't narrative-approved, of course. It wasn't white supremacists committing all the crimes. Instead, more black Americans than their percentages were responsible for the awful incidents. It was just one of many factoids kept off the front pages.

Still, anyone who told anti-Asian jokes, or those simply perceived as such, were suddenly on warning. So, Leno decided to fess up before the woke mob came for him, too.

It's worth noting Leno is obscenely rich after decades in the business. He famously bragged about keeping his spending habits modest, by superstar standards. His signature vice—his car addiction—meant "Jay's Garage" was to automobiles what Willy Wonka was to sugary confections.

Leno apologized all the same for cracking wise about Koreans eating dogs.

> "At the time I did those jokes, I genuinely thought them to be harmless," Leno said in a joint press release with MANAA [Media Action Network for Asian Americans] leader Guy Aoki.... "Whenever we received a complaint, there would be two sides to the discussion: Either 'We need to deal with this' or 'Screw 'em if they can't take a joke.' Too many times I sided with the latter even when in my heart I knew it was wrong."[86]

Said heart stayed silent until the woke culture ran to the aid of Asian Americans.

Did it matter that Leno was right? Here's an Associated Press report from 2019, years after Leno had signed off from his NBC show, confirming that Koreans do, indeed, consume dogs.

Dog meat is neither legal nor explicitly banned in South Korea. Dog meat restaurants are a dwindling business as younger people find dog meat a less attractive dining option. Pets are growing in popularity, and a survey last year indicated that about 80% of South Koreans had not eaten dog meat in the previous year.

Once again, Jim Treacher at PJ Media offered a sober analysis of Leno's plea for forgiveness and the critical context.

The consumption of dog meat is so commonplace in Asia that Barack Obama bragged about it in one of his various autobiographies, and nobody blinked an eye until his presidential campaign (with the eager assistance of the media) decided to turn Romney's dog into a campaign issue. Then some miserable blogger dug up that factoid about Obama and turned it into a whole thing.[87]

Truth Trailer: MANAA never said a peep about gay Asian journalist Andy Ngo's bravery while reporting on Antifa. Ngo suffered a brain bleed after one encounter with the fascist group, and he kept on reporting. Meanwhile, the media relentlessly slandered Ngo, discounted his tireless work and maligned him as a right-wing zealot, and worse. Somehow Ngo didn't come into the woke mob's protection circuit despite his Asian heritage. Odd!

Meanwhile, notable industry cads like Alec Baldwin, Johnny Depp, Charlie Sheen, and others keep working without a single hostage apology.

Of course, in some cases the apology isn't enough. The woke mob wants the scalp, and it typically gets it.

Roseanne Barr shattered the sitcom glass ceiling with her signature '80s show. *Roseanne* revolutionized TV, giving blue-collar Americans a voice and women a champion to call their own.

Even more astounding? Barr threw her weight around behind the scenes, calling the shots and flexing her industry muscle. That was unheard of in sitcom circles prior to *Roseanne*.

One of many consequences from her self-driven ascent? Colleague Norm Macdonald said Barr would court black female writers for her show, eager to diversify her crew.

All of that got memory-holed by two seismic actions.

Barr embraced Trump Nation in 2018, giving MAGA supporters a voice when ABC rebooted her sitcom. Barr's politics, up until then, were all over the proverbial map. She even starred in a 2015 documentary dubbed, *Roseanne for President!* The film followed the comedienne as she ran against Jill Stein for the Green Party's presidential nomination. The Green Party is to the Left of the current Democrats. 'Nuff said.

Liberal film site RogerEbert.com captured the spirit of both the documentary and Barr with this trenchant paragraph.

> She pays lip-service to a single-payer universal health-care system and berates Wall Street bankers regularly, going so far as to say they deserve to face the guillotine.[88]

So, Barr's transformation from socialist to Trump backer was a head-scratcher of epic proportions. Her switch didn't matter, though. What did? She "normalized" Trump at a time when too many Hollywood denizens were in the grip of Trump Derangement Syndrome.

She had a measure of protection due to her reboot's massive ratings, but when it comes to anti-Trump fervor, that wasn't enough.

So, when Barr unleashed an awful, racially charged tweet, we all knew what would happen next.

"Muslim brotherhood & planet of the apes had a baby=vj," Barr tweeted of former Obama advisor Valerie Jarrett, who is black.

Barr backpedaled instantly, saying she didn't know the light-skinned Jarrett was black and that she was on Ambien when she sent the tweet. Her apology didn't mimic the hostage-like tone of her fellow stars. Perhaps that helped seal her fate. Her sitcom got canceled, then reborn without her. ABC killed off her character, and her colleagues happily carried on with *The Connors*.

Roseanne made stars out of Sara Gilbert, Michael Fishman, Johnny Galecki, and Lecy Goranson. That group, along with John Goodman and Laurie Metcalf, showed zero solidarity with Barr by continuing the franchise without her.

A very select group of stars avoid the Apology Tour entirely. Some make it a point of pride, like British comedian Ricky Gervais.

Podcaster and comedian Adam Carolla raised the non-apology to an art form. The comic's 2020 book, *I'm Your Emotional Support Animal*, starts with this confession:

> I'm starting with a warning. I'm not going to apologize for anything in this book. I'm not going to qualify anything in this book. If you don't like something in this book, you can kiss my hairy ass. I'm like a country that lets the world know it doesn't negotiate with terrorists who take hostages. Guess what happens? Less hostages get taken. So I'm making a mark now. No f***ing apologies. As the great Dr. Jordan Peterson said on my podcast, "You can't apologize to a mob."

Of course, Carolla has a bulletproof way to back up his claim. He built his own "pirate ship," a self-driven company where he calls all the shots. Here's betting Carolla would stick to his fighting spirit with, or without, his signature ship.

Joe Rogan also stands in the "no apologies" camp. The sitcom star turned podcast titan dared to speak to anyone at any time via his wildly popular show. That enraged the Left, for all the obvious reasons.

Even after Rogan inked a massive ($100 million by some reports) deal with Spotify, he kept on interviewing anyone he pleased. The company's woke employees freaked out, held multiple meetings with their supervisors, and threatened walkouts (that never happened).

Rogan stuck a thumb in their collective eyes by inviting conspiracy monger Alex Jones back to his podcast after he officially switched over to Spotify.

Rogan DID apologize for getting some facts wrong during a conversation about wildfires raging in parts of the country.

I f***ed up on the podcast with Douglas Murray and
said that people got arrested lighting fires in Portland.
That turns out to not be true. I was very irresponsible
not looking into it before I repeated it. I read one story
about a guy getting arrested for lighting fires…turned
out to be true, but the other s*** I read about people
getting arrested for lighting fires in Portland was not
true. I repeated it without looking into it and it was a
really f***ing stupid mistake that won't happen again.
I'm sorry.[89]

The press pounced on Rogan for the error, including the network
which rigorously spreads erroneous information—a.k.a., CNN.

Yet these same bold, brave fact checkers stand down as liberal stars
stain social media with lie after lie after lie. Alyssa Milano jumps to mind,
poisoning her massive flock with Fake News without a hint of remorse.
She's far from alone. Most liberal stars aren't forced to make any apology,
hostage-style or otherwise. Liberal celebrity privilege is real, even if the
stars won't admit it.

Let's end with the saddest Hostage Apology possible.

The Bachelor host Chris Harrison shared his thoughts about show
contestant, Rachael Kirkconnell, who once attended a party with a
pre-Civil War South theme.

News reports of the party didn't show any slavery-themed elements,
just the fashions associated with that part of the country at the time.
Harrison touched on the matter with the first black "Bachelorette,"
Rachel Lindsay.

"Well, Rachel, is it a good look in 2018, or is it not a
good look in 2021? Because there's a big difference,"
Harrison responded to Lindsay when asked about the
photo. "Where is this lens we're holding up, and was
this lens available and were we all looking through it
in 2018?"[90]

The backlash proved considerable, so Harrison apologized.

"To the Black community, to the BIPOC community: I am so sorry. My words were harmful," Harrison wrote in an apology posted to Instagram. "I am listening and I truly apologize for my ignorance and any pain it caused you."

Apology not accepted. He lost his high-profile gig anyway, because the woke mob is a caring, forgiving bunch eager to make the world a better place.

CHAPTER 4:
Progressive Stars Feel the Burn

THE WOKE RULES DEFY simple definition, and that's no accident. Roseanne Barr's career ended the day she sent one racially vile tweet while ex-husband, Tom Arnold, can tweet virtually anything without repercussions.

And boy, has he tested those boundaries. Need just one example? Arnold sent this lovely note to Diamond & Silk, a pair of black female pundits who adore President Donald Trump.

> "I'd like to investigate every crack curve & crevice of you two tons of fun's heavenly bodies," he tweeted. "I'll start with intensive oral examination of your naughty bits. So take off all yo clothes & get your big booties butts back into Big Daddy's hot tub. Don't bring Streisand. Too freaky."[91]

Alec Baldwin's toxic track record means he should have been cancelled more times than a Forever stamp. His homophobic rant against a photo journalist alone could do the trick.[92]

And that's just the tip of the anger management iceberg. Yet he's failed to endure any blowback from the usual social justice suspects.

In 2020 actor/singer/TV host Nick Cannon called Caucasians the "true savages," part of a lengthy, idiotic rant that also slammed Jews. He was briefly suspended by Viacom, but the two sides reunited in 2021. He never even lost his *Masked Singer* gig on Fox.

Confused? Of course, but imagine how the following progressive stars feel when Cancel Culture knocked on their eco-friendly, sustainable doors.

Sarah Silverman once sang the praise of the woke Left's comedy rules. The nasty progressive said we must heed the young generation's enlightened take on humor. That's a 10.5 on the Woke Meter.

Her position softened after her own Cancel Culture kerfuffle. Silverman's Comedy Central series, imaginatively titled, *The Sarah Silverman Program*, once featured her in blackface, a bit meant to highlight the cultural forces lined up against black Americans.

She said the sequence earned her positive attention at the time it originally aired in 2007. Few, if any, complained, and she soaked in the adulation.

The culture changed dramatically since then. Suddenly, any variation of black face, no matter the context, is no longer allowed.

In 2019 Silverman lost a plum movie role at the literal last minute once someone on the film's team saw a still of her in the blackface sequence.

> I didn't fight it. They hired someone else who is wonderful but who has never stuck their neck out. It was so disheartening. It just made me real, real sad, because I really kind of devoted my life to making it right.[93]

What does that even mean? Did she ditch her comedy career, film work, and touring to boost black representation? Or did she send a few BLM-friendly tweets and call it a day?

Suddenly, Silverman sounded afraid of what she dubbed "righteousness porn."

> "It's like, if you're not on board, if you say the wrong thing, if you had a tweet once, everyone is, like, throwing the first stone," she continued. "It's so odd. It's a perversion. It's really, 'Look how righteous I am and now I'm going to press refresh all day long to see how many likes I get in my righteousness.'"

To this author's knowledge, Silverman didn't rush to Barr's defense after that one awful tweet. Barr's personal life may be messy, but she shattered glass ceilings with her iconic, blue-collar sitcom.

You could argue female comics like Silverman owe Barr a sizable debt, much like they should thank Joan Rivers and Phyllis Diller for breaking new ground in stand-up circles. It took a call from the woke mob before Silverman realized Cancel Culture may not be all it's cracked up to be.

Fellow progressive comic Tina Fey knows the feeling.

Fey famously pummeled Sarah Palin with her devastating *Saturday Night Live* impression of the vice-presidential candidate in 2008. Fey's been a reliably left-of-center figure over the years, although one not afraid to tweak her own side in shows like *30 Rock*. She still caught holy heck for co-producing *Unbreakable Kimmy Schmidt*. This BuzzFeed subhead on the topic says it all:

> The Netflix series, created by *30 Rock's* Tina Fey and Robert Carlock, brought audiences a nuanced (and hilarious) black gay man, but its Asian-American and Native American characters are far from perfect, as are the jokes about them.[94]

"Far from perfect" jokes—summon the guillotine! Imagine being a comedy writer and realizing your jokes have to be "perfect" in order to avoid a hashtag campaign against your career.

What was Team Fey's thought crime or crimes? Caucasian actress Jane Krakowski's character is revealed to have Native American roots, even though she isn't Native American in real life.

(Pssst, Outrage Mob: the character's rich, affected privilege was part of the joke.)

Some of the ensuing gags were insensitive and stereotypical, according to the show's critics. Amazingly, Fey held her ground, although had the kerfuffle happened more recently, she would have done the Official Apology Tour™.

All the way back in 2014, though, Fey stood up to the Thought Police:

> "Steer clear of the Internet and you'll live forever," Fey told Net-a-Porter magazine in a wide ranging inter-

view. "We did an *Unbreakable Kimmy Schmidt* episode and the Internet was in a whirlwind, calling it 'racist,' but my new goal is not to explain jokes."[95]

Kimmy Schmidt co-star Gil Birmingham, a Native American actor, laughed off the controversy.

"Often the criticisms come without knowing the context to what's being portrayed," he told this reporter for an interview tied to *Hell or High Water*. "That's what happened there…when they find out the plot, the way it's structured, it's pretty damn funny."[96]

It wasn't Fey's only brush with the Woke Police. Her *30 Rock* series had its own blackface moments, bits instantly memory-holed following 2020's BLM ascension.

This time, Fey did as the woke culture told. Context? Comedy? Intent? Irrelevant.

Fey might have thought her days in the progressive trenches would shield her from her far-Left critics.[97]

She was wrong.

Fey could have given fellow *Saturday Night Live* alum Will Ferrell a heads-up on the subject. The PC Police didn't pull the *Elf* star over when he flirted with an Alzheimer's comedy about President Ronald Reagan, one of the more egregiously offensive projects in recent memory.

That might be a legit reason for cancellation…or at the very least a contrite apology.

Instead, they lit their torches over a Ferrell comedy co-starring Kevin Hart…who is black, for the record.

The 2015 comedy *Get Hard* found Ferrell's crooked Wall Street type getting prison-ready by hiring a car wash owner (Hart) to toughen him up. The joke is obvious, with Ferrell's character the target. This out of touch fool assumes Hart's character is a thug because of his skin color.

The film proved moderately funny and partially successful, netting $90 million at the U.S. box office. The reaction to *Get Hard*, though, tainted its rollout.

The script featured the "n-word" (something most Quentin Tarantino films do…and then some!). Another problem: as *The Independent* put it, Ferrell's character "expressed distaste towards homosexuality in prison."

> It remains to be seen whether America, coping with the aftermath of the Ferguson unrest and still engulfed in a cultural battle over gay marriage, is ready for the film.[98]

America, land of the free, home of the brave, and the world's lone superpower, cowering before a problematic Ferrell/Hart romp.

Sadly, Ferrell had to explain how comedy works to the publication's dubious writer.

> While *Get Hard's* gay and racial jokes are causing offence, Ferrell proudly declares the intention was to lampoon the elites. "With all due respect to anyone who went to Harvard, including our director [*Tropic Thunder* co-writer Etan Cohen], I was thinking Harvard a**hole," says Ferrell, a graduate of the University of Southern California, when asked who he based the role on. "As much as my character knows about financial dealings and how to make a lot of money, he really is completely ignorant about the rest of how the world works."

Ferrell's previous work on behalf of the Democrats, highlighted by his never-ending George W. Bush impression, didn't shield him from the woke brickbats. Nor did co-creating "Funny or Die," an aggressively liberal humor site.

Still, Ferrell never apologized for the film, nor did Hart. The movie rolled out as expected, and the early version of the woke mob moved on to other potential victims.

Again, this was back in 2015…a lifetime in culture-war terms. Then again, Ferrell has steered clear of projects that might inflame the woke mob since then. His film career is also in freefall, following duds like *The House*, *Downhill*, and *Watson & Holmes*. Is it a coincidence?

Cancel Culture doesn't care how inoffensive an artist might be. If you step over the line, and said line can be virtually any transgression, they'll let you know it. That includes film critics, an aggressively woke community eager to police content as they see fit.

It's why liberal comedian Jim Gaffigan cried foul after his movie *Being Frank* hit theaters. The indie black comedy found the stand-up character playing a patriarch to not one but two families, but the story focused on Frank's ties to one particular son.

> "A lot of the reviews ... there was a tone of like, 'how dare this white male [laughs] have two families,'" he said. "They couldn't get beyond...they would insert, like, a social commentary onto a platform that was not for that....
>
> "Some reviews were like, 'they under-served [the female characters]!' You know, the movie was really about my character and his son," he said. "Because of the day we live in, it had to be deciphered through this kind of social critique that is just absurd. And it wasn't here and there. It was a lot of reviews like that."[99]

Gaffigan subsequently turned into a frothing Trump Derangement Syndrome sufferer, forgetting about the connection between his liberal peers and unfair critiques like those *Being Frank* pans.

The most shocking, and extended, attack on a liberal star came after Amy Schumer's *Trainwreck* made her a bankable movie star. At least for a spell.

Schumer's progressive shtick often overshadowed her career accomplishments. She donned a you-know-what hat for various Women's Marches, used her *Inside Amy Schumer* to promote anti-gun memes, and weaponized social media to smite the Right whenever possible.

None of that protected her from a one-two punch from critics and social naysayers, tied to her follow-up features.

It started with *Snatched*, the 2017 movie featuring Schumer and screen legend Goldie Hawn. Their mother-daughter bonding offered a blast of feminism, heightened by a subplot involving a friendly gay couple. What could be more empowering?

Sadly, Team Schumer set the film in a foreign land and made the story's villains members of the local community. Here's *New York Times* critic A.O. Scott hammering the film, and by extension, Schumer, for racist tropes.

> "*Snatched* is one of those movies that subscribes to a dubious homeopathic theory of cultural insensitivity by which the acknowledgment of offensiveness is supposed to prevent anyone from taking offense," Scott wrote. "The idea is that if you use variations on the phrase 'That's racist!' as a punch line a few times, nothing else you say or do could possibly be racist. Including, say, populating your movie with dark-skinned thugs with funny accents and killing a few of them for cheap laughs."[100]

And he wasn't alone. The *Village Voice* doubled down on that sentiment, saying *Snatched* dabbled in "offhand xenophobia" and "soft racism."

Schumer clearly hoped her follow-up comedy, *I Feel Pretty*, might get a better reaction from critics. What she didn't realize is the woke fury present during her *Snatched* rollout had grown even stronger by the time *Pretty* hit theaters two years later.

Schumer stars as a woman who looks a lot like...Amy Schumer: a curvy blonde who bonks her head and suddenly thinks she's supermodel thin. The trailer alone caused a social media backlash, leading to the film's grim reception.

Schumer treated her press tour as an extension of her feminist brand.

> "I said, 'Do not retouch me in this movie. Do not retouch anything,'" Schumer told King at the Fishbowl Bar in New York City's Dream Hotel. "You see my cellulite. You see my, my rolls, whatever.... It's like, I feel great. And I just want, I want other women, other people to—to feel good about themselves. And I think walking out of this movie you really do."[101]

That's when things got comical.

Schumer began by attacking her own movie. Note: this isn't a made-up quotation. It's real, it exists, and it's amazing:

> It would be great if my role had been played by a woman of color and there were more trans people in it, more people with disabilities.[102]

She's both the star *and* producer on the film, so she might have had some say in the final casting, no?

Katie Walsh, a syndicated critic better suited for *The Nation* or *HuffPo*, given her woke reviews, got personal with her *Pretty* critique.

> Schumer might not be a supermodel, but she still benefits from being an average-size blonde white woman, and therefore, isn't quite the right performer for the role.[103]

The *New York Post's* Sara Stewart, a liberal critic toiling for a right-leaning tabloid, similarly attacked Schumer for being white, straight, and able-bodied.

> With seemingly no understanding of how tone-deaf it might be to cast a straight, white, able-bodied blonde like Schumer as victimized by society's judgment, the lazily written *I Feel Pretty* takes a talented comic and casts her in the worst possible light (and I don't mean that literally—she looks fine).[104]

The *L.A. Times's* Justin Chang joined the frenzy.

> If the idea was to feature a woman marginalized by her appearance, wouldn't a bolder, more progressive version of this story have cast a relative unknown, perhaps even a woman of color, someone without Schumer's distracting white-feminist baggage and celebrity profile?[105,106]

Is it any wonder Schumer eventually left the *Barbie* movie project and hasn't anchored a comedy feature since? It's far easier to send out a few woke tweets than pitch a movie likely to get you called the worst names possible.

The expanding woke mob would much rather cancel conservatives, but it has no qualms taking down voices on their own side.

CHAPTER 5:
How Taylor and Jimmy Got Woke

TAYLOR SWIFT IS A once in a generation talent, a pop superstar whose songs speak to millions of adoring fans.

Jimmy Fallon became a household name on *Saturday Night Live* before taking over the iconic *Tonight Show* desk.

Two talented, affluent stars at their top of their respective professions. Neither had a nasty track record or closets full of skeletons waiting to spring open. No arrest records, embarrassing financial scandals, or exes with juicy stories to spill.

Each got bullied by the woke mob anyway, a cautionary tale for peers to consider. Talent, ambition, and results are no protection against the woke mob. In short, you could be next to little through no fault of your own.

Let's start with Swift, whose meteoric rise left her wealthy beyond measure in her teen years. Her bank account has swelled considerably since then, as had her megastar status.

She's the biggest pop star in the world not named Beyonce.

While other superstars rise and fall, Swift's fame appears here for the long haul. She proved that by segueing successfully from lite country to pure pop, earning endless praise and awards glory at every step.

Swift owns ten Grammys, as many as the Beatles and Rolling Stones… combined.

Yet in 2016 the media found a critical flaw in her squeaky-clean persona. She hadn't chosen a side in the Trump/Clinton presidential race. In fact, Swift remained resolutely apolitical for much of her young career. She made music, not stump speeches.

That was once the cultural norm. Some stars waded into political waters over the years, but they were the exception, not the rule. Think John Lennon, for example. That's far less the case today, as celebrities from virtually every field vie to be as political as possible.

***

Many stars still conduct their careers without political consideration. It's the old normal, but one that feels increasingly out of step with modern times. They stand out in today's divisive climate. Think Kevin Hart, Gal Gadot, Chris Pratt, and Dolly Parton. Although by the time this book hits the press, one or more may have changed their mind on the matter.

Swift's "just the songs, ma'am" approach became unacceptable to the Mainstream Media and the woke mob, parties with sizable overlap. They demanded she choose a side in the presidential matchup, and hurry.

They never actually said "which side," of course, but that went without articulating. Reporters weren't badgering her to join the MAGA movement and start singing odes to a "big, beautiful wall."

Just imagine the reaction had she done just that.

Swift did send a chipper "I Voted" message out on social media on Election Day 2016, but even that enraged select members of the press. It was too late by then. Why hadn't she weaponized her "Swifties" to make Hillary Clinton the nation's first female president?

When Trump won the White House, the pressure on Swift only intensified. Reporters started to turn on the beautiful singer, whose only crime was to stay out of the culture wars and entertain countless fans. The same press outlets that would recoil at bullying efforts elsewhere did just that to Swift, with no awareness of the irony.

The ACLU, a group now disinterested in the fight to save free speech, demanded Swift's legal team stand down after it went after a blogger. Why would Swift Nation recoil over a press article? The blog post had argued that lyrics in Swift's recent single "Look What You Made Me Do" seem "to play to the…subtle, quiet white support of a racial hierarchy."

That's as nasty as it gets. Except the minor publication wasn't alone. *Fast Company* similarly demanded Swift renounce "White Supremacists":

> …wouldn't it be easier to just come right out and publicly denounce her neo-Nazi fans and their dubious claim on her? Put another way: Swift chose to threaten to sue a progressive blog rather than speak out against white supremacy.[107]

Another blogger wrote a "think piece" with this racist headline:

> Why I'm Afraid of White Women…and Taylor Swift[108]

Over at *BuzzFeed*, the liberal site screamed, "Taylor Swift's Persona Is Not Built for 2017":

> The Nazi connection is not one Swift has ever courted, at least not in any active, provable, or logically tangible way. But it's not one she can seem to shake off, either. And as white supremacist groups take center stage in the news cycle more and more throughout 2017, the connection grows more troublesome for Swift….[109]

> Swift's relative silence on politics may have worked for the majority of her career so far. But by the time the 1989 era came to a close, a lot of Swift's standby strategies had already proven themselves outdated. And as a sizable portion of the US entered panic mode[110] politically, the perceived stakes[111] of anyone's silence seemed to grow exponentially.[112]

Get woke, or else.

The Daily Beast, which can be enlightening, subversive, and utterly mean at random intervals, doubled down on Swift's Nazi "problem."

> The pop superstar is worshipped as an "Aryan goddess" by the white supremacist community. In the wake of Charlottesville, the least she could do is speak out.[113]

Really? "Nazis are bad," proclaims Swift. Talk about dog bites man stories. What's next? "Cardi B. takes bold stand against child abusers, rapists, and people who cut in line at Starbucks"?

These attacks don't exist in a vacuum. The media love to weaponize celebrities in order to push their approved points of view. Conservative pundit and radio show host Derek Hunter spelled that out beautifully in his 2018 book, *Outrage, Inc.*

As cartoonishly biased as modern reporters are, they can't come right out and say what they want to about various candidates, Hunter argued. They have come very, very close as of late, but they still can't unleash on GOP targets as much as they wish.

So…when Robert De Niro attacks President Donald Trump for the forty-eighth time, they consider it breaking news and repeat every last syllable he utters, without a fact-check or tsk-tsk for salty language.

Reporters didn't want Swift to get politically active in the traditional sense. If she'd started raising money for UNICEF or clean water in Africa, it wouldn't be enough. They needed her to embrace the Left and all its tenets. Today, that means going woke without restraint.

It's why the media turned so viciously against *Harry Potter* author J.K. Rowling, a loud and proud liberal who dared to take one step off the progressive plantation when she questioned elements of the trans movement.

For Swift, the media demanded she act as an arm of the Democratic party.

What's interesting about the *Fast Company* attack is what it revealed about the singer's PR machinery at that moment.

> The letter Swift's team wrote to *PopFront* reads, "Ms. Swift has no obligation to campaign for any particular political candidate or broadcast her political views, and the fact that her political views are not public enough for your taste does not give you the authority to presume what her political opinions may be or that her political views correlate to the support of white supremacy."

But that apolitical pose had a limited shelf life. The constant media bullying clearly impacted Swift.

She spoke out repeatedly against Republican leaders, including President Donald Trump. She pushed for Democrats around election time, leveraging her massive social media flock to the cause. And it had some impact. Vote.org claims one such effort inspired 65,000 people to register to vote, thanks to Swift's social media nudge.[114]

A young woman with beauty, talent, wealth, and global adulation eventually caved to media bullying tactics.

Or did she? A case could be made that her progressive embrace happened by choice, much like her previous, apolitical pose. Any PR team knows it's almost impossible to stay at the top of the celebrity mountain indefinitely. For every Tina Turner and Stevie Nicks there are Paula Coles and Fiona Apples whose fame burns brightly but fades even faster.

Perhaps Swift's management team realized going woke was the best way to keep the positive headlines flowing. In any case, she did just that.

That isn't all that changed about Swift. The formerly sweet superstar bared her teeth, saying she was "on the right side of history" with her actions. That, of course, meant part of her fan base stood on the "wrong side."

Meanwhile, she no longer gets challenged on any of her political views by the fawning press. Yes, they fawn now because she does what she's told. Only journalistic softballs come her way today.

She was so proud of her transformation she even starred in a documentary about it.

The Netflix film *Miss Americana* captured her progressive journey while reporters, who by now had her in their pocket, lauded the film without reservation. Here's how the far-left *Hollywood Reporter* capped its review.

> Near the end of the film, Swift says she wants to be able to still wear pink and talk about politics seriously, and the film sees her finding her way toward creating an aesthetic that marries elements cohesively. If she gets bored with being America's pop princess in the next few years, perhaps she could consider using her ample gifts for messaging and grassroots coalition-building in

the political realm outright. After all, by 2024 she'll be 35 and eligible to run for president. It's about time we had a cat lover in the White House.[115]

And yet everything wasn't perfect for the newly woke Swift. Social Justice types are never fully satisfied, and you could be more woke than Lena Dunham at a BLM rally and still attract some naysayers.

So, it went with Swift, who wrote a whole song, "You Need to Calm Down," wagging her finger at rubes who aren't lined up with the progressive movement. Still, that song rubbed some on the Left the wrong way because—all together now—"you never can be woke enough." *The Atlantic* decried the video and song, saying Swift had "hijacked queerness."

> Swift and Perry, dressed, respectively, as French fries and a hamburger, hugging. The two onetime rivals didn't do the classic stunt lesbian kiss, but they did splashily end one of the most epic celebrity feuds in recent memory. Thought this video was about gay rights? Nope, it's primarily narrative management for superstars....

> Writing off bigotry as negativity—the word Swift used to describe what her song is attacking—probably isn't helpful either. Homophobia is a real ideology with a real history. Telling homophobes they're boring downers probably won't sway them, and it's hard to imagine that such a message will comfort many of the people they target.[116]

Vox decried Swift for trying to monetize her LGBTQ support.

> But when a major celebrity like Swift decides to take on social causes, she is also able to monetize them. This isn't a coincidence; Swift is our most business-driven pop star. She took an artistic risk by going edgy for her last album, Reputation, but immediately returned to her hyperfeminine princess aesthetic when that failed

to translate into early sold-out stadiums or match her previous blockbuster record sales; she does not do anything that is unlikely to turn a profit. And right now, during Pride Month in the year 2019, is a very good time to make money by aligning oneself with queer causes.[117]

Swift initially drew the woke mob's wrath without actually doing something wrong. Critics couldn't point to anything cruel, or hateful, in Swift's bag of tricks. No, her "silence was violence," and that's why they pounced.

Fallon, by comparison, did commit an act so heinous, so cataclysmically bad, it's a wonder he wasn't thrown in jail then and there. He treated then-presidential candidate Donald Trump *like a guest* on his *Tonight Show*.

Even worse, he messed up Trump's signature 'do for yuks.

Yes, mere weeks before Election Day 2016, Fallon actually laughed it up with Trump, and the press went to DefCon 4. It wasn't the banter that bothered them, though. Reporters and the Left went apoplectic when Fallon playfully tousled Trump's legendary coif.

It's real, and a big-time TV star proved it for all to see.

Critics wailed Fallon had *humanized* Trump—let that verbiage sink in. Reporters spent week after week hammering Fallon following Trump's electoral win.

The Guardian led the charge:

> Not only was it not funny. It didn't do anything to take Trump down a notch (if it was even meant to). Instead, it humanized him, boosting him on that stupid metric so many Americans use when choosing a president: "Hey, he's a guy I'd want to have a beer with! Look at him, letting Fallon have fun with him!"
>
> Fallon had real power last night and squandered it. I can't imagine Chelsea Handler, Trevor Noah or the recently departed Larry Wilmore building up Trump like that.[118]

The author isn't wrong about that last paragraph.

The "not remotely biased" Associated Press called the moment a "cringeworthy interview." Has that AP scribe ever watched Stephen Colbert suck up to a Democrat?[119]

Still, a major TV personality can withstand a few critical news articles, right?

Apparently not. He was "devastated" by the negative reaction to the interview. Perhaps the pressure Fallon faced behind the scenes was far more than a few scathing reviews.

Had Fallon read the reviews for his Queen Latifah comedy *Taxi*?

Here's how much the blowback hurt him, and his show, according to his mea culpa:

> "If I let anyone down, it hurt my feelings that they didn't like it. I got it."

> But in the podcast, Fallon reveals the backstage fallout to the criticism that he had been too soft on Trump. "It's tough for morale," he said. "You go, 'Alright, we get it. I heard you. You made me feel bad. So now what? Are you happy? I'm depressed. Do you want to push me more? What do you want me to do? You want me to kill myself? What would make you happy? Get over it.'"

> He said he works hard and is one of the "good people," but faced a "gang-mentality" online. "People just jump on the train, and some people don't even want to hear anything else. They're like, 'No, you did that!' You go, 'Well, just calm down and just look at the whole thing and actually see my body of work.'"

Imagine being so jelly-spined that you can't just say a variation of "bite me" after people complain about a five-second segment on your iconic TV show.

Apologies don't actually register with the woke world, though. They're admissions of guilt, at best, and they keep the "kick me" sign stapled to your back.

That's why Fallon wasn't freed by his mea culpa. He was still viewed with suspicion by the woke mob. So, when his twenty-year-old blackface episode "resurfaced," he was more vulnerable than your average star. Fallon's impression of fellow *SNL* performer Chris Rock had floated in the ether for two decades without anyone noticing. Or caring.

Now? It was time for a full-on apology on *The Tonight Show*.

> "I had to really examine myself in the mirror this week because a story came out about me on SNL doing an impression of Chris Rock in blackface.... And I was horrified. Not of people trying to 'cancel' me or cancel this show, which is scary enough. The thing that haunted me the most was, how do I say I love this person?"

> "I respect [Chris Rock] more than I respect most humans.... I'm not a racist. I don't feel this way."

The feeling, alas, wasn't mutual. Why didn't Rock instantly rush to his good friend's side? You know, with something like: *"Hey, I get where we don't do blackface anymore, but the rules were different then. And I know Jimmy...he's got a good heart and this doesn't reflect it...at all,"* Rock said in a statement.

Easy, right?

Instead, Rock let Fallon twist, and twist some more, in the wind. Only months later, when the groveling was long over and the brand damage done, did Rock at last admit to the *New York Times* there wasn't a racial crime in the first place.

> "Hey, man, I'm friends with Jimmy. Jimmy's a great guy.... And he didn't mean anything. A lot of people want to say intention doesn't matter, but it does. And I don't think Jimmy Fallon intended to hurt me. And he didn't."[120]

> *Truth Trailer:* Rock is one of comedy's most respected stand-ups, but one of the quietest voices on the

free speech front. While Ricky Gervais, Adam Carolla, and John Cleese lead the fight to preserve creative expression, Rock sits on the sidelines. His brand of take-no-prisoners comedy could clearly be hurt by the woke police, but he refuses to take a stand. Silence is complicity, as the woke mob says—right?

Back to Fallon's *Tonight Show* apology:

> I realized that I can't not say I'm horrified and I'm sorry and I'm embarrassed.... I realized that the silence is the biggest crime that white guys like me and the rest of us are doing, staying silent. We need to say something. We need to keep saying something. And we need to stop saying "that's not OK" more than just one day on Twitter.

Guess who *wasn't* forced to make a similar groveling apology? Jimmy Kimmel.

The angry, far-left host repeatedly employed blackface makeup to imitate basketball great Karl Malone and Oprah Winfrey.

It took months after Fallon's grovel-fest for the media to oh, so gently turn on Kimmel. The former *Man Show* host eventually served up an apology, of sorts, via a press statement. He spent more time sniping at his critics than expressing real remorse.

> I have long been reluctant to address this, as I knew doing so would be celebrated as a victory by those who equate apologies with weakness and cheer for leaders who use prejudice to divide us.

> That delay was a mistake.... There is nothing more important to me than your respect, and I apologize to those who were genuinely hurt or offended by the makeup I wore or the words I spoke.

I've done dozens of impressions of famous people, including Snoop Dogg, Oprah, Eminem, Dick Vitale, Rosie, and many others. In each case, I thought of them as impersonations of celebrities and nothing more…. Looking back, many of these sketches are embarrassing, and it is frustrating that these thoughtless moments have become a weapon used by some to diminish my criticisms of social and other injustices.

I know that this will not be the last I hear of this and that it will be used again to try to quiet me…. I love this country too much to allow that…. I won't be bullied into silence by those who feign outrage to advance their oppressive and genuinely racist agendas.[121]

Actually, the woke mob is on the far left, and they're the ones pulling the Cancel Culture strings. It didn't help that Kimmel lashed out at those on the Right, without evidence, during his statement. Conservatives were hopping mad, and rightly so, at the gargantuan double standard Kimmel enjoyed, and let him have it.

Kimmel continued bashing the Right and Trump, and ignoring easy targets on the Left.

As for Fallon? He became Colbert, Jr., trashing President Donald Trump at every monologue turn. His rants became increasingly one-sided, with little comic energy left for anyone on the Democratic side.

Guess what happened next?

His ratings sank. Why? Liberals rightly viewed him as a false progressive voice. He didn't hate conservatives with the fury Colbert and Co. He was following the progressive pack, but begrudgingly so. As for viewers, his few Trump devotees drifted away, while everyone else stuck to the more authentic Colbert.

And there you have it. Two mega stars successfully forced to bend the knee.

The next time a formerly apolitical star starts sharing progressive talking points, you won't have to ask yourself why. Chances are it's just career self-preservation.

CHAPTER 6:
#OscarsSoWoke

THIS CRITIC DREADS one movie event more than any other each year: Oscar night.

How is that possible?

As a youngster I remember booing my TV screen as *Annie Hall* defeated *Star Wars* for the Best Picture Oscar. (For the record...I wuz right.)

Roughly a decade later I cheered so loudly I probably woke my neighbors when Kevin Kline accepted a statuette for playing Otto in *A Fish Called Wanda*.

> "So, the old lady's gonna m-m-m-meet with an accident, eh K-K-K-K-Ken?"

Yes, that Oscar-winning performance wouldn't pass muster today because Kline's villainous Otto mocked a stutterer. But I digress.

Back then, I loved Oscar night. And why not? The ceremony teemed with Movie Stars, the kind you could only see all dressed up together once a year. Frequent Oscar host Billy Crystal made the night fun and frivolous, turning that year's nominees into a frothy musical number. Crystal's good cheer reigned supreme, but he never nudged the solemnity of the awards off screen.

They mattered.

An Oscar win changed a star's career, at best. At worst? They achieved a feat few of their peers could match. And you could feel that excitement in every Oscar speech.

Actors can't fake that emotion. An Oscar win humbled the biggest, brightest stars. All their glamour and hubris melted away as they stood before the nation, the world, holding their new trophy aloft.

Suddenly, the biggest names in Hollywood, more glamorous than anyone I'd ever meet, were just hard-working folks who made it to the top of the mountain against insurmountable odds. Think Jack Palance doing one-armed push-ups. Tom Hanks thanking his gay teacher as part of his Best Actor speech for *Philadelphia*. The tender team behind the musical *Once* getting the premature curtain nod before they completed their acceptance speeches, something host Jon Stewart personally righted on live TV.

And, through it all, was Jack—there's only one "Jack" in Hollywood—sitting in the front row, ready to cock his signature eyebrow at a moment's notice.

Heck, I tuned in just for moments like that, Oscar moments you couldn't see anywhere else. Those moments were real, raw, and relatable.

I didn't "know" these celebrated stars. They sure seemed nice, though. They were attractive, well-coiffed, and spoke beautifully on the biggest night of their careers.

Today?

The Oscar telecast is a bloated, insufferable affair that gets worse every year. The dull, self-important showcase fails the one task it's meant to achieve: sell us on loving movies.

That's no longer part of the Oscar mission statement. The modern telecast is about virtue signaling, far-left political speeches, laugh-free monologues (assuming they have any), and rage against half the country. If you're reading this book, you know which half I'm talking about.

A few years back, Woke Hollywood killed the concept of hiring a funny comedian to host the annual event. Kevin Hart, one of Hollywood's few bankable stars, got picked to do the honors in 2018. What a perfect choice, and he confessed he'd dreamed about such a gig for years.

His euphoria lasted as long as an NFL halftime show.

Someone dug up some of Hart's past "jokes," a few of which flashed anger and disdain for gay people. They were jokes, of course, but they had a nasty bite to them. The bits in question weren't funny, but they were also a decade old and hardly captured Hart's current state of mind.

Few stars are as positive, and uplifting, as Hart is today. That didn't matter. Nor did the fact that the Oscars had previously given a statuette to an admitted child rapist, while the toast of the industry gave him a standing ovation.

You know who we mean.

The woke crowd smelled blood over HartGate, and they wanted a pop culture scalp. It helped that Hart offered a decidedly apolitical persona, avoiding partisan bickering on and off social media. The mob got its scalp in near-record time, with few comedians going to bat for him.

Since that disastrous moment, Team Oscar doesn't even bother finding a comic to host the Oscars. Why try? The gig doesn't pay handsomely. Critics roast whoever helms the event, regardless of their abilities or performance.

Even if a host goes the full woke, you know it can't be woke enough.

And any comic who agrees to the gig will go through a vetting tougher than any gumshoe detective might offer. Vice presidential nominees aren't X-rayed as thoroughly as a potential Oscar host.

"I'm sorry, Mr. Chappelle, you once poked fun at a trans celebrity. Your genius, skill, and comic legacy aren't welcome here."

Who needs that?

We do, actually. The best way to enliven a super-serious event is to let a comedian guide our path. It's what they do best, say funny things on the fly and roll with the tension-filled punches.

But the Oscar institution is no more, with former iconic hosts like Crystal (nine times) and Johnny Carson (five times) a distant memory. The shows themselves are three-plus hours of sanctimony, hard-left speeches, and jokes meant to enlighten more than entertain.

It's the Lousiest Show on Earth, and the Academy of Motion Picture Arts and Sciences doesn't have the slightest interest in changing that.

A few years back, *The New York Times* published a behind-the-scenes look at the annual show. It revealed far more than its producers likely realized. We learned how they track the show's ratings moment by moment (ain't technology grand?), which sounds both creepy and helpful. If they could see where the show was flailing, they could set about fixing it.

Or so you'd think.

Turns out the night's political speeches saw the show's ratings droop time and again. *The Times* either got a fresh source to confirm that revelation or recycled it anew in 2021, as experts feared another massive rating drop.

> Increasingly, the ceremonies are less about entertainment honors and more about progressive politics, which inevitably annoys those in the audience who disagree. One recent producer of the Oscars, who spoke on the condition of anonymity to discuss confidential metrics, said minute-by-minute post-show ratings analysis indicated that "vast swaths" of people turned off their televisions when celebrities started to opine on politics.[122]

Give credit to the *New York Times*, famously derided as "a former newspaper" by author/podcaster Andrew Klavan, for at least mentioning how progressive lectures push plenty of people away from the show.

In a sane Hollywood, that might lead producers to gently advise nominees and presenters, "ix-nay on the olitics-pay," for the sake of ratings…and Hollywood's incredibly shrinking brand. Either that speech never happens, or the stars hear it and silently mutter, "Nah, I'm good." The results are the same, though, no matter how many new producers promise an extreme Oscar broadcast makeover. Show after show plays out like a parody written by Ben Shapiro or Dennis Prager.

Then again, neither Shapiro nor Prager could have predicted that when Joaquin Phoenix won in 2020 for his bravura turn in *Joker*, he'd use his acceptance speech to say, "We feel entitled to artificially inseminate a cow and steal her baby."

Some of the telecast's problems aren't the fault of the show or the stars. The modern awards season is longer and more widely reported on than in the past. That means if a star wins, say, four Best Actress awards, prior to Oscar night chances are she'll be making room on her mantle for a fifth trophy. So much for any sense of surprise when the envelopes are ripped open.

The very nature of celebrity isn't the same as when I was a lad, either. Back then, it felt special to see Mr. Jack Nicholson lording over the event.

Today? Actors are everywhere, literally. We see them on social media, read all about their Keto-friendly diets in glossy magazines and web listicles, and hear them on any number of late-night interviews.

Some of this carpet bomb-style PR is unavoidable. The modern actor must do tons and tons of publicity to bring attention to their films in our noisy digital age. It's no longer special seeing Tom Hanks or Halle Berry on an Oscar stage. We just saw them moments ago in one platform or another. *Ho hum.*

Their personas are often less than flattering, too. Stars do plenty of damage to their own brand, one of many ways they've made Oscar night a chore. Even Sean Penn's ardent admirers, and there are many, recoil at his word salad speeches and politically incoherent ramblings.

Or take Robert De Niro, a superstar who avoided interviews for years. *GQ* magazine once wrote an entire article based on the Oscar winner's reluctance to be interviewed. Perhaps he wanted his performances to speak for him. Or, he understood the mystery he created by being less available to the press. I met him oh so briefly at a public event, and he declined my attempt to question him. I knew he would, but I gave it the ol' college try. It *is* De Niro, after all.

To be precise, it was the *old* De Niro. The new version talks to any media outlet that will shove a microphone in his face. And, as it turned out, he has little of value to share. He spent four solid years savaging President Donald Trump in terms that would make a pre-teen boy blush. The great Robert De Niro reduced himself to a caricature. Here's betting even liberal movie lovers feel little excitement when they see him today, be it on MSNBC or an Oscar podium. The thrill is gone. And, in its place, widespread public rage against a celebrity who can't stop insulting a politician many care deeply about.

Some stars retain their sense of glamour and prestige despite our woke age. Think Denzel Washington, Julie Andrews, or Angelina Jolie. However, Oscar night rarely features the best and brightest stars. Instead, we're given disposable talent and youngsters with microscopic IMDB. com credits. Perhaps the producers hope the latter "stars" will lure young viewers to the show. Yeah, your seventeen-year-old niece will sit through a three-hour snoozefest to catch a glimpse of Miley Cyrus or Post Malone.

I had the unique fortune to watch one Oscars telecast with Andrew Breitbart and the late mogul's team. Andrew cracked wise about the event, bringing a cynicism to his commentary that clashed with his Happy Warrior persona. Even he couldn't stomach the cavalcade of self-importance. That night opened my eyes to the event it truly had become, not the one I watched every year as a lad. He was right. I had been in denial far too long.

The Oscars of my youth were long gone. The modern Oscar ceremony is awful. Boring. Sanctimonious.

Somehow, the night has only gotten worse since then.

You can partially blame the #OscarsSoWhite hashtag.

The press and social media didn't think that year's Oscar nominees were diverse enough, a problem so profound our towering moral leaders, like the Reverend Al Sharpton, weighed in on the tragedy.

> We are not going to allow the Oscars to continue. This will be the last night of an all-white Oscars.

Hollywood felt a deep, stabbing pain of guilt, and for good reason. The industry had done a horrible job of including minorities and women in its ecosystem up until recently. The numbers bore it out at the time. A 2018 study by the Ralph J. Bunche Center for African American Studies at UCLA found some progress, but plenty of work remaining.

> Minorities remain underrepresented in film leads (13.9%), film directors (12.6%), film writers (8.1%), broadcast scripted leads (18.7%), cable scripted leads (20.2%), broadcast reality and other leads (26.6%) and leads for cable reality and other leads (20.9%).[123]

That study wasn't an outlier.

> The report from the University of Southern California (USC) Annenberg Inclusion Initiative, which analyzed the top 100 films each year since 2007, found that only 31.8% of characters with dialogue were women last year, roughly the same ratio that has persisted for

the last 11 years. Only four women of color were leads in 2017, and white actors were cast in 70.7% of all speaking roles.[124]

Confronted by those ghastly stats and collective guilt, the industry brought virtue signaling to the Oscars telecast. Rather than do the hard work necessary to ensure all voices are heard, it went woke, setting up diversity mandates that pushed artistic excellence to the back of the bus.

A dull show suddenly got much, much worse. Out went the stinging barbs at the industry's expense. In came jokes meant to shame Hollywood for not being inclusive enough. Little by little, the night's remaining joy drained from the telecast. And the audience fled the extravaganza slowly, surely, year after year.

Here's *Variety's* assessment following the 2020 telecast.[125]

> The 2020 Oscars ceremony was watched by the smallest audience the awards show has ever received.
>
> 23.6 million viewers tuned in on Sunday night to see *Parasite* sweep to a surprise victory. That's a 20%, 6 million viewer drop-off from last year. The Academy's second hostless show in a row scored a 5.3 rating among adults 18–49 in the fast national ratings, a 31% dip from 2019.
>
> For comparison, last year's Oscars delivered a 7.7 rating in adults 18–49 and 29.6 million viewers. That viewership figure, while up 12% from 2018, represented the second smallest audience ever for an Academy Awards telecast at the time. 2018 delivered the previous smallest viewership tally with 26.5 million viewers.

For context, the Oscars hovered between thirty and forty million viewers for eleven years—from 2001 to 2012. The 2001 awards telecast drew 42.9 million viewers who saw *Gladiator* win the night. Eleven years later, *The Artist* won while 39.3 viewers caught the black-and-white film's signature moment.[126]

The Oscars weren't alone, though. Competing awards show felt a similar slippage. The 2021 Golden Globes telecast saw its ratings plunge 62 percent from the previous year. The 2021 Screen Actors Guild (SAG) Awards sank 52 percent from the prior year. The Critics Choice Awards dropped a whopping 69 percent from 2020's numbers, and the 2021 Grammy Awards plunged 53 percent.[127]

To no one's surprise, the 2021 Oscars telecast dropped an alarming 56 percent from the previous year. Suddenly, a Super Bowl-sized event drew roughly 10 million viewers.

And, once again, for those who decided to watch, the show was a bore. The woke virtue signaling continued, but the hostless gala felt like watching paint dry, with apologies to drying paint. Presenter Regina King broke a land-speed record by politicizing the show's first minute, virtue signaling over Derek Chauvin's guilty verdict in the death of George Floyd.

National Review's Kyle Smith compared the dour telecast to *The Sorrow and the Pity*.

> It was as if it set out to deliver, in the form of a glitzy gala, all the repetitive, irksome, frustrating, embittering endlessness of 2020–21. If a single five-minute period went by without someone reminding us of something horrible, I guess I missed it. When your comedy highlight is Glenn Close's butt dance, you've got a little problem.[128]

Comedian Joe List tweeted mid event, "I can't wait for the 'In Memoriam' so we can lighten the mood a little."

Who knows how low the show's ratings will sink once the *new* woke rules go into full effect?

What rules, you ask?

In 2020 the Academy released its latest attempt to "fix" the Oscars. The new rules, which are not officially enforced until the 2024 gala, will require studios hoping to win Best Picture to meet certain criteria to be eligible for the night's biggest prize. That means making the nominees and winners more "diverse."

***

Now, a Best Picture hopeful will have to check off a number of boxes in order to start dreaming of Oscar glory. It could mean hiring a diverse set of crew members. Or touching themes that the woke rules demand to be covered.

A film following a gay man's rise to political glory? Check!

The tale of a father seeking justice for his daughter's death at the hands of an illegal immigrant? Sorry, better try the Golden Globes! What about the Best Picture simply being the best picture?

How foolish to even think such things!

Consider this snippet from a helpful *Variety* "explainer":

> *I'm producing an Oscar hopeful that Sam Mendes is directing about two British soldiers in northern France during World War I. Do I have to scrap it?*

> No, you do not. First, even if the film were to not meet the threshold, it can still be submitted to the Academy in all categories except for best picture. But "1917" is a useful illustration of how the new standards would apply. Although it might not qualify for the A category of diversity in lead roles, ensemble cast or storyline, it could easily qualify in the required two of the four categories. In the case of that 2020 nominee, it would be eligible under Standard B1 (creative leadership and department heads) and B2 (other key roles)—with only one out of the two categories required to qualify. Mendes, who is part West Indian, would qualify, along with his co-writer Krysty Wilson-Cairns. Mendes' film also has Naomi Donne as makeup department head, Rachael Tate as sound editor and Pippa Harris and Jayne-Ann Tenggren as producers.[129]

How many youngsters read those paragraphs and thought, "Man, now I wanna make movies, too!"

You might be thinking, "Well, at least if the Oscars suddenly care about disadvantaged groups, it'll make way for some conservative-themed stories or talent…right?"

Dream on! It would require another entire book to detail how conservatives are treated like second-class citizens in Hollywood, and that's being generous. Right-leaning stars cower in fear lest their voting preferences go public. It's a stain on the industry that few media outlets will accurately describe.

It's also a key reason why so many Oscar fans no longer watch the annual event. Why would you submit yourself to stars who savage your political views for three…straight…hours? The modern Oscar ceremony actively pushes conservative viewers away, and then Hollywood wonders why the night's ratings crash year after year. Some media reports, like this laughable *L.A. Times* piece, mention the matter deep within the story, but then compare the current state of affairs to one-off political speeches like Marlon Brando's virtue signal from the 1973 Oscars ceremony:

> Additionally, while there is no way to quantify the impact on viewing, networks have conducted research showing some audience members don't want to hear stars presenting their political positions on the programs.
>
> Although stars have used the Oscars as a political forum going back to the time when Marlon Brando sent a Native American activist[130] to the stage to refuse his best actor award in 1973, today's politically polarized audience has plenty of other viewing options.[131]

Yes, they do. Personally, I'd rather watch one of those insufferable "Bake-Off" competitions than the annual Oscars borefest. If the ceremony chased this life-long movie groupie away—someone who forged his career to follow every film industry nuance—imagine how many more casual viewers similarly refuse to be insulted by Hollywood's "best and brightest?"

CHAPTER 7:

Two Thumbs Down for Woke Critics

SISKEL & EBERT made it hip to bicker about movies.

The Chicago-based film critics brought their outsized opinions to TV screens beginning in 1975 and kept the act going until Gene Siskel's death in 1999. (Roger Ebert carried the TV torch until his passing in 2013.) They weren't movie-star handsome, but their passion for film made them famous.

And rightly so.

Siskel & Ebert rendered their verdicts with the now-iconic "thumbs up" or "thumbs down" decree, distilling their complex views into an easily accessible symbol. Studios craved putting "Two Thumbs Up" on their movie posters and DVD covers.

This critic always found it funny when a movie poster had a single Thumbs Up, which all but screamed the other critic hated it!

Movie criticism flowered in their wake. The Internet gave every wannabe Siskel or Ebert the chance to share their reviews with the world. And plenty did just that.

Every online critic owes a debt to the duo. I know I do.

Still, no one critic could compare to *Siskel & Ebert* in terms of fame or influence today. And, in an undated clip from their series, the pair shared a chilling warning about the future of movie criticism. (Spoiler alert: We didn't listen.)

The pair broke down an emerging cultural trend that spelled doom for their profession.

"There's a whole new world called political correctness that's going on," Siskel said. "That is death to a critic to participate in that."

"You've really put your finger on something," Ebert jumped in, but Siskel was just warming up.

"Just personally wanting to be liked, wanting to go along with the group, is death to a critic. Take your best shot," Siskel said. "I've been given this lucky break to say what I think. If I censor myself, I'm gonna regret it, I'm gonna regret it."

Ebert cautioned how aspiring writers of the era were falling victim to the growing P.C. mentality. Remember, the movie *P.C.U.*, a film mocking the rise of politically correct universities, hit theaters in 1994. (Few movies demand a remake more than that one.)

"A lot of college writers are either working for their student papers or they're writing papers that are gonna be read out loud in class," Ebert said. "Political correctness is the fascism of the '90s. It's this rigid feeling that you have to keep your ideas and your ways of looking at things within very narrow boundaries or you'll offend someone."

Anticipating the ideological conformity in the mainstream press today, he went on.

"One of the purposes of journalism is to challenge just that kind of [P.C.] thinking," Ebert said. "Certainly one of the purposes of criticism is to break boundaries. It's also one of the purposes of art.

"If a young journalist…tries to write politically correctly, what they're really doing is ventriloquism. They're not saying what they think. They're projecting their ideas into another politically correct persona and trying to pretend that persona reflects their ideas, and that's tragic."

"You're training yourself at a very young age to lie, to lie," Ebert added for emphasis.

It's like the duo took Doc Brown's time machine into the future, took furious notes, and then returned…much the wiser.

Ebert looked back at his own college days at the University of Illinois, when his school newspaper featured voices from the Left and the Right.

"Let's have a lot of opinions, and that's very important," he said, not knowing the website that carries on his reviewing tradition today lacks a single, openly conservative critic on staff. "Today, on the campus, there's such tunnel vision when it comes to political correctness that people are afraid to use terms or to have feelings that haven't been approved."

Imagine what the famous duo would think of the modern film critic. Yes, some still abide by the gig's core tenets—no spoilers, just a smart sense of whether audiences will like a particular film.

A growing number of modern critics, though, fall into the sad description shared in that undated show clip. They act as both the woke movement's advocates and their unofficial enforcement arm. They count up the number of minorities in films, attacking the production should it come up short in their estimation. They rail against stories that suggest right-of-center themes, as if such ideas shouldn't be considered in the creative process.

Some use the term "white" as a pejorative.[132] Forbes.com's far-left film scribe Scott Mendelson used the word "white" four times in the opening paragraph for his review of the 2018 political biography *Vice*.

> Yet the movie, which itself is a cinematic mediocrity that is being hailed as a potential Oscar contender partially due to its subject matter and the established pedigree of its white male filmmaker.[133]

Here's more:

> The film offers a seething indictment of who we automatically presume to be competent and worthy of leadership roles (white guys of a certain age).

TheWrap.com's liberal critic, Candice Frederick did the same for *Vice*:[134]

> If there's one thing writer-director Adam McKay's *Vice* does well, it's highlight how white mediocrity has thrived in American politics and pop culture. But McKay also does this by way of making a mediocre movie about mediocre politician Dick Cheney played by a surprisingly mediocre Christian Bale. At some point, and at some level, you wish the white mediocrity could be reined in, but it never is.

She does it again later in the review:

> And that's pretty much how a mediocre white man,
> whose own wife at one point remarks how disastrously
> unappealing he is as a public speaker, rises to power.
> The narrator of the film (Jesse Plemons, in a thankless
> role) notes that Cheney has "an ability to make his
> wildest ideas sound measured."

Other critics clearly grade feminist movies on a curve. Or they might
moan that a particular film ruined its "girl power" appeal by having a
heroic male figure.

Even if said figure is a male robot as in this review of *Terminator:
Dark Fate*.

> And it is sort of depressing in the end to find the film
> putting these badass ladies in the position of needing
> rescue from a man—even if he is an android—when
> they were doing just fine on their own, thank you
> very much.[135]

In short, they completely ignore both the *Siskel & Ebert* model, as
well as their advice regarding P.C. groupthink. And there's little sign this
will change anytime soon.

One movie review website purposely views movies through a woke
lens. MediaversityReviews.com is up front about its purpose.

> The Mediaversity grade does NOT just reflect the tech-
> nical aspects of a show or film. Cinematography, writ-
> ing, soundtrack, editing? That's what every other review
> site is for. Instead, Mediaversity examines the social con-
> text surrounding a program and grades how inclusive it
> is. In fact, something can be a critically acclaimed but
> if it isn't inclusive, it will score low at Mediaversity. And
> if that bothers you, you're probably in the wrong place.
>
> Our scoring system prioritizes intersectionality. While
> deep social impact for specific groups is crucial in the

ongoing fight for onscreen (and behind-the-lens) representation, culture blogs are already fantastic sources for
those types of discussions. Instead, Mediaversity takes
the macro view and measures how well a TV show or
film presents different and overlapping identities.[136]

That kind of transparency is both valuable and appreciated. Other
critics take the same approach without so much as a warning.

The Daily Beast's film reporter savaged Disney's 2020 hit *Soul*, a
movie luxuriating in black culture with black characters voiced by
black performers.

It wasn't enough:

> Pixar's latest film is a return to form for a company
> that has built a reputation for heartwarming stories
> with a creative twist, but these stories continue Dis-
> ney's tradition of giving Black leading bodies little
> screen time as they often morph into either an animal
> or something else inhuman. If you were looking to
> watch a very lively Gardner grooving to jazz through-
> out the film, as was suggested in various trailers and
> commercials, guess again. Expect to see a melanin-less
> soul with the voice of Foxx floating through much of
> the film instead; and if that weren't enough, Gardner's
> body is later overtaken by another soul, voiced by Tina
> Fey, while Gardner assumes the form of a cat.[137]

Remember, you can never, ever be woke enough.

Another critic complained that *Soul's* main character is briefly inhab-
ited by—gasp—a character voiced by a white actress.[138]

> And not just any woman, but Fey, who, earlier this
> year, requested that episodes of her show *30 Rock* be
> pulled from streaming because of blackface? The same
> show that still has episodes on streaming featuring
> brownface. Hearing her "trapped" in Foxx's animated
> body just felt insensitive, especially after this year.

Yes. A critic actually railed against Fey's inclusion in the film because, on an entirely different project, she wore blackface as part of a comedy narrative.

Another problem for the woke film critical community—and they have loads of problems they're eager to share—is the very nature of superhero films.

> Superheroes tend to maintain the status quo, however unjust, and villains who desire change tend to be depicted as unhinged radicals. Even if villains have a sympathetic grievance, or a strong point (*Black Panther's* Killmonger, *Spider-Man: Homecoming's* Vulture), they are always written to be violent, unhinged psychopaths—because they have to be.

> Superheroes, however admirable their character, are rarely agents of change. They tend to be comfortable with the status quo, and look down upon characters who express unhappiness with their lot in life, especially those who dare to do something about it.[139]

Thanks for nuthin', Superman!

A critic, in theory, could rattle off his or her (is that offensive?) take on a film's intersectionality scorecard while still keeping the film's principles in mind.

Is it funny? Scary? Thrilling? Well-acted? Joyful? Sad? Impactful? Entertaining?

Yet we often see the woke complaints factor into the reviews, often in a sizable fashion. One famously corrupt review gave an "F" to a movie because the story implied a pro-gun position.

Would the critic reverse that grade if the story packed a pro-gun-control message?

The 2018 movie *Kin* featured a young black male as the lead, but that clearly wasn't enough for *Entertainment Weekly*. The liberal site shredded the film via critic Chris Nashawaty, who objected to a fourteen-year-old character, the aforementioned black teen, using a space gun to defend his family from bad guys.

That's three years younger than Dylagn (sic) Klebold and Eric Harris were when they went on their killing spree at Columbine High School and six years younger than Adam Lanza was when he murdered 27 kids and teachers at Sandy Hook Elementary School in New-town, Connecticut. You can disagree with this review-er's take on Kin and what it's saying both explicitly and implicitly about guns. But I can't and won't recom-mend it in good conscience.

He doubled down on Twitter:[140]

If you think a movie with a 14 year old with a giant gun sounds cool, you'll love 'KIN'. Also, you're insane. My first 'F' review in some time.

Just remember. If your family is in jeopardy, do not pick up any weapon that might save them, especially a shiny space object. Let them die in peace.

Dear Chris: Is it a good film? Will we be entertained? Does the story move along, or is it plodding? Are the performances worthwhile? Do we care about the main characters?

What if we don't hold the same rigid, nay, maniacal, anti-gun beliefs you do? Do we still count? Are we insane for enjoying the film—or is that a wee bit of projection?

None of that matters to this social justice scold, or to countless oth-ers like him. And, in his political crusade, he ignores what a film critic should do: advise readers whether a film is engaging enough to spend ninety-odd minutes watching it.

Heaven help a film that espouses a pro-life or openly conservative spirit. The makers of *Roe v. Wade* knew film critics wouldn't be kind to their film. Still, consider the following review of the movie and see if the critic is going over the top:

Roe v. Wade is not just sure to be the worst film of 2021, it's among the worst films of the past several years. Barely a movie, it's not even particularly coherent as conservative propaganda. Without question, it fails on every single level. Cinema is tangibly worse for its existence. If I see something worse this year, I'll truly be despondent about the state of the industry. For now, let's just pretend this never existed. You certainly never have to see it. Consider this my service to you all. I saw it so you don't have to.[141]

To be fair, this critic found *Roe v. Wade* wanting, too, although I wouldn't have pulled a muscle slamming it like that critic did.

What about a better film, one that's an unabashed B-movie, but told with verve and humor?

Run Hide Fight dared to depict a teen fighting back after a team of school shooters enters the building. The movie offered a strong, empowered lead (Isabel May), crisp action beats, and very little messaging. You can see a glimpse or two of it, that's all.

So how did critics react to the movie? Hold on.

> [Thomas Jane] didn't survive three biogenetically enhanced backwards-swimming super sharks so that he could live to help sell the "good guy with a gun" fallacy from Redbox kiosks in red state gas stations....

> Rankin is uninterested in gun fetishism, white nationalism, YouTube radicalism, or any of the other clear and present dangers that dangle over America's classrooms like a scythe—and he sure as hell isn't interested in starting "a conversation." If the willful obliviousness of his movie's relationship to the real world implicitly aligns it with Republican ideology, Rankin's only legible goal is to imagine what John McClane's daughter might do if some pubescent terrorists took over her school.[142]

One quip from the comments section of the site was worth repeating:

> Nice to see you didn't let your political biases cloud your review....

The Hollywood Reporter noted the movie was "slick and compulsively watchable." So that's a Thumbs Up in the grand Siskel/Ebert tradition, right?

Not quite.

> [Director Kyle] Rankin (*The Battle of Shaker Heights*) knows his way around efficient thriller construction, getting capable assists from Darin Moran's prowling camera, Matthew Lorentz's nervy editing and the ominous score by composing duo Mondo Boys, which includes a moody cover of the '60s protest song "Eve of Destruction" on the end credits.

> But a numb detachment takes hold as you realize sensationalism is being flimsily packaged as social commentary on the kind of scenario that has caused America immeasurable suffering. What's next, a pulse-pounding action thriller about a fierce transgender warrior thwarting a deadly assault on a gay nightclub in Florida? Please, no.[143]

Woke film critics get to say what subjects are appropriate for filmmaking, and what ones aren't.

Perhaps the funniest part of this exhausting trend is reading feedback from readers who have had enough of this trope. Here's a few comments attached to the *Kin* review mentioned above.

- I've had my fill of these type of reviews. I have plenty of places to go to talk about the need for better gun control measures. Does the character actually go on some crazed killing spree? No? Then why even bring up Columbine?

- I know! What is a fact? Millions of teens use guns every year hunting with friends and family or at ranges.

- What a joke of a review. I think this guy just watched the trailer and used it as a soapbox to spout his anti-gun rhetoric. Hopefully *EW* will take this nonsense down and replace it with a reviewer that actually reviews the movie.

These outlets don't care, of course. Indiewire.com, a far-left film and TV site, routinely uncorks uber-woke think pieces that get shredded in the comments section. And they only double down.

It's like starting a business, realizing customers hate your product, and shouting to the assembly line, "Keep 'em coming!"

Critics should be on the front lines of the current free speech fight. Instead, they're often cheering for the wrong side. That was never truer than when *No Safe Spaces* hit theaters at the end of 2019. The docudrama couldn't be more prescient about how the anti-speech forces on college campuses would, sooner or later, leak into society at large.

The film wasn't dogmatic or partisan, just eager to protect our right to think and speak freely. That triggered more than a few film critics.

Common Sense Media uncorked this doozy of an argument against the film.[144]

> The crux of *No Safe Spaces'* logical hole is that although Carolla and Prager work really hard to convince us that curtailing free speech is tantamount to fascism, they're making their points on a stage, to an audience, with microphones—freely. If free speech is truly in such terrible danger, where are the protestors and police to stop this not-so-dynamic duo?

Actually, protesters very often do just that. Just ask Ben Shapiro and many others like him.

The far-left AV Club, the entertainment hub of the far-left *Onion* satirical site, savaged the film for daring to defend free speech.[145]

Really.

> With regards to colleges, the protest is that students are supposed to be intellectually challenged by ideas, objectionable and otherwise, they'd otherwise never

encounter. Given that this stuff is everywhere, it's a weak argument—the marketplace of ideas is sorting itself out, just not in the direction Prager and Carolla would like.

Woke critics also cover the TV landscape with predictable results. Probably the best example came courtesy of Dave Chappelle. He's arguably the most influential, well-respected comedian of our age, and rightly so. Yet when he delivered *Sticks and Stones* to Netflix in 2019, critics recoiled at the content.

Why?

Chappelle savaged the woke mob, made us reconsider our opinions on issues that we often do little self-examination over, and otherwise zigged while nearly every one of his peers zagged.

RottenTomatoes.com tallied the "professional" critics on the special, an anemic 35 percent "rotten." The general audience, meanwhile, gave the very same content a 99 percent "Fresh" rating.

The specific reviews couldn't be more revelatory.

> *The Atlantic*—*Sticks and Stones* registers as a temper tantrum, the product of a man who wants it all—money, fame, influence—without much having to answer to anyone.

> *Vanity Fair*—Ultimately, though, it feels like stale work from a comedian who was once known for truly boundary-pushing comedy—the kind that actually understood nuance, particularly where famous and powerful men were concerned.

Stale? Telling an anti-Trump joke when every single one of your peers does that is the epitome of stale. Critics can loathe Chappelle's special if they deem it so, but let's traffic in the realm of reality. Please.

Sebastian Maniscalco, an absurdly gifted comic who recently moved into character work on the big screen, isn't the provocateur like Chappelle. Yet when he did what any MTV freelancer should do, make us uncomfortable, woke critics wouldn't have it.

Maniscalco hosted the 2019 MTV Video Music Awards and took a few light-hearted shots at the millennials who allegedly make up the channel's demographic.

> The 2018 VMAs didn't have a host, and ten minutes into the 2019 VMAs, fans were wishing this year's show didn't either.
>
> Comedian Sebastian Maniscalco—already the host who launched a thousand SEO-optimized "Who is...?" posts—opened the show with a series of jokes punching directly down at the crowd in front of him, and not in a particularly clever way.[146]

The hard news site dredged up a series of tweets, because that's how journalism rolls today, to back up their critique.

The saddest part of it all?

Who knows if Siskel and/or Ebert would be brave enough to repeat their '90s lecture on woke film criticism...or if they would have given two thumbs up to the mob?

CHAPTER 8:

Believe All, Most, or a Fair Percentage of Women

THE PRECIPITOUS FALL of producer/predator Harvey Weinstein led to something unabashedly good from *La La Land*...for a *New York Minute*.

The #MeToo movement.

Weinstein's downfall allowed the culture at large to reconsider other famous men and their behavior toward women. In a matter of months, stars like Matt Lauer, Charlie Rose, Brett Ratner, Kevin Spacey, Senator Al Franken, Danny Masterson, Dustin Hoffman, and others found themselves accused of a variety of sexual improprieties.

Some of the more recognizable names lost their careers in a flash, like Spacey and Lauer. Director Ridley Scott literally erased Spacey from his 2018 film, *All the Money in the World*, replacing him with Christopher Plummer. That iconic star snagged an Oscar nomination for his troubles.

Others, like Hoffman, found decades of steady work suddenly dry up.

The #MeToo movement spread far beyond Hollywood, of course, as it well should. Men abuse their power across the culture, be it in a muffler shop or the set of a blockbuster Hollywood film.

Still, Tinseltown helped lead the debate, a conversation that was long overdue. Stars leveraged their social media accounts, celebrity cachet, and other platforms to spread the word that enough is enough.

Hooray for Hollywood...right?

Something felt wrong about the movement from its earliest days, even if few could safely express the reasons why out loud. A man could be accused of wrongdoing in this new climate and be found guilty in both the court of public opinion and every studio in Hollywood.

No judge. No jury. Just a career execution. Simply expressing an un-approved viewpoint could lead to a virtual shaming session.

Consider what happened to liberal actor Matt Damon. The Oscar winner weighed in on the movement, offering comments as obvious, and benign, as possible. Here's what he said:

> "I think it's wonderful that women are feeling empow-ered to tell their stories, and it's totally necessary," Da-mon said in an interview on ABC's *Popcorn with Peter Travers*.[147]

> "I do believe there's a spectrum of behavior. There's a difference between patting someone on the butt and rape or child molestation, right? Both of those behav-iors need to be confronted and eradicated without question, but they shouldn't be conflated," he said.

> "When you see Al Franken taking a picture putting his hands on that woman's flak jacket and mugging for the camera…that is just like a terrible joke, and it's not funny. It's wrong, and he shouldn't have done that," Damon said. "But when you talk about Harvey and what he's accused of, there are no pictures of that. He knew he was up to no good. There's no witness-es. There's no pictures. There's no braggadocio. That stuff happened secretly, because it was criminal and he knew it. So they don't belong in the same category."[148]

The reaction was fast, furious, and utterly unhinged. The argument crashed headfirst into the feelings-not-facts crowd, and Damon got the worst news cycle of his overwhelmingly positive career.

So, Damon did what any red-blooded male would do when con-fronted with a deeply false narrative.

Just kidding! He buckled.

"A lot of those women are my dear friends and I love them and respect them and support what they're doing and want to be a part of that change…. But I should get in the back seat and close my mouth for a while."

In a way, that's the perfect summation of the woke mentality. Shut up. You're not allowed to have an opinion unless it mirrors ours. Perfectly. Syllable for syllable. And try rhyming. It wouldn't kill you.

The great Jim Treacher at PJ Media shared this context on Damon's "hostage"-style apology, made on an NBC program.

Keep in mind that Damon is begging for women's forgiveness in the very same building where, up until two months ago, Matt Lauer had an office with a secret button to lock women inside so he could attack them. And somehow, none of Lauer's co-workers knew anything about it? Yeah, right. Maybe the *Today* show isn't the best venue for Matt Damon's struggle session on sexual assault.[149]

Vox, the far-left outlet which feels the need to "explain" everything to its readers, shouted, "Why Won't Matt Damon Stop Talking?" in its headline.

Vulture piled on: "Matt Damon Just Shared All His Bad Opinions on Sexual Misconduct."

Even his former co-stars got into the act. *Good Will Hunting* star Minnie Driver cried foul. She told the UK *Guardian* that men "simply cannot understand what abuse is like on a daily level." That meant they cannot differentiate the various levels of abuse?

Gosh it's so interesting (profoundly unsurprising) how men with all these opinions about women's differentiation between sexual misconduct, assault and rape reveal themselves to be utterly tone deaf and as a result, systemically part of the problem.[150]

Here's a quick thought experiment. Your daughter just told you she suffered a sexual assault. Would you rather learn she was gang raped…or that someone gave her bottom a long, disgusting squeeze?

It's ironic that Bill Maher attempted a similar framing on his *Real Time with Bill Maher* show on March 5, 2021. The host and guest Charlamagne the God argued over the sexual allegations lobbed at Governor Andrew Cuomo.

> "It's kinda hard to ask Cuomo to resign when you voted for Joe Biden. If you weren't more upset with Joe Biden, who had more serious allegations," Charlamagne said.

> Maher interjected saying he was unaware of any more serious allegations against Biden. When Charlamagne reminded Maher about Tara Reade—who accused Joe Biden of sexual assault while she was an employee in his Senate office—the host dismissed the allegation.[151]

> "Well, I don't believe that," he said.[152]

This exchange, however, caused no Damon-sized blowback. The Women's March didn't hold an emergency session. Amy Schumer failed to weigh in on the matter via her all-powerful Instagram page.

After all, we previously learned the "Believe All Women" card could only be played against politically *select* targets.

Other stars found their careers put on hold by that early #MeToo momentum but managed to scrape back a semblance of their good names.

That's the fate that initially befell Chris Hardwick, a comedian who created his own geek empire with his Nerdist website. Hardwick's rise to fame seemed improbable and a real-life example of *Revenge of the Nerds*. He was the pudgy guy who drank too much and worked out too little, who finally had enough. He straightened up his act and became a digital age mogul.

None of that could protect him from what happened at the peak of his career. An ex-girlfriend, Chloe Dykstra, unleashed on Hardwick, and suddenly his lucrative gigs disappeared. Slowly, Hardwick's career came back from the dead as an investigation cleared his name, or at least it indicated Dykstra's story wasn't strong enough to officially erase Hardwick's career.[153]

Still, the mere accusation could stall, if not permanently damage, a star's livelihood. That's dangerous territory, an ecosystem ripe for misuse. Comedian Norm Macdonald said just that.

> "The model used to be: admit wrongdoing, show complete contrition and then we give you a second chance. Now it's admit wrongdoing and you're finished," Macdonald told the trade publication, later adding: "I do think that at some point it will end with a completely innocent person of prominence sticking a gun in his head and ending it."[154]

Guess what happened next? Macdonald apologized, of course.

Something else came up, though, that far eclipsed that fear in the eyes of conservatives.

What if the #MeToo movement, powered by starlets like Amy Schumer, Chelsea Handler, and others, looked the other way depending on a person's political party? Why, that would be a death blow to the cause, no? People would quickly see the partisan nature of the movement, permanently staining all the good it originally brought about.

Yes, and no.

The movement savaged candidate Donald Trump, for example, after several women shared stories of the real estate mogul sexually accosting them.

#MeToo's Hollywood division screamed in rage, demanding he be held accountable. That screaming continued for four straight years. That also sparked the Women's March, an annual event with its own troubled history.

The same Hollywood crowd grew even louder when President Donald Trump nominated Brett Kavanaugh to the highest court in the land. During the contentious nomination process, a woman named Christine Blasey Ford said Kavanaugh had attempted to rape her when they were both teenagers.

She couldn't share the date, time, or place of the incident. She had no corroborating witnesses. Her story sounded frightening and real, but it lacked the kind of details that would make it credible. The more you looked at her tale, the less plausible it became. And that was before *The Federalist* compiled a damning list of twenty-one reasons not to trust her story.[155] Number five is a doozy: "Ford's Father Supported Kavanaugh's Confirmation."

Yet Hollywood's #MeToo contingent rushed into battle, spending week after week savaging Kavanaugh in the nastiest ways possible. Amy Schumer purposefully got arrested protesting Kavanaugh, to show she meant business.

She was far from alone. Hollywood stars and starlets raged against Kavanaugh, ignoring decades of glowing notices and testimonials, for one of the flimsiest charges ever shared in the public arena.

Ron Perlman signaled his feminist commitments by sharing these reflections on the future Justice and how his Catholicism compared to Sharia Law.

> The move back to Medieval Values, Shariah Law even, where old, bitter men get to tell women what is best for their bodies, lives, and well being is as done a deal as this is Twitter. Unless we say NO! NO![156,157]

None other than Matt Damon, still smarting over his shaming on abuse issues, played a cartoonish guilty version of Kavanaugh on *Saturday Night Live*. He might have performed that sketch regardless, but don't tell me the verbal beatdown he suffered at the start of #MeToo mania didn't influence his decision.

The reaction to Kavanaugh's 50–48 confirmation vote was just as hyperbolic.

> "I've been on a plane all morning. Just landed. Trying to make it home. Feel like I want to scream. And rage. And cry," Ava DuVernay tweeted.[158]

> "Another gross day in the history of our country, but the midterms are coming. We are stronger than this bulls—. We can fight and fight and we may not see the results right away, but we will see them. Our daughters

will see them. Don't give up. Fight harder," Chelsea Handler, 43, tweeted.[159]

Obscure actress Sophia Bush of *One Tree Hill*, but better known of late for ladling hate on conservatives, shared this gentle thought after Kavanaugh's confirmation:

> "My sternum feels like it's going to crack in half," she added. "I'm holding friends and loved ones close today. And tomorrow, I'm ready to #RAGE."

Yet a few years later that same movement fell silent when former Vice President Joe Biden's lengthy history of making women uncomfortable resurfaced in the worst way possible. You could hear a pin drop. Amy Schumer didn't even get re-arrested!

Protest marches mysteriously vanished once Biden took the oath of office. Never mind all the women Biden sniffed, or far worse. The patriarchy had apparently toppled…just like that.

Former Biden staffer Tara Reade told a detailed story of how then-Senator Biden digitally assaulted her, and she had far more to back up her claim than did Ford. Several friends recalled Reade telling them that story at the time. Her mother appeared on CNN's Larry King talk show and described a very similar incident involving her daughter.

The media, well into its transformation into an adjunct of the Democratic Party, ignored the story for weeks upon weeks while it raged, yes, raged, across social media. It was shocking to see, even for those who understood just how deeply biased most reporters are.

Their silence was matched by that of Hollywood's #MeToo movement. Its signature line, "Believe All Women," suddenly acquired an asterisk. The far-left Deadline.com gave actress-turned-activist Alyssa Milano editorial space to try to explain her inexplicable double standards, which she did in stupefying fashion:

> Believing women was never about "Believe all women no matter what they say," it was about changing the culture of NOT believing women by default.[160]

Pretty sneaky, eh? At least she addressed the matter head on. Other stars fell silent, realizing that to do anything more would jeopardize their party's chances of defeating President Donald Trump.

Western Journal did us all a service when it tallied up the number of celebrities who railed against the Kavanaugh nomination and fell silent after Reade's allegations went public. Nearly one hundred, by the website's final tally.[161]

The #MeToo movement unofficially ended with the Biden/Reade affair, even if no one posted an obituary or otherwise marked the occasion. Clear-eyed people saw right through Hollywood's faux outrage and realized the movement was a political creation. We had our hunches about it, but the end still felt like a shame. The media, of course, admits nothing of the kind.

It's hardly the only time Hollywood's #MeToo contingent fell silent after a Democrat faced charges of sexual abuse. Virginia Lieutenant Governor Justin Fairfax got accused by not one but two women of sexual assault, and all of a sudden, the Schumers of Hollywood lost their voices.

Silence isn't violence, but it sure is damning.

That's also true for Time's Up, the nonprofit established in the #MeToo movement's wake. The organization, replete with celebrity supporters like Eva Longoria and Ashley Judd, vowed to cut big checks for women to fight back against their accusers.

Again, a noble impulse, given societal woes that didn't fade to black following Weinstein's defeat.

Need more #MeToo fails? Let's revisit New York Governor Andrew Cuomo, who celebrated his victory over COVID-19 in 2020 by writing a book about what an amazing leader he is. And by "victory," we mean overseeing one of the country's largest death tolls from the virus.

Cuomo was a fraud, a blowhard, someone playing the anti-Trump card to distract the media from his transgressions. And it worked.

The media and Hollywood competed to see who could fete him more enthusiastically. They even coined a new term for participants in the contest: "Cuomosexuals." Everyone from Chelsea Handler to Ben Stiller lifted hosannas his way. The erstwhile King of All Media, Howard Stern, similarly sucked up to Governor Cuomo. As a former Stern fanatic, that turn of events hit me hard.

The house of Cuomo soon came a tumbling down as the media couldn't hold back the truth forever. Still, a more insidious part of Cuomo's reign of error directly impacted Hollywood's #MeToo contingent.

Woman after woman after woman came forward to allege the governor sexually harassed them. This wasn't rape or sexual assault, just a man in power abusing it by making the women in his inner circle feel like meat.

Truly, totally awful.

And guess which Hollywood sub-group once more stayed silent on the matter?

Yes, the Hollywood #MeToo movement. Once again it became completely clear what the problem was: wrong political party. Someone should have told that to the women Cuomo allegedly harassed.

The Time's Up Campaign did step up to demand answers about the Cuomo accusations, but briefly at first—and then its voice faded into nothingness. It burned many more calories attacking the Golden Globes for not having any black members in its elitist club.

We later learned Team Time's Up coached Cuomo on the scandal, going so far as to help him discredit one of his accusers. This reporter asked eight celebrities, all of whom served on one of two Time's Up boards, for their reaction to this news and other disturbing accusations against Time's Up.

No response.

Time's Up all but imploded in September of 2021, with most celebrity board members resigning in protest.[162]

None of this legacy of hypocrisy would be complete without sharing how the media enabled it all.

If a celebrity uttered a joke a decade ago that no longer fits with the modern comedy landscape, you'll see dozens of news articles excoriating them and demanding an Apology Tour™.

If a group like #MeToo fails to raise its voice when the perpetrator is a Democrat, those same journalists suddenly forget the passwords to their laptops.

It's that simple.

***

To be fair, one actress with a personal stake in Weinstein's downfall stayed true to herself, the movement, and #MeToo's prime directive.

Rose McGowan.

The *Charmed* veteran accused Weinstein of raping her in 1997, and she served as one of the key voices that drove him from public life.

Later, as starlet after starlet undermined the #MeToo movement with their silence, McGowan refused to back down or mute her anger based on the political party in question.

> "It's all bulls–t.... It's a lie. It's a Band-Aid lie to make them feel better.

> "I know these people, I know they're lily-livered, and as long as it looks good on the surface, to them, that's enough." She added, "They're not champions. I just think they're losers."[163]

McGowan added it was "literally impossible" that Hollywood royalty like Meryl Streep were unaware of Weinstein's sexual antics. She even sided with Trump fans on one issue. Hollywood hypocrisy.

> "They hate Hollywood for being faux liberals—and they're 100 percent right about that," she explained. "It's a bunch of faux liberals. It's crap, and they know it is deep down, but they're living an empty life, and to me that's their punishment. They get to live the lives they live."

And so, years after Weinstein's fall from Hollywood's highest perch, the movement that helped topple him is one big, fat joke, but hardly the har-har kind.

CHAPTER 9:

The Ballad of Gina Carano

HOLLYWOOD IS ALL ABOUT female empowerment, when it's not telling actresses to lose weight and get Botox, or ignoring starlets on the "wrong" side of forty.

Yes, the industry's woke revolution is making sure all the sexism and inequality baked into the movie-making cake is replaced by strong, independent women and boundless opportunities.

Hollywood's Future is Female…to a point.

The saga of Gina Carano, groundbreaking MMA fighter and all-around "sweetheart," according to her *Mandalorian* co-star Bill Burr, will be written about for years to come. Or at least it should be.

Carano's rise to Hollywood glory could yield its own blockbuster biopic. Daughter of Dallas Cowboys quarterback Glenn Carano, she excelled at multiple sports before becoming an MMA fighter.

Her professional career wasn't long, but she amassed an impressive 7-1 record and became the first women to headline a major MMA event. Her beauty, bravery, and fighting skills helped the sport in ways that would make professional victim/soccer star Megan Rapinoe green with envy.

Glass ceiling, crashed into a thousand tiny shards.

That's when Hollywood came calling. Oscar-winning director Steven Soderbergh (*Traffic*) spotted her last fight, in which she lost to a competitor nicknamed Cris Cyborg (gulp), and she left an impression on him.

He offered to make an action movie around her, an offer any sane soul wouldn't refuse.

The 2011 movie *Haywire* gave Carano her big Hollywood break and proved she could hold the screen with the likes of Ewan McGregor and Michael Fassbender. Plus, she brought an authenticity to her action scenes, something other actresses couldn't match. How many times can we watch a 120-pound starlet take down thugs double, nay triple, her size in convincing fashion?

Or, as Soderbergh himself said at the time, "It's so satisfying watching her beat the s*** out of the cast."

An action star was born.

San Diego Entertainer Magazine's Nathalia Aryani dubbed the "strong, sexy" Carano just that in her review.[164]

> Carano looks natural for a first-timer and this is the ideal vehicle for her. Her scenes do not require in-depth acting and she's at her best during the physical ones. She brings certain credibility to the fighting scenes. Her running, leaping, kicking, punching, choking, shooting look real. She goes toe-to-toe with the guys and really does look like she's capable of doing these things. The fact that she also falls and doesn't spring back up adds a sense of realism. No special effects, just old-fashioned, hard and brutal hand-to-hand combat shot in close range.[165]

Carano worked steadily following *Haywire*, an up-and-down career that seemed on the verge of a straight-to-video future at times. For every plumb gig like *Deadpool* and *Fast & Furious 6* there were blink-and-you-miss-'em titles like *Madness in the Method* and *Scorched Earth*.

Then Team Disney came calling.

Lucasfilm sent her to "a galaxy far, far away" to co-star in 2019's *The Mandalorian*. The Disney+ series came along at the perfect time. The *Star Wars* brand had been brought down, in part, by a woke storytelling turn.

The 2017 film *The Last Jedi* stopped the narrative cold, mid-movie, to trot out a class-inequality subplot that went nowhere. Conservative critics dubbed new heroes like Rey (Daisy Ridley) and Rose Tico (Kelly Marie Tran) Mary Sues, perfect characters with little edge or flaws.

Neither could compare to Carrie Fisher's Princess Leia, a beloved figure universally embraced over the past forty years.

That, and a new trilogy that lacked the magic and splendor of the original *Star Wars* films left the saga on cultural dry dock.

The Mandalorian brought George Lucas's baby back to life, with an assist from Carano. She played Cara Dune, a take-no-prisoners type who quickly became a fan favorite.

The Mary Sue—the unofficial, online woke bible—couldn't praise her performance in the series enough. Here's just one fawning example:

> Seeing Carano take on Cara Dune wasn't just about seeing a woman in *Star Wars*. We've had that, and we've had it since the beginning, but it's refreshing seeing Carano bring this new strength to the screen where it isn't about being imposing, but rather just that she's a woman who is strong and powerful, but that doesn't have to be everything that defines her.[166]

Disney even talked about a possible Cara Dune spin-off series, the ultimate compliment, until some of Carano's social media messages went viral.

The woke mob rushed to grab its pitchforks.

Carano shared tweets that questioned the pandemic lockdowns and mask mania. She also pleaded for more voter security, arguing the public would have a greater trust in the electoral process if safeguards like Voter ID were employed.

Insane. Crazed. Out of control. Or, to a sober-eyed observer, reasonable arguments that put her gently to the right of center.

The crooked media quickly went to work, bending her social media musings to fit its agenda. That means a tweet asking for better election security was akin to saying President Trump crushed Joe Biden before the Democrats stole the election.

> *Truth Trailer:* A great way to spot media bias is to see how often reporters don't cite the material in question.

> If a star like Carano tweets something beyond the
> pale, they'd better quote from it exactly. If they don't,
> chances are the paraphrasing is meant to distort the
> actual meaning.

Worst of all, she poked back at those demanding we all add our personal pronouns to our Twitter bios. Carano did as told, except her pronouns read, "Beep/bop/boop."

Brilliant.

She explained her comments with this thoroughly rational message, one Dr. Jordan Peterson would heartily approve.

> Beep/bop/boop has zero to do with mocking trans
> people & to do with exposing the bullying mentali-
> ty of the mob that has taken over the voices of many
> genuine causes.

She later expounded on the move during her *Sunday Special* interview with *The Daily Wire*'s Ben Shapiro.

"It was one hundred percent to go to the Twitter mob that was telling me what to do, and it had zero to do with trying to go after the transgender community. I would never do that…. I'm not trying to target anybody or go after anybody."

She didn't bow to the woke gangsters. Instead, she oh, so gently told them to take a hike.

A publicist insisted she put out an apology, but she did it her way.

"Can I just do my own research?" she told them.

That wasn't good enough.

"I don't have any hate in my heart for anyone…. I stepped on a land mine," she told Shapiro.

Meanwhile, Lucasfilm employees were savaging Carano on social media without repercussions. The company wanted her to go on a Zoom call with forty-odd colleagues, some of the same folks saying awful things about her on Twitter.

She refused.

"I think it's a bit abusive that you want me to talk to forty people… forty people…a lot of them had been [slandering me]. I don't feel like I really deserve this."

Remember, Hollywood is all about female empowerment!

The media took it from there, amplifying any and every #FireGinaCarano hashtag campaign they could find. Each time, Carano's tweets got twisted, distorted, and/or altered to make her sound like a sarlacc. (See what I did there?)

Hacky movie blogs feasted on anything tied to Carano, hoping to generate clicks and a possible pink slip from Disney. Other allegedly more mature sites, like the far-left *Men's Health*, piled on as well.[167]

> Slowly but surely, the ever-expanding Star Wars universe has started to resemble the diversity of its fans. Viewers who aren't straight, white men can see themselves reflected in a growing roster of inclusive characters. Unfortunately, that can be a fraught process, as Star Wars die-hards are finding with the case of Gina Carano and *The Mandalorian*.

Just make sure that "diversity resemblance" doesn't include half the country.

Most stars would have handed their social media accounts over to their publicists to avoid future problems. Others would hit the "delete" button or even quit Twitter in the grand Alec Baldwin fashion. Or, they would have done some serious virtue signaling to repair the "damage."

Black Lives Matter! Men can have babies! Trump is Hitler! The options are endless, and each one could have spared the actress from further digital grief.

Not Carano.

She said,

> My whole perspective on this is, I've seen people get bullied off of Twitter on both sides. I don't like bullying, and if I don't stay present, which I don't even necessarily want to stay present that often, I want to make art, art is my passion, but if I don't stay present then other people win.[168]

For the record, that's the sound of an empowered woman speaking.

From that perspective alone she should have earned Feminist Nation's grudging approval. That's not how it works, of course. She wasn't a feminist role model, much like Candace Owens isn't actually black-black to the hard-Left mob.

So, when Carano sent out an Instagram post comparing how Germans treated Jews in public during the 1940s to a growing mistreatment here in the states, Disney had the cudgel it needed to crush her *Star Wars* career.

Here's her actual verbiage:

> Jews were beaten in the streets, not by Nazi soldiers but by their neighbors.... Even by children. Because history is edited, most people today don't realize that to get to the point where Nazi soldiers could easily round up thousands of Jews, the government first made their own neighbors hate them simply for being Jews.

Yes, after four solid years of liberals calling both President Donald Trump *and* his fans Nazis, this proved too much for Disney.

Let's remember how Sarah Silverman stomped onto Conan O'Brien's TBS show stage dressed as Der Fuhrer prior to the 2016 presidential election. No outrage. No cancellations.

It gets worse.

Did it matter that fellow *Mandalorian* star Pedro Pascal played the Nazi card on his social media account, but in an angrier fashion that insulted nearly half the country? Just spit-balling here, but you think there's a good chance that half might want to pay a monthly fee just to watch *The Mandalorian*?

The Mouse House called Carano's comments "abhorrent" weeks after we learned how the company kissed up to China for letting it shoot portions of the live-action *Mulan* near the Uyghur Muslim concentration camps.

You literally cannot make this up, but it's par for the gaslighting course in today's culture.

And, of course, the media took Disney's side and couldn't wait to escort Carano out of Hollywood. Even more female empowerment!

It wasn't enough to fire Carano from arguably the most popular TV show in the galaxy. Disney temporarily erased her appearance on the Discovery Channel's *Running Wild with Bear Grylls*, taped prior to her *Mandalorian* dismissal. Disney would neither confirm nor deny the move, but a listing of the show's upcoming season showed her name missing from new episodes. Corporate cowardice run amok.

Cooler heads prevailed, and the Carano episode eventually aired.

The erasing didn't end there. The toy manufacturer Funko stopped producing their Pop! Vinyl figure based on Cara Dune. Hasbro, in turn, ended its Black Series and Vintage Collection toys fashioned after Carano's character.

Disney, toy manufacturers, and the corrupt mainstream media did all they could to "un-person" Carano, and they would have gotten away with it, too, if it weren't for those rascally kids at *The Daily Wire*.

Mere days after Carano's termination, she teamed with the conservative news empire co-founded by Ben Shapiro, bringing her career back from the grave. Carano would produce and star in a new movie for the website, part of its efforts to build an alternative Hollywood where empowered women could speak their minds *and* stay employed. Shapiro, the man so many liberals want banned from college campuses nationwide, did more for true feminism than any other public figure.

Who didn't come to Carano's rescue during the debacle?

Certainly not her cast mates. They'd initially praised her after she caused some initial ruffles on social media. Here's Carano showering love on co-star Ming Na Wen via Twitter months before Disney canned her:

> I just adore this woman. you can feel her heart exploding with happiness. SO deserving! Shining bright over there @MingNa I'm geekin out for you too

The response from Wen?

> I love love love you, girlfriend!!! Thank you for geeking out with me! I'm so happy @themandalorian not only got me into @starwars, but also bringing you into my life. Let's keep kicking butt!![169]

Once the Mouse House laid down the hammer, though, Wen and Co. fell silent. Dan Rather's famous "courage" sign-off took a knee in response.[170]

The Mandalorian co-star Bill Burr clearly wanted to speak out about Carano's mistreatment. He's been very vocal about Cancel Culture and the vicious nature of the woke mob. His 2019 Netflix stand-up special, *Paper Tiger*, excoriated Cancel Culture.

Feminism: "Feminists are not as smart as they're coming off, I'm telling you."

The "Believe All Women" #MeToo standard: "That's a little open-ended, huh?" he said. "What about the psychos?"

"It's exciting to be doing stand-up outside of my own country.... Every f***ing joke you tell, 'Well what did you mean by that? I didn't go the gym today, are you calling me fat?'"

"'I feel f***ing triggered,'" he whined, in character.

Burr segued into addressing the heat Bryan Cranston faced for playing a disabled man in *The Upside*.

"'Why is there an able-bodied person playing a quadriplegic?'" Burr cried, using a beta-male tone not unlike the one Rush Limbaugh uses to mock the far left. "It's called acting, you dumb f***."

"Why didn't you have a murderer play a murderer? And how come the guy he shot showed up in another movie? What the f*** is going on?" he continued.[171]

Still, as a comedian straddling the line between stand-up clubs and sound stages, he understood how quickly he could be canceled next.

So, he probably wasn't happy when his podcast partners brought up Carano during an episode of *The Bill Bert Podcast*, which he records with fellow comedian Bert Kreischer. Burr wasn't fully open about the situation, but he captured both Cancel Culture and how the stacked deck against those who waver from liberal groupthink.

> "She was an absolute sweetheart. Super-nice f***ing person...and you know, whatever, somehow someone will take this video and they'll f***ing make me say something else and try to get rid of my bald action figure!"

"Unless you did some truly horrible s***, you know…
if you're saying overtly racist s***, yeah," Burr said,
opining more broadly on the empty concept of cancel
culture. "If you make a bad comparison…"[172]

Who else didn't come to Carano's rescue? The Women's March. The
National Organization for Women (NOW). Chelsea Handler. Sarah Silverman. Amy Schumer. Piper Perabo. Scarlett Johansson. And, by this
reporter's calculations, groups dedicated to empowering women in film
and TV.

At HollywoodInToto.com, I reached out to five such organizations
for their thoughts on Carano's dismissal. It's a journalistic trick I often
employ at the website, reaching out to special interest groups that I know,
beyond a shadow of a doubt, won't so much as respond to my inquiries.

Why? The victims in play embrace the "wrong" ideology. They're
conservatives.

So why bother? I'm partial to displaying their hypocrisy for all to see.

Note: Gay rights groups went silent when liberal comedian Jimmy
Kimmel used homophobic slurs against conservatives, this time Sean
Hannity and President Donald Trump.[173] Sure, a few random Twitter us-
ers called Kimmel out, but where were GLAAD and like-minded groups?

Here are the female-centric film groups who couldn't bother to respond to my query concerning Carano:

- Women and Hollywood

- Women in Film & Media Colorado

- New York Women in Film & Television

- Women Make Movies

- Women in Film

The following shouldn't surprise anyone who watches *Saturday Night Live* in the modern era: not only did the show not rush to Carano's side, it joined her critics in piling on. Today's "Not Ready for Prime Time Players" earn their name over and again, misconstruing Carano's Nazi tweet to create a limp laugh line. Oh, so predictable.

It took a Disney shareholder to put the company on blast for its behavior. Disney CEO Bob Chapek got a tough but fair question during a virtual shareholder's meeting about Carano's dismissal.

David W. Almasi, National Center for Public Policy Research's Free Enterprise Project (FEP), challenged Chapek on the matter.

> It's clear there's a new blacklist punishing conservatives in the entertainment industry. Disney+ actors Pedro Pascal and Gina Carano tweeted similar analogies of current political events to Nazi Germany, yet only Carano—who is considered conservative—was fired from *The Mandalorian*. Disney and the blacklist: This is the way?"[174]

Chapek had an evasion ready.

> "I don't really see Disney as characterizing itself as left-leaning or right-leaning, yet instead standing for values, values that are universal," Chapek said. "I think that's a world we all should live in, in harmony and peace."

For those scoring at home, that's a dodge and a lie all wrapped in one dishonest package. And we all know the bigger picture when it comes to Disney in the modern era. The company owns both the *Star Wars* and Marvel Cinematic Universe, two mega-franchises that took a turn for the woke in recent years.

The MCU's head honcho, Kevin Feige, is all in on the series going woke, an about-face from the apolitical tone of the saga's first, and wildly successful, decade of films.

And Disney threatened to boycott the state of Georgia in 2019 after it passed abortion restrictions deemed beyond the pale by the Left.

"I think many people who work for us will not want to work there," [former Disney CEO Bob] Iger told Reuters, "and we will have to heed their wishes in that regard. Right now we are watching it very carefully."[175]

Thank goodness today's stars have no problem making movies in China, home to the previously mentioned concentration camps.[176]

What happened next to Carano was more sticks and stones, but it also showed how media lies fuel additional hate. It's almost as if the Instagram message that got her fired was even more accurate than she imagined.

Bill Maher invited former U.S. Senator Heidi Heitkamp on his HBO show in March 2021. The subject was Cancel Culture, which Heitkamp turned into an excuse to assassinate Carano's character with lies.

The North Dakota politician claimed, without evidence, that Carano "was a Nazi" who hung "with white supremacists."

Maher objected, to his credit. Heitkamp, who may have realized in "Real Time" the legal trouble she might be in, answered, "I suppose I get subject to defamation."

Carano's Twitter response was…perfect.

> Here we have more of the dehumanizing phase of cancel culture. -Repeat lies over and over until the population takes them as "truth". False, disturbing & disgusting language coming from a former US Senator.
>
> @HeidiHeitkamp
>
> You knew as soon as you said it you were liable.

Journalists stood down, once more, proving they don't care a damn about female empowerment. How Hollywood.

CHAPTER 10:
Insider Horror Stories

ARTISTS WORKING ANYWHERE near the woke beast must tread carefully these days.

The industry is openly hostile to right-leaning creators and has been for some time. The same is mostly true for people of faith, even as select studios gently embrace the Christian film genre in their own ways.

While Sony's Affirm boutique label produces faith-friendly films (*Risen*, *Heaven Is for Real*), most Christian movies flow from outside traditional Hollywood.

The election of Donald Trump in 2016 arguably made matters worse for both beleaguered groups.

The woke revolutionaries apply a new level of restrictions on what can and can't be said. Ideology is less important than adherence to the ever-changing woke rules. It doesn't matter if you're conservative, liberal, or a dyed-in-the-wool centrist. Contradict the woke groupthink and watch your career suffer as a result, if not sink entirely.

It's one thing for a superstar to issue a "hostage" apology for sharing the wrong social media message. It's another for those who work tirelessly behind the scenes, or lack the name recognition of a Scorsese or Spielberg, to find their careers clipped for sharing inconvenient truths. It's why we're hiding the identity of several artists here so they can speak freely without fear of career cancellation.

That fact should be alarming in and of itself.

One prominent producer recalls entering a Netflix office prepared to "seal a deal" for his project to stream on the service. "Jim's" optimism slumped as he spotted a massive, metallic art display within the company's hallways.

The assembly had a simple message: "Stay Woke."

The meeting, as it turned out, let Netflix gently reject the proposed title, one that clashed with woke sensibilities.

Jim says he's grown accustomed to making movies that are punished for their ideological point of view. If one of his movies scores a 49 percent rating at Rotten Tomatoes, or higher, he feels he's done his job well.

"Forty-nine means it's great, but it's being punished for other reasons," he explains.

Jim says he's hearing both whispers and outright examples where white artists are being told their skin color is stopping them from getting work in the industry.

"It's out in the open now," he says.

He's not ready to cede defeat, though. In Hollywood, tenacity often matters as much as other attributes. Artists must assume Hollywood's woke sentiment, combined with an aggressively liberal mindset, before getting their work approved, shared or greenlit.

"I feel like you can join the 'Whiners Club,' you end up never succeeding," he says.

A veteran actor, "Lou," is fed up with the kinds of roles offered to him of late.

"If you're a white guy in his sixties, you're the racist guy...that's all I get," in between gigs to play the occasional boss or grandfather, Lou said. "You're the old generation that has to be done away with.... It's not stuff that I'm interested in."

Those roles may, in part, reflect Lou's demographic, but he doesn't remember it being this way up until recently. He appreciates that diversity in art can be important, but it shouldn't override the prime storytelling directives. What he sees now are scripts where race is the key driver of a character, as opposed to what the character's function in the story might be.

It is identity politics run wild, and the art is suffering.

Lou recalls pitching a project he co-wrote, an action film set on the U.S.-Mexico border. The tale followed a rancher fighting back against a drug cartel, akin to the most recent *Rambo* sequel.

The pitch meeting went well before the executives suggested a sizable change.

"Is there a way to change it, to make it more attractive to China?" Lou recalls them saying to him.

"I thought they were kidding," he said, but soon realized it was no joke. They even suggested making the film's villains Japanese because of China's animosity toward that country.

More recently, he reports, pitching a story to a Hollywood studio comes with its own complex rules.

"It's impossible to get a movie done in Hollywood that isn't overtly woke right now.... You have to have a gay character, a trans character, all ethnicities [represented]," he says. One exception: historical films can get away with less diversity based on the historical record.

Still, that didn't stop some wokesters from blasting 2017's *Dunkirk* for featuring a predominantly white cast.[177]

Lou says the woke and progressive worlds in Hollywood are "intertwined," making matters worse for anyone who may be either unwoke or right of center. The results? Oscars so woke, the death of the movie star as a cultural institution, and a divide between Tinseltown and large swaths of America.

"I think Hollywood is gone," Lou said. "They've destroyed their credibility with the audience.... Everything they do is to tear down the American dream and reinforce the ridiculous idea that America is a racist country and full of hate...anything that doesn't reinforce that is suspect."

Lou says he isn't alone in his thinking.

"A lot friends come up to me and say, 'I agree with what you're saying but I can't take a public stance. It would destroy my career.' These are guys working in the industry as long as I have.... They're afraid to stick their heads up and say what they believe. They know they'll pay a price."

The animation field offers a wealth of ways to indoctrinate young minds into the new woke world.

Nickelodeon showcased a 2021 special about "environmental racism" as part of its Earth Day celebration. The one-hour special, *Nick News:*

Kids and the Impact of Climate Change, featured John Kerry and overt messaging some parents may not cheer.[178]

> What do these cities have in common? They're all examples of environmental racism, a form of systemic racism where minority and low-income communities are surrounded by health hazards because they live near sewage, mines, landfills, power stations, [and] major roads.[179]

The messaging runs much deeper.

"John," who works within Disney's animation division, is a twelve-year industry veteran. He says the company's 2016 film *Zootopia,* a whimsical tale brimming with lessons about prejudice, kicked off the Mouse House's new woke agenda. Since the positive cultural message in Zootopia was met with awards and success, specifically for adding in social commentary, it incentivized Disney to push that even further in upcoming projects, and their messaging took a hard left turn.

Disney movies now regularly insert progressive messages into the finished product, "instead of focusing on creating content that families will enjoy and are okay with," John says. "We're now always pushing for some kind of messaging."

It doesn't end there behind the scenes, though. John describes frequent business meetings tied to "diversity" and "inclusion," events that lean overtly to the Left. He said one such meeting repeatedly referenced the January 6, 2021 Capitol protests as an "insurrection," for example.

"It kind of feels almost cultish," he says of the gatherings, which occasionally included former Disney CEO Bob Iger. "They only have one side of the view on what's happening.... There are no opposing views, no one contradicting that narrative."

"It's infuriating to go to those things and waste my time," he adds, noting issues surrounding "white guilt" frequently crop up. Even worse? Visual aids used to highlight the issues in play routinely feature white male figures committing the various offenses.

"Before this recent shift, Disney didn't talk about political issues from only a single perspective and didn't force-feed that viewpoint to employees and viewers. We just tried to make good movies," he says. That's no longer the only directive, he says, with stories now focusing on LGBTQ elements and other progressive topics. "They're pushing an agenda that not all families want to have pushed on their kids, especially at an early age." A few fellow employees "in high-ranking positions" decided to leave Disney rather than work on projects that didn't align with their worldviews.

The corporate culture is one that doesn't leave much space for right-leaning employees. "Going against the leftist narrative would probably cause you to be shunned at Disney," he says.

"Scott," a veteran filmmaker, found making a dream project nearly impossible, for reasons of skin color. The film in question, a biography of a famous black musician, got put on hiatus recently, its future uncertain. The musician's estate was on board with the project, down to hand-selecting the director to bring the tale to life.

"The estate saw the filmmaker's previous film and loved elements of the story—the style, the certain way the story was told," Scott said.

However, the icon in question was black. The director was not.

"He had some hesitation directing a film about a black musical figure even before all the George Floyd [protests] happened," Scott says. "He loved this individual's music."

Scott took an active role in pitching the project to several major studios. The initial interest seemed promising.

"They were almost unanimously thrilled to be talking to us about this," he says. "They saw the pedigree from which the producers and director came from."

The pandemic made face-to-face meetings all but impossible, which meant they turned to Zoom to push the conversations ahead. That's when the trouble began.

"There was sort of a shift in tone once we got onto these Zoom calls," he says. "We started to get the implication that they were uncomfortable with him being a white guy. We heard the word, 'optics' a number of times. 'The optics wouldn't be right for us to do this.'"

One studio meeting spelled out the obvious to them.

"We have a mandate, we aren't allowing white director projects with [films featuring] people of color….

"Making a movie is already challenging in and of itself," he adds. "We get that Hollywood is left leaning. [The skin color issue] was the added obstacle that we couldn't have possibly predicted."

The irony of the situation struck Scott.

"They were trying to promote stories about people of color, but we can't honor this musician because your director is the wrong skin color."

Scott toyed with the idea of adding a black co-director to the project, but that seemed unfair to whoever might be chosen.

"It would be so insulting to that filmmaker, to tokenize him," he says.

Scott says he knows several black filmmakers who have never been in higher demand than now.

"I'm very happy for them," he says, adding they know why their phones suddenly can't stop ringing. What they fear, though, is what happens when the story in question doesn't involve black themes or characters. Will those same phones suddenly stop buzzing, even though they're fully capable of directing stories outside their world view? There's a concern about that," Scott says.

Another veteran filmmaker who requested his name be withheld grapples with the self-censorship that comes with the current creative climate.

"You go through the process. Okay, am I going to have a problem with X, Y, or Z? Do I have to be careful? Am I going to have to change it? Self-censorship and self-doubt come into play, and that's self-defeating to any artist," he says.

The current woke push threatens to upend the great content produced in recent years, particularly for the small screen.

"We're just going to get bad shows that are very plain-wrapped, very safe, very conventional, and yet they're thinking they're unconventional," he says. "Where's the drama?"

Demands for diversity at all costs, he adds, is having an impact beyond a more inclusive Hollywood.

"'Talent' seems to be moving down the ledger of importance in these conversations, and that's sad," he says. "I think talent comes from all colors, from all kinds of sources. I do think it's difficult for some [minority groups] to break through, no doubt about it."

He contends, after his long tenure in Hollywood, that ability will eventually come out on top.

"I don't care what color you are or your origins, talent wins out in the end," he says. "It does take incredible persistence."

The filmmaker says that receiving feedback from studio executives is a natural part of the Hollywood eco-system. More recently though, the nature of those exchanges has evolved.

"You deal with notes on every level of your work, and usually they're expected to be dramatic notes," he says, referring to various aspects of the story. "The art of navigating this crazy minefield of a business is how you deal with the notes.

"Now," he says, "they're notes of a different sort. 'Hey, what if this character were Native American?' I'm fine with that, if we can find a great actor to play that role."

The filmmaker says his fellow artists are sensing the trouble with the aggressive woke push, but they keep those opinions to themselves.

"There's such huge risk to speaking up publicly about it. The way [Cancel Culture] can destroy lives and careers overnight, there are very few people willing to take that risk. It takes balls of steel."

He says the current climate is so toxic even an auteur like Quentin Tarantino might struggle if he came of creative age today. "Tarantino would be shot down in today's Hollywood." Movies like the director's *Pulp Fiction*, with its intense use of the "n-word" and other challenging elements, wouldn't be made now.

"Somebody's gotta be like Tarantino was twenty-five years ago, and be that bold today, and flip the bird at all the chatter," he says.

Dallas Sonnier makes it a habit of sticking his neck out in Hollywood. The indie producer behind mesmerizing films like *Bone Tomahawk*, *Run Hide Fight*, and *Dragged Across Concrete* says he saw the woke writing on the wall all the way back to President Barack Obama's first term.

Sonnier says the country's first black president lacked a stirring record to run on in 2012, in part due to a recalcitrant Republican Senate. Obama needed a Plan B—giving rise to a combination of wokeism, Identity Politics, and victimhood as ways to recast his re-election hopes.

The film producer realized those sentiments would soon flood into the culture at large, including left-leaning Hollywood. It's one reason why he eventually packed up his family and moved back to Texas to work on movies there, on his own terms.

"By 2014 it was game on, in terms of just feeling like the tidal wave was coming," he said, calling his move a "pre-emptive strike against the changing tides in Hollywood."

At the time, he noticed slight but stealth messaging enter Hollywood films, while indie filmmakers shifted aggressively to the Left. Said messaging is no longer slight, nor is it stealthy.

What Sonnier is building, though, is a studio aimed at giving a voice to artists, on the left, center, and right, who just want to tell a compelling story.

Should Bonfire Legend, the name of Sonnier's new studio, succeed, along with other emerging platforms like *The Daily Wire*'s entertainment hub, some of the aforementioned voices here won't have to protect their identities any longer.

CHAPTER 11:
Those Lady Ghostbusters

BLAME BILL MURRAY.

The *Saturday Night Live* icon refused to play by modern Hollywood rules.

One such rule? Have a gargantuan hit on your resumé? Make a sequel, stat, no matter how old the original film might be. Sequels beget all sorts of professional perks, from massive paychecks to fawning media coverage, assuming you don't make another *Caddyshack II* or *Son of the Mask*.

And Sony Pictures, which owns the rights to all things *Ghostbuster*, understandably craved the franchise's revival. That's a no-brainer in show business. Never mind that an actual sequel to the 1984 original existed. The film, ingeniously titled *Ghostbusters 2*, killed the franchise in 1989—and for good reason. The reputation of this clumsy cash grab has only grown worse over the years.

Still, time heals old wounds, as does nostalgia. So, the idea of a new *Ghostbusters*, with an older Bill Murray, Dan Aykroyd, and Co. passing their proton packs on to the new generation had "hit" written all over it.

The painful part came in waiting for the principals to sign on the dotted line. Aykroyd and co-star Harold Ramis appeared game for the ghostly reunion, with the former penning scripts he hoped would spark a third *Ghostbusters* romp.

Except Murray wasn't having it. He refused to step into his gray *Ghostbusters* suit again, bucking all industry norms. And you can't get the gang back together again if the funniest gang member stays home.

Rumors circulated that Murray shredded one script and sent it back to Aykroyd and Ramis, accompanied by a nasty note. Aykroyd torched that gossip; the two maintain a professional and personal respect that precluded such behavior, he said. The "Blues Brother" did confirm Murray had little interest in another sequel.

Aykroyd wouldn't let go of the project, though. He even teased a third *Ghostbusters* film without Murray's Peter Venkman character, assuming most of the other key players returned. The show must go on, along with the accompanying paychecks and career boosts.

On and on it went, and even the passing of Ramis in 2014 couldn't crush the project. Eventually, Sony came up with a Plan B.

Enter Paul Feig. The hot comedy director (*Freaks and Geeks*, *Spy*, *Bridesmaids*) would reboot the property for today's audiences, with a twist. The boys weren't back in town. Four comic actresses got the call, instead.

It smelled like Hollywood's nascent gender-swap template, where old properties are brought back with the leads' sexes reversed. Feig famously said he went out and found the four funniest people he could, and said group just so happened to include Leslie Jones.

Hollywood *is* the land of make believe.

Still, co-stars Kristen Wiig, Melissa McCarthy, and Kate McKinnon are bold talents, and perhaps their take on Slimer and friends could bring the *Ghostbusters* spirit back from the grave.

Feig explained he had the chance to work with something similar to the original concept but opted to go in a different direction.

> "I just kept turning it down because I didn't know how to do it," he told *AlloCiné*. "The scripts had been written, but I couldn't figure out how to do it. I wasn't excited about it....
>
> "I'd rather do it as a reboot so I'm not tied to the old movies," he said. "The old movies are so good, I didn't want to mess with them. And I also want to see the beginnings of this group. I want to see people seeing ghosts for the first time, and how they're going to fight them for the first time, how they develop their technology."[180]

That's not a bad idea, but it discarded what made the I.P. such a cultural touchstone. What happened next drew cheers from a Sony executive...for a while.

Woke Hollywood was just warming up at the time, and the *Ghostbusters* project aligned with it better than any other film could.

You must adore the Lady Ghostbusters, or else.

Why?

Because little girls can't dream of becoming scientists if they don't have role models on the big screen.

Yes, that was part of the fanciful logic attached to the female *Ghostbusters* project:

> But when it comes to the gender representation in *Ghostbusters*, there's something even more significant going on: It features women who move the action forward with their scientific know-how....
>
> Carl Sagan, Neil DeGrasse Tyson, and Bill Nye the Science Guy all worked wonders for popularizing science—but they're all men. *The Big Bang Theory*, which remains one of the sole popular, long-running shows to focus on scientists, pits feminine Penny against the awkward male scientists. Silicon Valley too has a serious gender representation problem.[181]

So, when some online fans trashed the film, sight unseen, for ditching the male leads, the response was swift and predictable: If you hate the new *Ghostbusters*, you hate women.

The Washington Post, a newspaper that would transform from left-leaning to unabashed liberal advocacy in the age of Trump, led the charge, but many other news outlets followed right along.

It's worth noting that these kinds of pre-release outrages, especially with Comic Con-friendly fare, happen all the time. Remember when Tim Burton's *Batman* cast Michael Keaton—*Mr. Mom!*—as the Dark Knight? Even in the pre-social-media age the response was furious, unrelenting. Had that casting news hit in 2020, not 1988, Keaton might have been sent packing before cameras rolled.

Back then, fans had little sway over controversial casting decisions. Online petitions weren't a thing, and audiences lacked the collective power to change hearts and minds.

There weren't even hashtag campaigns at the time.

As fate would have it, audiences cheered Keaton in the signature cowl. The movie, and Mr. Mom's performance, spoke for themselves.

The same could have been true for the new *Ghostbusters*. Make a funny movie and the mockery fades to black. It's why so much rode on the film's first trailer, Sony's chance to change the mood from outrage to anticipation.

Take that, basement dwelling misogynists! Who's laughing now, Comic Book Guy?

Yet no one was laughing after the trailer dropped with a thud. The clip quickly became the unofficial worst trailer of all time, according to intense viewer feedback.

The Washington Post rushed into battle once more, savaging anyone who didn't dissolve into laughter during the two-minute clip. The headline itself is a howler: "People hate the 'Ghostbusters' trailer, and yes, it's because it stars women."[182]

Sony's PR arm, let alone NOW, couldn't have done it any better. Except spin control can only do so much. The trailer was weak, at best, and the negative momentum continued despite reporters' best efforts on the movie's behalf.

That captured the media's general response to the film prior to its July 11 release date. Protect, defend—and destroy its critics. Movie journalism today is as corrupt and biased as "straight" news coverage, and the journalists covering *Ghostbusters* proved that anew:

Sexist "Ghostbusters" Backlash Coincides with 2016 Gender Divide[183]

Why the "Ghostbusters" Backlash Is a Sexist Control Issue[184]

The Real Reason Men of a Certain Age Hate the "Ghostbusters" Remake[185]

Rather than letting their film speak for itself, Team *Ghostbusters* leaned into the woke movement. The female leads appeared together on *Ellen* along with—what a coincidence!—presidential candidate Hillary Clinton.

The movie itself even featured a scene where the Ghostbuster-ettes fire back at YouTube trolls. Talk about anti-empowerment.

Finally, *Ghostbusters* hit theaters nationwide.

Deadline.com, a far-left entertainment site, couldn't bury the bad news. The film's $46 million opening weekend, while great for most movies, represented a disappointing yield for a hotly anticipated franchise reboot. And the word-of-mouth factor wouldn't give those numbers any help.

> PostTrak "definite recommend" fell to an OK 57%, below the awesome 70% figures we saw for *Finding Dory* and *Captain America: Civil War* this summer.[186]

Deadline confessed an even more surprising reason for the film's deflating returns. (For the uninitiated, film journalists routinely hide inconvenient truths that betray progressive narratives, like a dog burying a bone he never intends to find.)

> Despite the old saying that there's no such thing as bad publicity, some believe that Sony and the filmmakers made too much out of the anti-feminist controversy. One major studio executive criticized Sony for continually addressing its bullies instead of ignoring them: "The media thrived on that anti-feminist through-line. That message doesn't work for Hillary Clinton in regards to getting her elected. It should never be about supporting or not supporting a movie just because it stars women. If the movie looks good, people should just go." If *Ghostbusters* had more heat than hate, it would have climbed to greater heights.

Simple. Direct. Now, is that so hard? Nowadays, it is. Here's betting if a female-led *Ghostbusters* launched today, Deadline.com might just bury that cold, hard truth. Back then, some facts wriggled free.

Film critics rallied to the film's side, delivering a shocking 73 percent "fresh" rating at Rotten Tomatoes. Except veteran film critic Richard Roeper, no conservative he, smelled a rat.

> I find it hard to believe that after having sat through that dreck, that three quarters of the critics out there really saw that as a fine example of a reboot of a pretty classic, legendary motion picture. It was just bad.[187]

Back in 2016, critics occasionally let their biases influence their reviews. Today? It's rarer when they don't. Consider this confession from A.O. Scott about the movie. You can almost smell how hard he's working to praise a mediocrity.

> I think what pleased me most about this *Ghostbusters* was how matter-of-fact—how chill—the movie was, notwithstanding the bombast of the climactic battle. I think we all agree that it has a generic, middle-of-the-road quality. That's something it shares with the original, by the way, which far from being a transcendent masterpiece of cinematic imagination was a nice paycheck for the artists involved and an easy, inoffensive night out for the audience.[188]

Yes, a movie that spawned a sequel, a reboot, an animated series, a Billboard-topping single, and decades of cult-like devotion was merely a "nice paycheck" for all involved. That's what you have to say in order to build up a lackluster reboot.

> Mr. Feig, like Ivan Reitman before him, has assembled a workmanlike action-comedy about people at work. Professionalism may be the opposite of gonzo, but I think there's something (dare I say it) radical about how job-focused this story is.

That's the epitome of grading on a curve.

Reaction to the film also predated a far more insidious trend, one that's ripe for humor if we had any comedians willing to tackle it.

You never, ever can be woke enough.

So, while Sony tried to make a female-led blockbuster, brimming with empowerment, it wasn't enough in select circles. *The Guardian*, for example, worried that the film cast Jones as a transit worker who ends up "answering the call," besmirching black female scientists in the process.

> But for all the character's great qualities, this felt like a missed opportunity. Representation really matters, and often, black women and girls are stereotyped on screen as the sassy, angry loudmouth, and never as the intellectual, professional or scientist.[189]

Jones also became a flashpoint for some ugly, racist Twitter comments. That's sad and disgusting, of course, but the media singled out the attacks both to defend the actress and to further smear *Ghostbusters* critics with one large, nasty brush.

Prior to the film's release, Team Sony saw the film as the gateway to a new *Ghostbusters* "universe," the term studios use for films with huge franchise potential.

> "While nothing has been officially announced yet, there's no doubt in my mind it will happen," said Rory Bruer, president of worldwide distribution at Sony.

But the *Ghostbusters* relaunch fizzled, and with it plans for a whole crush of "Ghost"-themed film products. The media cheerleaders put their pom-poms away when the bill came in. The film would set Sony back $70 million.[190]

Sony eventually licked its wounds, jettisoned the ladies, and asked the son of the original film's director, Jason Reitman, to revive the tattered brand with *Ghostbusters: Afterlife*. This time around, Sony avoided insulting the fans, vowed the new film would be a true sequel, and hoped the stench from the reboot wouldn't impact future box office receipts.

Clearly Sony realized the error of its ways and tried to revive the franchise one last time. So, did Hollywood in general take similar lessons from the debacle? ·

Of course not!

Feig partly blamed the *Ghostbuster* flop on the theory that the "white male patriarchy" felt threatened.[191]

That line is funnier than anything uttered in his movie.

~~Why does a single, underwhelming reboot matter in the big Holly-~~ wood picture? Because we would see a similar blueprint play out in the ensuing years.

Consider 2019's *Terminator: Dark Fate*.

It's the franchise that won't die, even though audiences stopped caring about it long ago. Arnold Schwarzenegger had returned to the series with *Terminator: Genisys*, the 2015 dud that couldn't crack the $100 million mark at the U.S. box office. Even *Ghostbusters* crossed that barrier.

The latest *Terminator* sequel lured original director James Cameron back to the franchise, albeit in a producer capacity. Schwarzenegger returned, too, and so did Linda Hamilton. The original Sarah Connor served up an extra blast of nostalgia and gravitas. Hamilton gave sterling performances in the first two features, and her return clearly thrilled the fan base.

Cameron. Schwarzenegger. Hamilton. It felt like old times.

Then the woke marketing kicked in.

The first official image from *Dark Fate*, an important part of any film marketing campaign, featured three of the film's female characters in a forced pose.

The image looked airbrushed and false, including two actresses with very little name recognition. More importantly, where was Ah-nold? He's the face of the franchise, hands down. *Terminator* isn't *Terminator* without the former Mr. Olympia.

The film itself proved more entertaining than many expected, but it leaned into its woke sensibilities. The story overlapped a clumsy immigration subplot replete with factory-ordered, far-left messaging, and Mackenzie Davis's character did much of the muscular heavy lifting with Ah-nold relegated to a mid-movie introduction. He steals the movie anyway.

Like its predecessor, *Terminator: Dark Fate* flopped in theaters. The movie opened to a pathetic $29 million en route to a $69 million final tally.

The film's woke marketing and far-left themes didn't crush the box office entirely. This was a spent franchise, no doubt. Those factors didn't help, though.

One movie avoided the woke defense entirely. A year after "Ghostbusters-Gate" came *Wonder Woman*, brimming with many of the same feminist themes. We'd seen plenty of superheroines before, on screens large and small, but DC's Wonder Woman stood at the top of the superhero heap. She mattered, and the film's success could mean more female-led super romps.

Yet neither Warner Bros. nor the team's key players—star Gal Gadot and director Patty Jenkins—resorted to victimization tropes.

No "girl power" shrieks on *Ellen*. No "journalists" doing pre-release damage control. No whining about the pressure placed on the film. The finished product didn't need any of it.

Wonder Woman delivered a strong trailer capped by a memorable score refrain, and the best super casting since Christopher Reeve first donned his blue tights. Gal Gadot *was* Wonder Woman, and the film opened to a majestic $103 million on route to an eye-popping $412 million U.S. haul.

Team *Ghostbusters* lacked confidence in their product, and for good reason. That helps explain the protracted battle to pretend an ill-advised reboot was anything but a misfire.

CHAPTER 12:
Gender Reboot Mania

AUDIENCES COMPLAIN HOLLYWOOD has officially run out of ideas, and they're partially right. The industry runs on reboots, sequels, origin stories, re-imaginings, and remakes.

Lather. Rinse. Recycle.

When you hear whispers of either a *Hunger Games* or *Twilight* reboot a few years after the original properties wrapped, you know there's a problem.

When it comes to repurposing I.P.s (intellectual properties), Hollywood is as green as Kermit the Frog.

The 1991 feature *The Silence of the Lambs*, for example, gave way to a sequel (*Hannibal*), a prequel (*Red Dragon*), an origin story (*Hannibal Rising*), a TV reboot (NBC's exceptional *Hannibal*), and, most recently, a TV spin-off dubbed *Clarice*.

Can we expect *Hannibal: The Musical* next?

Not bad for one movie, right? Who knows how many more Hannibal-themed stories we'll see over the next decade? There might be a few in production as you read these words.

Each *Lambs* off-shoot generated copious media coverage and, more often than not, viewer intrigue. It's human nature to wonder how a beloved property will be extended, or damaged, in the process. Or perhaps we're starved for comfort food.

What's the alternative, anyway? Drop an original, $100-million adventure on an unsuspecting culture, and it could bomb bigly, to quote a certain former president. The 2021 megaton dud, *Chaos Walking*, is a prime example, despite "name" players (Tom Holland, Daisy Ridley) and a veteran director (Doug Liman).

Does anyone remember *Jupiter Ascending* with Channing Tatum and Mila Kunis? Didn't think so. How about *Valerian and the City of a Thousand Planets*? Box office tally for that 2017 original: $41 million domestic, $225 million international.

Do the same with a *Dune* remake, though, and you're insulated against the worst-case scenario—even if the movie itself is a dud-ski.

It's one reason Hollywood went all in on gender reboots in recent years. These projects, which span both big and small screens, swap out established male characters for female ones, settings and circumstances be darned. Some are positioned as pure female empowerment—think *Ocean's 8* and 2016's *Ghostbusters*. Others exist to continue a theme or story in a slightly fresh direction. Or so they claim.

A few are so awful it's hard to know what to make of their germinal DNA.

The results are often creatively vacant, proving their entire existence was based on a concept, not inspiration. Even more dispiriting, the box office tallies are typically tame.

That likely won't shut the gender reboot spigot anytime soon. It took a gazillion anti-war movies bombing during the Dubya years for Hollywood bean counters to finally say, "Hey…maybe audiences don't want to see our troops treated like dirt…."

When Hollywood clings to a narrative, it's like a Rottweiler and her favorite chew toy. You could lose a finger trying to separate the two. And if a half-dozen gender reboots give producers a shot of social media dopamine, their attitude is "Keep 'em coming!"

The *Ghostbusters* 2016 reboot stood as the most anticipated gender reboot of the modern era (see previous chapter). Director Paul Feig is obsessed with female-led projects, but he never shared a firm reason to swap out the genders in that long-awaited reboot. And it showed.

The gender switcheroo added little, if anything, to the story. For many, entertainment value and *Ghostbusters* proved mutually exclusive. Here are other gender-swap remakes and how they fared with the American consumer.

What Men Want

Mel Gibson got in touch with his feminine side with the 1999 hit *What Women Want*. Part of the project's appeal was that Gibson represented the prototypical alpha male. Tough. Strong. Handsome. Rugged. He's *Mad Max* and a *Lethal Weapon*, for crying out loud. The sight of Martin Riggs tugging on nylons and getting inside a woman's head proved to be intrinsically funny.

And successful. The comedy scooped up $182 million at the U.S. box office alone. That's massive, both for the year in question and even today. Comedies don't make half of that amount these days. It's hard to tell a joke in woke Hollywood. (Heck, someone should write a book about that.)

So, to power the *What Men Want* remake, they cast Taraji P. Henson, a gifted performer, but with no comparable cinematic reputation to be leveraged.

The reboot earned $54 million, not a terrible amount but a far cry from the original property. The reviews were poor—42 percent "rotten" at Rotten Tomatoes—and it quickly joined the cable and streaming universe for those hungry for mediocrity.

The Hustle

Dirty Rotten Scoundrels (1988) was actually a remake of *Bedtime Story*, the 1964 comedy starring Marlon Brando and David Niven. The fear of stepping in for two film legends clearly didn't rattle two cinematic "scoundrels"—Steve Martin and Michael Caine.

The second remake's stars are no slouches, either, though neither brings the comedy chops of their predecessors. Anne Hathaway does own an Oscar, and Rebel Wilson excels at creating laughs out of wafer-thin scripts. That skill came in handy here, but not enough. The comedy's opening scene tells you up front you're in for a long, long ninety-four minutes.

The Hustle proved to be one of the worst remakes of the modern era, with or without the gender component. This stinker sunk like a stone, netting $35 million at the U.S. box office and even-more-withering reviews—13 percent "rotten" at Rotten Tomatoes.

Life of the Party

This 2018 gender-comedy remake did an impressive job of hiding the source material. It's not a beat-for-beat retelling of Rodney Dangerfield's *Back to School*, nor does it directly replicate any of that film's signature moments. That's a shame, since it might be fun seeing Melissa McCarthy attempt the "triple Lindy" dive.

The premise is close enough to conjure thoughts of that 1986 classic. Big mistake. McCarthy is playing a middle-aged mom who goes back to school to help out her daughter. A review snippet, courtesy of the *Chesapeake Family Magazine*, tells you everything you need to know:

> Melissa McCarthy stars in *Life of the Party*, which uneasily tries to mix messages about female empowerment and body positivity with clichéd jokes about aging.

Once again, the reviews weren't kind and neither were the box office receipts ($52 million). Trying to send a woke message in the middle of a comedy is rarely a path to success.

Ocean's 8 (2018)

Easily the most successful of the gender reboots, this quasi-sequel carried on the anti-hero tradition Frank Sinatra kicked off in the 1960s. Old Blue Eyes' film gave way to George Clooney's all-star version, guided by Steven Soderbergh.

Now, it was the ladies' turn to make high-stakes robbery look chic. They got the right actresses for the gig, including Sandra Bullock, Cate Blanchett, and rising star Awkwafina. She's as talented as her name is contrived.

The film kept the woke nonsense to a minimum, focusing on the fashions, the bonding, and the intricate heist at the heart of the film. That, and movie stars who know how to carry a scene, did the rest of the heavy lifting.

The movie earned loving reviews and a cool $139 million at the box office. Oddly enough, no one has attempted an *Ocean's 9*...yet.

High Fidelity

Hulu regularly cranks out woke content for its platform, sometimes literally, in the case of its comedy series, *Woke*.

For Nick Hornby's beloved novel, the streaming platform decided to retell the story with a female main character. Zoe Kravitz got the call to replace John Cusack, the star of the 2000 film of the same name.

Reviewers were mostly kind, although Kravitz's inescapable beauty made her sad sack schtick harder to buy. The show clearly didn't connect with audiences. The ten-episode first season proved to be its last.

Overboard

If you squint hard enough, you can be outraged by the 1987 original, starring Goldie Hawn as a cruel heiress who stiffs a carpenter (Kurt Russell), whose crime was doing a job to her specifications. When Hawn's character suffers amnesia after—wait for it—falling overboard from her yacht, the carpenter hatches a scheme to get his money back from her.

He convinces her she's his wife, and has her work off her debt by taking care of his home and kids. Naturally they fall in love, right?

Yes, this movie actually exists as a romantic comedy. Suddenly, *How to Lose a Guy in 10 Days* feels like a documentary.

Overboard remains a lark, powered by two game stars who we know love each other off-screen. That knowledge helped power one of the '80s overrated films.

So…let's do it again!

This time, Anna Faris plays a hard-working parent trying to juggle motherhood and two jobs. Mexican comic Eugenio Derbez plays the snooty rich dude who loses his memory and ends up working for Faris's character.

The film earned awful reviews (24 percent "rotten" at Rotten Tomatoes) and couldn't even please the woke minded. Here's the *Daily Telegraph* administering last rites to the film's comedic potential:

> Manages to feel far more dated, regressive and stale than the film it's based on.

The original *Overboard* netted $26 million, a tidy sum for an '80s comedy. The remake roughly doubled that amount, a decent return especially given the scathing reviews, but far from a comedy blockbuster.

American Pie Presents: Girls' Rules

Who needs teens humping pies when you can have girls, well, doing something truly empowering? This straight to VOD/Netflix offering barely made a ripple in pop culture waters. The future of lame sex comedies is female.

It didn't help that the "Pie" series evolved from a trio of Jason Biggs/ Eugene Levy romps to a low-rent, direct-to-video franchise.

Critics savaged *Girls' Rules*, with audiences following suit (30 percent "rotten"/15 percent "rotten"). Naturally, critics complained that a bunch of dudes—yes, dudes!—helped make *Rules* possible.

> …the problem is that it envisions itself as a progressive reboot of the original merely because it stars women. Sadly, there's nothing resembling a human female in this tasteless (but mildly tender) rom-com. Dashed together by a male director, two male screenwriters and a half-male producing team, the film appears to be the cinematic equivalent of two straight girls making out at a party for some bro's attention.[192]

I hope the female half of the movie's producing team hangs this notice on her fridge!

***

Gender reboots aren't new, per se. The early 1980s saw *The Incredible Shrinking Woman* with Lily Tomlin, a satirical re-imagining of the sci-fi classic. It was different enough to matter, giving Reagan era audiences a genuinely clever story.

Others seem as strained today as they were back then, like *The Next Karate Kid*, starring then-unknown Hilary Swank. Suffice to say that film didn't spawn any sequels. Swank survived, though, scoring a pair of Oscars in her impressive career.

The current mania, though, reflects a far different dynamic, one that too often yields inferior product.

Just don't expect Hollywood to give up on the gender-swap concept. What we're starting to see is a broader approach to the gimmick, making it even more woke—if that's possible.

The upcoming *Father of the Bride* remake features an all-Latino clan headed by Andy Garcia. Or "Latinx," to be more politically correct. The new version will focus on a Cuban-American family and will take its cues from the Spencer Tracy/Elizabeth Taylor original from 1950 more than Steve Martin's 1991 version.

> "I'm very excited to join *The Father of the Bride*, a beloved film that has brought so much joy to so many over the years and to represent my Cuban culture and heritage in this story," Garcia said in a statement after the project went public.[193]

Let's hope for his sake the film mirrors precisely what the woke mob demands of said culture. Otherwise, it'll be "problematic," not a diversity score.

The shock success of two *National Treasure* films had Disney dreaming of a third entry in the saga. For some reason that project dragged on for years and years, before the Mouse House tried something different.

Yes, it's another ethnic reboot.

Disney is moving forward with a new take on the franchise, one that originally featured Nicolas Cage and Jon Voight. The update, slated for Disney+, will scrap the Cage/Voight combo for one that better reflects the diversity of America.

Here's how the far-left *Hollywood Reporter* captured the new show's sentiment. The reboot will "reimagine the franchise through the eyes of its lead character, a 20-year-old DREAMer named Jess Morales":

> Mira Nair (*Monsoon Wedding, A Suitable Boy*) is attached to direct. The series will explore the ideas of identity, community, patriotism and who gets to write history as Jess and a diverse group of friends embark on an adventure to uncover her mysterious family history and recover lost treasure."[194]

Woke on steroids. Will the film drop the lectures long enough to entertain us? That's the only question worth asking at this point.

CHAPTER 13:
Canceling Classic Movies

THIS JUST IN...MOVIES from the '30s, '40s, and '50s reflect the values of their respective eras, and not those of twenty-first century America.

It's stating the bloody obvious, and yet social justice warriors need help grasping that. So do network executives frightened that a beloved film will suddenly become "problematic" and a problem for their PR team. *Quick, somebody do something before we're undone by a hashtag campaign!*

It's more than mere criticism, though. We've already seen one of the most cherished movies of all time, *Gone with the Wind*, briefly disappear from a major streaming service after a single screenwriter slammed its depiction of Southern slavery.

The latest rage is slapping warning labels on content, from classic WWF wrestling matches to Disney cartoons that allegedly share racist and/or bigoted material.

That trend hit *Gone with the Wind*...hard. The film now merits a trigger warning of sorts for anyone watching the film on HBO Max. The label treatment extends to select home video versions of the film, too, meaning even those clinging to physical media can't avoid a cultural "expert" finger-wag their choice in movies.

Perhaps the most chilling phrase of late finds people mentioning a classic film or TV show closely followed by a variation of this lament:

"Boy, you couldn't make that film today."

It's a statement that should send shivers down the spine of any artist who cares about free expression. Too often it doesn't, though. It's part of the New Numb Normal, where Americans simply accept the stupefying status quo.

The great Mel Brooks rightly says you couldn't make his brilliant western satire *Blazing Saddles* today.

> "It's OK not to hurt the feelings of various tribes and groups," he said. "However, it's not good for comedy.

> "Comedy has to walk a thin line, take risks. It's the lecherous little elf whispering in the king's ear, telling the truth about human behavior."[195]

The same holds true for many other films, and the list will keep on growing.

Mariel Hemingway snared a Best Supporting Actress nomination for *Manhattan*, Woody Allen's black-and-white ode to New York and complicated romance. She, too, said the film's May-December romance wouldn't fly today, in part due to the allegations Allen sexually assaulted his young daughter, Dylan Farrow, in the 1990s.

Hemingway also meant the large age gap between her character and Allen's, even though those kinds of gaps exist in our culture, then and now.[196]

The site UltimateClassicRock.com curiously weighed in on this trend, coughing up a list of thirty comedies that couldn't be made today.

Think *The Bad News Bears* (the remake watered down its roughest edges), *Silver Streak*, *Life of Brian*, *National Lampoon's Animal House*, and *Airplane!*

Boy, life would be so much better without those movies, right?

A few films that fit into this category make some sense. The 1983 comedy *Mr. Mom* delivered some serious laughs, but the concept of a father who clumsily tackles laundry and dinner duty is now the norm for many families—but without the "clumsy" part. That takes the comedic elements out of the story. The culture changed since then, so the "fish-out-of-water" yuks no longer make sense. The movie still packs a comedic punch, though, assuming you abandon your safe space long enough to revisit it.

Other "couldn't make it today" films are unacceptable for dubious reasons.

USA Today lined up a millennial to whine about *Animal House* and, significantly, John Belushi's iconic Bluto character.

"In the Era of #MeToo Is It Still OK to Laugh at 'Animal House'?" wrote budding *New York Times* reporter Hannah Yasharoff.[197]

> But rewatching it in a time of hyperawareness about issues of sexual abuse, there are a handful of parts that don't sit well and make appreciating the movie as a whole frustrating and troublesome. There's a scene where Bluto climbs a ladder to watch a group of sorority women engage in a half-naked pillow fight.[198]

Let that sink in. We're no longer allowed to see rapscallion characters behaving...like rapscallion characters. Think of how that diminishes a storyteller and his or her toolkit. What's funnier? Bluto's ladder plummeting to the ground at the end of that scene, or a sequence showing him tutoring a younger student in calculus?

Is anyone asking us to vote for Bluto for Congress? Should we make our moral decisions based on what a drunken college student does or says? Can we find bad behavior funny, even if we'd never do something quite like it?

No, according to Yasharoff, and she has plenty of company.

Comedy can be cruel. Think pies in the face, slips on a banana peel, or getting pushed into a pool. Take the cruelty away, and your comedy toolkit looks a lot different than before.

It's no wonder big screen comedies are on life support, crushed by both the 2020 pandemic and screenwriters frightened to death of "offending" the wrong group or subgroup.

At least *USA Today*'s wunderkind reporter is giving us some wiggle room, for now.

> By today's standards, *Animal House* would have a tough time getting greenlit by any studio, and would face inevitable wrath on Twitter if it did. That doesn't necessarily mean that we need to ban this movie from

being watched ever again, but we do need to become more mindful about the entertainment we consume and be especially cognizant of what it's telling us about acceptable social behaviors. For now, we'll just put *Animal House* on double secret probation.

Oh, thank you for not banning the film quite yet! (But you know that's precisely what she'd like to see happen.)

To paraphrase another comedy classic, "Lighten up, Francis."

Molly Ringwald, of all people, helped spearhead this new woke tactic, penning an op-ed attacking the very films—John Hughes's *Sixteen Candles, The Breakfast Club,* and *Pretty in Pink*—that made her one of the '80s' biggest stars. Two-plus decades later, she lashed out at the late Hughes and his Brat Pack filmography:

> John's movies convey the anger and fear of isolation that adolescents feel, and seeing that others might feel the same way is a balm for the trauma that teenagers experience. Whether that's enough to make up for the impropriety of the films is hard to say—even criticizing them makes me feel like I'm divesting a generation of some of its fondest memories, or being ungrateful since they helped to establish my career. And yet embracing them entirely feels hypocritical. And yet, and yet..."[199]

Sorry, Molly, your woke revisiting of classic films to get back in the headlines, and to assuage any regrets over characters who behaved badly, won't dislodge these films from the public's imagination.

Quite the contrary. Hughes's films endure because he intuitively understood the American teenager—the pain, the hubris, the sexual appetites, and more. What you did, though, Molly, was usher in a new era of woke revisiting, one that could make other great films vanish sooner or later.

There's an easy-peasy way to show how absurd this all is. Some of today's most popular movies and TV shows highlight men and women who behave terribly.

- Walter White, the high school teacher turned meth cooker

- Tony Soprano, an unrepentant mobster and murderer

- *The Hitman's Bodyguard* franchises

- John Wick ('nuff said)

Countless movies feature death, destruction, and mayhem, and we're often asked to sympathize with those doing the worst of the worst. In fact, we're occasionally told such behavior is empowering, as in the case of 2019's overrated *Hustlers*. That film featured heroines who drug and steal from perfect strangers. *You go, criminal girl!*

So many characters. So many terrible actions. And there's nothing wrong with any of it to the woke mob.

You'd think an august channel like TCM (Turner Classic Movies) would be rushing to protect classic films from the woke pitchforks. And, once again, you'd be wrong.

The month-long series *Reframed: Classic Films in the Rearview Mirror* tried to complete two different tasks at once. The first is admirable: to mount a defense against those eager to "cancel" some of Hollywood's most admired films for sharing the wrong views. The other task, sadly, is less honorable. The very existence of *Reframed* legitimizes the woke culture warriors stalking classic movies.[200]

TCM's Ben Mankiewicz, Alicia Malone, Eddie Muller, Dave Karger, and Jacqueline Stewart—not a right-leaning soul in the bunch—attempted to view classics through a modern prism...a very woke prism.

Among the films deemed problematic? *The Jazz Singer* (1927), *Gone with the Wind* (1939),[201] *Dragon Seed* (1944), *The Searchers* (1956),[202] *The Children's Hour* (1961), and *Breakfast at Tiffany's* (1961).

The Searchers, the classic 1956 John Wayne western, commits several woke sins, according to the TCM.

> The Wayne character is overtly racist, and many argue
> that the label also applies to the film itself, as the char-

acterization of Indigenous people is both stereotypical and underdeveloped.

Oh, are we declaring underdeveloped characters "problematic" now? That might wipe out half the films in Hollywood history, including nine-tenths of all horror films.

National Review's Armond White, arguably the most contrarian voice in film circles, blasted the program upon its 2021 arrival.

> Not quite cancel culture, TCM's *Reframed* still steps in that direction. It follows the same revisionism that distorts the history of Hollywood's late-'40s to late-'50s blacklist: Everything is seen in terms of victimization and offense....
>
> Like the justice commissions appointed by progressive politicians, TCM's *Reframed* looked for flaws, errors, and offenses. Filmmakers were judged unfairly as guilty or naïve but never credited for their principles or convictions—the reasons that art endures, the qualities that keep viewers fascinated, attentive, and loyal.[203]

Of course, it isn't just movies from Hollywood's Golden Age up for a re-evaluation (and possible dismissal). A single scold in Oregon waged Twitter war against the harmless 1990 comedy *Kindergarten Cop* in 2020…and won.[204]

The NW Film Center scrapped an outdoor screening of the Arnold Schwarzenegger romp after a single social justice type dubbed it comparable to *Birth of a Nation* and *Gone with the Wind*.

The film had been chosen, in part, because it was shot in Astoria, Oregon, nearly thirty years prior. But Portland author Lois Leveen wasn't amused. Her six-tweet-long rant featured the following:

> What's so funny about School-to-Prison pipeline? Kindergarten Cop-Out: Tell @nwfilmcenter there's nothing fun in cops traumatizing kids. National reckoning on overpolicing is a weird time to revive Kindergarten

Cop. IRL, we are trying to end school-to-prison pipeline. There's nothing entertaining about the presence
of police in schools, which feeds the "school-to-prison"
pipeline in which African American, Latinx, and other
kids of color are criminalized rather than educated.

Yes, *Kindergarten Cop* is only a movie. So are *Birth of a
Nation* and *Gone with the Wind*, but we recognize films
like those are not "good family fun." They are relics of
how pop culture feeds racist assumptions. KINDER-
GARTEN COP romanticizes over-policing in the U.S.

The film center denied Leveen's complaints influenced its decision,
but Fox News noted the statement announcing its decision came as a direct reply to Leveen's tweets. The group cited an "overwhelming demand"
for the film's removal without showing the math or receipts.

Color me skeptical. Now, though, here comes the comedy. You'd
think Leveen would be:

A. Satisfied

B. In the middle of a victory lap

C. Looking for other innocent films to censor

Instead, she shared this indignant response in another tweet:

I think what you meant to type was, "Yes, we made a
grave error in not realizing the implicit racism in that
programming decision. We apologize and are rethink-
ing who makes our programming decisions hereafter."
How deep a white normativity hole will @nwfilmcen-
ter keep digging?

Leveen's pop-culture scalp-taking is notable. So, too, is a 2020 *Variety*
article in which various classic films are listed as needing warning labels.[205]

The usual suspects got the call, including *The Searchers, Holiday Inn,* and *The Children's Hour.* Also name-checked? *Forrest Gump* (1994), *The Silence of the Lambs* (1991), and *Me Before You* (2016). Those latter films are "hostile to protesters, activists and the counterculture," transphobic and insensitive to the disabled community.

The article opens with a howler, a vivid example of a bubble-dwelling journalist:

> It's now widely accepted that despite being a beloved classic, "Gone with the Wind" needs an explanation of its context when it's screened on TV or in theaters.[206]

Yes, "widely accepted" now means, "everyone I follow on Twitter."

The reasons for the trigger warnings are funnier than any Stephen Colbert monologue. Here's the rationale for adding 1994's *True Lies* to the label list.

> James Cameron is a rare filmmaker: a brilliant storyteller and a true visionary. But even a genius can make a misstep. The film is entertaining and has some terrific set-pieces, but the Arab characters are religious fanatics or terrorists, or both.

Imagine—making a movie in which an Arab character is one of those two types, when we never, ever see them in real life!

The best example, however, is picking a movie less than a year old for the "warning label" treatment. Yes, *Once Upon a Time…in Hollywood* by Quentin Tarantino is also a meany to hippies.

> It's about two middle-aged white guys who long for the old days in Hollywood; in other words, MHGA (Make Hollywood Great Again). The film is set in 1969, when some Americans felt the status quo was being threatened by minorities, hippies and newly liberated women. From the controversial depiction of Bruce Lee—one of Hollywood's rare Asian stars—to the fact that Black people seem non-existent and "the

Mexicans," as they're called in the film, are car valets or waitresses, Tarantino's film seems to have several blind spots. And Charles Manson's white supremacist agenda is ignored.

That might be the wokest paragraph ever written, requiring its own book to properly unpack. You'd think *Variety* would be embarrassed to publish a piece that reads like something a first-time blogger might type, before thinking better of it and hitting "delete."

Nope.

There is a glimmer of hope on the horizon, and it's both audacious and capitalistic to the core. A U.K. company, Mirriad, offers sports technology that allows advertisers to insert product placement into classic films.

> "The technology can 'read' an image, it understands the depth, the motion, the fabric, anything. So you can introduce new images that basically the human eye does not realise has been done after the fact, after the production," Mirriad's chief executive Stephan Beringer says.[207]

Traditional product placement is commonplace in modern film and TV shows, and has been for some time. Now, companies can weaponize some of Hollywood's most trusted titles to push their products.

Some placements might not work for practical reasons. You don't want Rhett Butler texting, "I don't give a damn" to a frazzled Scarlett O'Hara.

Other product placement possibilities, like adding old-school Coke logos to '60s era spy movies, might be a better fit.

Here's betting if this is Hollywood's new cash cow, the woke mob will pressure studios to steer the profits to the social justice cause du jour.

The mob would rather line their own pockets than protect us from "problematic" films. At the end of the day, Cancel Culture is about power (and, whenever possible, cash).

CHAPTER 14:

From Freedom Rock to Woke Rock

THERE'S A REASON THAT rockers like The Beatles, Pink Floyd, Fleetwood Mac, and Billy Joel still crush the music charts.

What modern bands are threatening their legacies?

The Fab Four sold the most records of any rock band in 2020. Greatest hits records featuring Elton John, Creedence Clearwater Revival, and Journey also moved briskly that year, with few signs of slowing down.[208]

Any quick peek at the Top of the Charts shows R&B, hip hop, and pop superstars pushing the most product. Drake, BTS, and Ed Sheeran were the top three artists of 2020, and no rock-style outfit cracked the Top 10. Rock isn't dead, but it's resting comfortably and not allowed out after 9 p.m.

Perhaps that's why we're seeing rock musicians, along with other genre artists, either embrace the woke revolution or stand down. Sure, it's the antithesis of the rock mentality, and John Bonham spins in his grave with every social justice gesture.

Who's out there pushing rock's irrepressible spirit? Where are the rebels?

We're not pining for overdoses and trashed hotel rooms, but how about singers willing to risk something, anything, by sharing a fresh opinion not formally approved by Lena Dunham? Spotify even has its own WOKE playlist for the social justice warrior on the go![209]

Music's biggest night of the year, the annual Grammy awards, is now a woke emporium (with the falling ratings to show for it). The 2021 edition had more Black Lives Matter messaging than a Portland coffee klatch.

Previous galas also leaned heavily on woke platitudes, especially the 2018 edition. That night featured Janelle Monae honoring the new Time's Up movement, black dancers "dying" as gun shots ricocheted around the theaters.

You know, just like what happens every weekend in Chicago that woke activists can't wait to ignore.

Grammy speakers that night referenced the political fight over DACA immigrants and the show began with celebrities reading from the anti-Trump book du jour. Because nothing screams music better than a progressive political screed.

Gosh, with so many inclusive moments, it's a mystery so few people tune in to watch these awards shows.

Comedian Dave Chappelle topped the night off by saying, "The only thing more frightening than watching a black man be honest in America is being an honest black man in America."

Tell that to Thomas Sowell, assuming he won't be censored for speaking his mind. Or Supreme Court Justice Clarence Thomas. His documentary *Created Equal: Clarence Thomas in His Own Words* got "canceled" by Amazon during Black History month in 2021. But we digress…

The woke histrionics stretch far beyond the Grammy stage, sadly. That punk rock sentiment is a thing of the past, something to be observed through a historical lens. Rock stars now apologize for their messaging or even sharing a simple book recommendation.[210]

The band Big Thief offered up a mea culpa for, get this, a T-shirt design. One of the band's shirts featured purple arms and hands grasping jail cell bars. That was offensive, apparently, coaxing the band to use Instagram to apologize.

Imagine how many rockers of yore would use social media to fess up to trashing hotel rooms or imposing their toxic masculinity on groupies? That may happen soon, but for now, Big Thief is big-time sorry.

> The jail cell was meant to be a metaphor symbolising imprisonment of the mind and spirit because of con-

structs, etc.... The arms were intended to be purple so as to avoid realism and race all together but we feel that that thinking was misdirected.

We believe that something as pervasive, horrific and insidious as incarceration can not lightly be approached and most especially in avoidance of the issue of race, as the entire incarceration system is fuelled by racism. The lack of attention we paid to this symbolism is, to us, is a reason to bring it up.

Letting this image get printed on a shirt is just another example of a symptom of being conditioned in a culture of normalised white supremacy and we apologise to anyone who may have felt hurt or uncomfortable with this image.

Is there anything less "rock 'n' roll" than a hostage-style apology for doing nothing wrong?

"The band is truly sorry for rocking as hard as we did last night in Cleveland. We understand some were traumatized by both the vibes and volume. We shan't let it happen again."

Left unsaid by Big Thief's mea culpa? The symbolism of a jail cell depicting how woke culture keeps free expression behind bars.

An obscure musician from Mumford and Sons got his fifteen minutes of fame via the least rock 'n' roll apology ever uttered.

The crime? Banjoist Winston Marshall praised a book written by a gay Asian journalist.

Wait? That's like Woke 101, right?

Sorry, this particular journalist isn't offered protection, even though he's in not one but two "protected" groups.

Andy Ngo's beat is Antifa, the violent, anti-American group that poses as a fascist-fighting force. It's a lie, of course, but one too many Americans believe thanks to our corrupt, dishonest media.

Marshall had read Ngo's recent book, *Unmasked: Inside Antifa's Radical Plan to Destroy Democracy*, about the history and mania behind Antifa, and he promoted the tome on Twitter.

That's it. That's his "crime." Once the woke mob let him have it on—where else?—social media, Marshall got the sads.

> "Over the past few days, I have come to better understand the pain caused by the book I endorsed," Marshall said in a statement Wednesday. "I have offended not only a lot of people I don't know but also those closest to me, including my bandmates and for that, I am truly sorry."[211]

Rockers offending their band mates? Roger Daltrey and Pete Townshend probably have three dustups before brunch on a random tour day. But Marshall continues:

> As a result of my actions I am taking time away from the band to examine my blindspots. For now, please know that I realize how my endorsements have the potential to be viewed as approvals of hateful, divisive behavior. I apologize, as this was not at all my intention.[212]

Left unsaid: what was hateful and/or divisive in Ngo's book.

Marshall later officially quit the band and rescinded his apology so he can keep speaking truth to power. Good luck!

Ozzy Osbourne, who in his career famously bit the head off a dead bat and two live doves, could not be reached for comment.[213]

The irony, beyond the fact that a rock musician behaved in such a fashion? Here's what Marshall had said in the original tweet:

> "Finally had the time to read your important book. You're a brave man."

He was right that first time. Ngo suffered a brain bleed following one altercation with Antifa (during, you know, a "mostly peaceful protest"). His continued reporting on the group keeps him in harm's way, something the average CNN "reporter" wouldn't dream of doing. Ngo's work educates millions on a subject the corporate media won't touch.

R.E.M.'s Michael Stipe hasn't made much music since leaving that Athens, Georgia band in 2011. He has been snapping pictures for a very long time, though, which led to a 2021 *Guardian* interview to promote his latest tome of photographs.

The long-ranging chat (It *is* the *Guardian*, after all) eventually touched on both social media and the one event that gave ol' Mikey the creeps.[214]

Twitter didn't ban President Donald Trump quickly enough. Really.

> "It's so upsetting to me that it took the end of the years of Trump as president for Twitter and Jack Dorsey to finally decide that Trump had said something that was offensive on Twitter, and [his account] needed to be suspended," he says. "That platform allowed Trump a voice that put wind under his sails, and allowed for the type of disgusting behaviour that earmarks those years, and allowed a pandemic to run ravage across our country and across the world. It's an embarrassing and horrifying chapter of our history. This stupid male idea of power, it's so dumb.... Americans, you know, we're particularly good at showing our asses publicly. But when I say we, I mean all of us. We're better than this."[215]

Yes, here's a veritable rock god crying out for speech censorship. Boy, there isn't a rock 'n' roll cell left in him, is there?

Other woke rock moments weren't as embarrassing, but simply showed how corporate even the biggest rock icons could become in our current climate.

Bruce Springsteen, after shooting a "unity" Jeep commercial that was rightly mocked on the Left and Right, got into the podcast business. After all, podcasting still has some cool cachet at this point.

Except his podcasting co-host was President Barack Obama.

It may be my duty to listen to a few episodes, but I already endure one Oscar telecast a year. How much torture can an entertainment scribe take?

It's only natural that today's pop stars, who desperately chase trends to keep themselves in vogue, would go woke.

Katy Perry dubbed her new woke-itude "purposeful pop," a name that thankfully didn't stick.

Yes, one of the richest women in pop has all the feels for the down-trodden. Only her intended audience recoiled at the messaging. Here's the liberal *Vulture* clapping back at the songstress.[216]

> Ineffectual messaging isn't a crime in the court of pub-lic opinion, but when wokeness is your stated aim, thoughtlessness is the result: Perry recently found her-self in hot water for a tasteless Barack Obama joke[217] and her choice of Met Gala dress,[218] a blood-red gown from Hitler-sympathizing Maison Margiela director John Galliano. Both gaffes brought back Perry's flor-id history[219] of cultural dress-up and raised questions about the seriousness of her social-justice initiative. Tellingly, the follow-up to "Chained to the Rhythm" is "Bon Appétit," a ditty about getting "spread like a buffet" with verses from guests the Migos.[220]

You just can't don a woke attitude like a dress, apparently. The woke mob demands true believers, and they're eager to surf through your entire life story to find evidence of your past thought crimes.

The site then targeted Miley Cyrus, another artist trying Woke 101 on for size. Cyrus's thought crime was pointing out that some rap songs reek of misogyny.

> It's a curious stance for her to take, as someone whose garish stage and award-show antics are singularly re-sponsible for introducing twerking to middle America.

Wait? Is this *Vulture* or a Christian website? See how the cultural goal posts move minute by minute, with little rhyme or reason?
Moving on…

> Longstanding suspicions[221] about her use of hip-hop culture as an accessory suddenly seemed confirmed, and fans pushed back.[222] Miley's single is ultimately refreshing, and her message isn't without value; but it's hard to receive a harsh word from someone who hasn't lived it.

Suddenly, you can't be an "ally" unless you've lived the messages you're sharing. Pretty hard for Cyrus, daughter of a mulleted music star and Disney Channel alum, to suddenly change her life story. What's her Plan B, Woke Nation?

How bad have things gotten? Don Letts, a musician and videographer for The Clash, penned a piece for *The Radio Times* warning the woke culture, moving forward, could dampen protest songs.

> For artists, the protest song is an increasingly difficult proposition. In a world so woke you can't make a joke, trying to navigate the minefield of fake news, conspiracy theories and information overload is made even trickier by the fear of being accused of cultural appropriation.
>
> In my day, getting into music felt like a rebellious, anti-establishment thing. Today, many see it as a way of becoming part of the establishment.[223]

Amen.

It took a seventy-something legend to show the kids how it's done in 2020. Legendary crooner Van Morrison took direct aim at the pandemic lockdowns with songs brimming with a hunger for freedom. "Born to Be Free," "As I Walked Out," and "No More Lockdowns" (subtle!) found Morrison questioning the extreme measures that crushed the music industry, among other institutions.

> I'm not telling people what to do or think, the government is doing a great job of that already. It's about freedom of choice, I believe people should have the right to think for themselves.

Morrison's lyrics in "No More Lockdowns" show what happens when you put the message in front of the art. It ain't pretty.

> No more lockdown/No more government overreach/ No more fascist bullies/Disturbing our peace/No more taking of our freedom/And our God-given rights/Pretending it's for our safety/When it's really to enslave.[224]

Naturally, *Rolling Stone* led the charge against Morrison for his rebellious streak. "Northern Ireland health minister says new songs are 'dangerous,'" the subhead reads.

And then there's rapper Tom MacDonald. The white Canadian shocked and rocked the charts with "Fake Woke," one of many songs that proved politically incorrect to the nth degree. He pounded the woke mob over and again with his music, which naturally meant the mainstream media either ignored his success or attacked him as a white supremacist.

Because, reasons. Or, more accurately, the woke mob cannot debate or reason. It's why they throw out "racist!" and "White Supremacist" with such fury. It's all they've got.

MacDonald gave just about everyone, save his fans, the middle finger. He's a literal one-man operation (with an assist from his talented girlfriend/videographer Nova Rockafeller). This author reached out to him via a contact email, to which he answered directly a very short time later. No PR team or handler. That approach lets him survive, nay thrive, while shaming just about every other working artist who refuses to stand up for free expression.

If the new wave of rockers can't be bothered to defend their right to rock, it's up to the old-timers to don the mantle.

Sex Pistols's front man Johnny Rotten (John Lydon) told the UK's *Sunday Times* what he thinks about the youth-powered woke revolution. Suffice to say it was less than delicate. He described its adherents as having "s*** for brains," for starters. And it's all the universities' fault:

> These people aren't really genuinely disenfranchised at all.... They just view themselves as special. It's selfishness and in that respect it's divisive and can only lead to trouble. I can't believe that TV stations give some of these lunatics the space.

> Where is this "moral majority" nonsense coming from when they're basically the ones doing all the wrong for being so bloody judgmental and vicious against anybody who doesn't go along with the current popular opinion.[225]

Of course, Lydon now leans to the Right, the true punk rock pose for the twenty-first century.

Other aging rockers prefer to stay unwoke, thank you. Alice Cooper won't be waving any BLM flags at his next concert. He's also not ready to get on a soapbox and tell fans which politician to support.

> When musicians are telling people who to vote for, I think that's an abuse of power. You're telling your fans not to think for themselves, just to think like you. Rock 'n' roll is about freedom and that's not freedom.[226]

Cool, man.

Morrissey stands out as another superstar unwilling to put on the woke trappings. He's pro-Brexit, for starters, a real no-no in celebrity circles. He quickly got called a racist for making that simple declaration.

> I don't think the word "racist" has any meaning any more, other than to say "you don't agree with me, so you're a racist." People can be utterly, utterly stupid.[227]

So much privilege!

The liberal *Paste* magazine did its very best to "cancel" Morrissey, compiling a listicle of his eight most offensive comments. What's next? "Twenty-One Reasons The Who Should Be Booted from the Rock 'n' Roll Hall of Fame (No. 14: Drummer Keith Moon trashed so many hotel rooms Holiday Inn banned him for life)."[228]

Yes, Morrissey says incendiary things. He's a musician, not a politician, and he's eager to poke and prod until your attention is his. Contrast the media reaction when Madonna famously said she dreamed of blowing up the White House, presumably with President Donald Trump inside. Yes, the same media detractors chuckled in response.

The most unwoke star of modern times may be Kanye West. He famously palled around with President Donald Trump, wore a red MAGA hat on *Saturday Night Live*, and repeatedly told anyone who would listen black Americans aren't slaves to the progressive mindset.

Chances are, though, that an industry known for building upon the work of black music pioneers like Chuck Berry and Little Richard won't be using Kanye as a role model.

CHAPTER 15:
That's Not Funny

WE SHOULD HAVE listened to Jerry.

The star and co-creator of *Seinfeld* warned us back in 2015 about the growing wave of woke Inquisitors swamping college campuses.

Seinfeld, a squeaky-clean comic who steers clear of political matters, told an interviewer at the time why he no longer performs for college students.

"I don't play colleges, but I hear a lot of people tell me, 'Don't go near colleges. They're so PC,'" Seinfeld told *The Herd with Colin Cowherd* about advice he's heeded from fellow comedians.[229]

Seinfeld wasn't the first comedian to share that frustration, but when it came from a beloved, spotlessly clean comic, it crashed the news cycle. It also spawned more than a few think pieces attacking Seinfeld for not being woke, like this one from far-left CNN contributor Dean Obeidallah:

> And where I greatly disagree with Seinfeld is that based on my experiences of performing on college campuses, I believe young adults for the most part really get racism, sexism, and other-isms.
>
> For example, I have been in shows where comedians told very sexist or homophobic jokes. These same jokes would elicit good laughs in comedy clubs, but were

met with numerous objections by college students.
The students have every right to voice their views
about these jokes.[230]

The veteran comic had a less sympathetic explanation for why young crowds are intolerant to humor.

"They just want to use these words: 'That's racist;' 'That's sexist;' 'That's prejudice,'" Seinfeld said of young people today. "They don't know what the hell they're talking about."

And he's right. What Seinfeld couldn't realize at the time was that no arm of the entertainment industry would be hit harder by the woke revolution than stand-up comedy. Comedians now work knowing a single joke can cost them a gig, a TV series, or a career.

Politicians often weigh their words carefully for fear of offending a special interest group or giving their opponents campaign fodder. That's part of the gig, and they behave accordingly. They do write laws that impact our daily lives, after all. A modicum of circumspection seems only right.

But now, stand-ups operate under a similar level of scrutiny.

Amy Schumer had to apologize after this crude joke: "I used to date Hispanic guys, but now I prefer consensual."

Here's her Twitter apology:

> I used to do a lot of short dumb jokes like this. I played a dumb white girl onstage. I still do sometimes. Once I realized I had more eyes and ears on me and had an influence I stopped telling jokes like that onstage.
>
> I am evolving as an artist.... I am taking responsibility and hope I haven't hurt anyone. I apologize [if] I did.[231]

The host of *Tosh.0* apologized after telling a rape joke from a comedy stage. Tosh's humor is bleak beyond most of his colleagues, and he routinely traffics in dark humor. Tosh joked that rape is "always funny," to which a female audience member disagreed—out loud.

"Wouldn't it be funny if that girl got raped by like, five guys right now? Like right now? What if a bunch of guys just raped her…."

"All the out of context misquotes aside, I'd like to sincerely apologize," Tosh tweeted later.

This, it's worth noting, happened in 2012. Flash-forward a decade later, and the very same *Tosh.0* host began pushing Black Lives Matter propaganda and doubling down on GOP targets via his Comedy Central show.

Comedians don't always apologize from the heart. It's often just an attempt to do PR damage control. In some cases, the stars admit it once the smoke clears.

Saturday Night Live star Pete Davidson riffed on Rep. Dan Crenshaw, a Republican who lost an eye in combat. Davidson dismissed the injury in his routine, and some conservatives did a fair impression of college snowflakes in response.

So, Davidson offered up an apology of sorts and even appeared with Crenshaw himself on a subsequent *SNL* episode. The latter wasn't necessary, but in an age of hate and invective, it still felt like a quality moment.

Then Davidson backpedaled.

"I didn't think I did anything wrong," Davidson said during a subsequent stage appearance. "It was like words that were twisted so that a guy could be famous."

"I kind of got forced to apologize."

The woke mob is unabashedly left of center, so Davidson could quickly backtrack with the full knowledge he wouldn't face any consequences. And he didn't.[232]

Others don't take that chance.

The 2020 hagiography, *Miss Americana*, fetes Taylor Swift for finally embracing her inner progressive. Part of the film turns serious as Swift describes the internal pressure she faces to stay trim in a brutal, looks-obsessed industry.

The documentary shows a brief clip of comedienne Nikki Glaser calling the singer "too skinny. It bothers me." Glaser used her Instagram account, after the film's release, to apologize for the crack. She added she struggled with her own eating disorder for nearly two decades.

"This quote should be used as an example of 'projection' in PSYCH 101 textbooks," Glaser wrote in the post. "I was probably 'feeling fat' that day and was jealous."[233]

Even progressive comics like Trevor Noah of *The Daily Show* aren't immune to offending folks.[234] His sin was riffing on escalating tensions between India and Pakistan. If war broke out, he said, it would be "most entertaining," mimicking a Bollywood dance number from his faux anchor chair.

Noah was dubbed racist and culturally insensitive. So, he backpedaled.

"I am sorry that this hurt you and others, that's not what I was trying to do," he tweeted.

The new, farcical "punching down" rules mean comedians must take great care in the groups they poke and prod from the stage. *BuzzFeed*, the unofficial arbiter of woke culture, declared "Punching Down Will Never Be Funny" in a definitive 2016 article.

> The real difference is that comedy shows or segments that are legitimately funny always punch up. Instead of wasting their time going after people who are typically in the minority, they go after people with tangible power that's being abused. A basic tenet of humor—and I mean real basic, we're talking ancient Greece here—is that your best stuff will come from going after people bigger than you.[235]

Yes, that's why several late-night shows mocked ordinary Americans who protested pandemic lockdown conditions that were crushing their businesses, and their lives. It's the epitome of "punching down," but the usual woke arbiters looked the other way.

When President Joe Biden took the oath of office, it wasn't long before two comedy referees (*The Washington Post* and *USA Today*) declared him so wise, so competent, that comedians had nothing to joke about with him.

Really? If you can't punch up at the most powerful man in the world, then the "punching down" rulebook is a fraud.[236]

Any gag aimed at the trans community is considered a hate crime of sorts. The biggest names in comedy aren't immune to that charge, be it

Dave Chappelle or Ricky Gervais. Each has been savaged by the hard-Left and the media—which is essentially one and the same in our current climate—for telling jokes about trans folks like Caitlyn Jenner. (For the record, both have shrugged off the slams and kept telling the jokes they want to tell.)

Of course, if you're poking fun at a conservative, you can punch down as long, and as hard, as you wish. Comedians teed off on former First Lady Melania Trump during her four years in the White House, sexualizing her and mocking her accent.

Comedians wouldn't dare mock, say, Michelle Obama in such fashion.

Jimmy Kimmel dirisively called Jenner "Trump in a wig," but the Woke Police never knocked on his door.[237] Hmmm.

Some comedians began fighting back against the new, oppressive rules. Chappelle made an entire Netflix special, *Sticks & Stones*, mocking the woke mob. Gervais shares free speech dictums on Twitter and refuses to back down.

Adam Carolla kicked off his 2020 bestseller, *I'm Your Emotional Support Animal*, by vowing not to apologize for any of the jokes contained within. His 2019 documentary *No Safe Spaces* similarly featured a crush of comedians sounding the alarm about woke culture. Tim Allen, Bryan Callen, and other humorists warned what happens when the hard-Left activists on campus run roughshod over free speech. They graduate into the "real world" and bring their censorious ways with them.

As a comedy manager, Keri Smith once helped woke comics snag gigs, record deals, and even late-night talk shows. Smith not so proudly admits to shepherding the first woke comedy series, *Totally Biased with W. Kamau Bell*, to FX in 2012. She considered herself a true believer at the time, someone who wanted woke comedy to influence the culture.

Slowly, surely, she had a change of heart in 2018. Now, she's dedicated to fighting back against the woke culture in any way possible, be it her *Unsafe Space* podcast or revealing the hypocrisies embedded in wokeness on social media. That's assuming she's still allowed on major platforms by the time this book is printed. Her *Unsafe Space* podcast's Twitter account got permanently banned early in 2021, something she says happened without a proper explanation.

YouTube also temporarily punished the video version of her podcast that same year.

Smith formerly worked for far-left comedienne Margaret Cho, an early adopter of woke material. That connection allowed Smith to see the future of woke comedy.

"As the culture started to change, the social justice stuff was getting bigger and more censorious," Smith told her *Unsafe Space* listeners during a March broadcast. She noted how even Cho was forced to abide by strict rules when telling jokes on stage. Allies, too, had to toe a very specific line.

"We got a letter from one of these events that had a list of things she wasn't allowed to joke about on stage," Smith recalled. "We hadn't seen that before, but it was very controlling about, 'you can't make these things the butts of jokes.'"

Smith understood that by divorcing herself from woke culture she'd end her reign as a comedy manager. However, she couldn't ignore the lessons she learned by listening to Jordan Peterson, among others who criticized the social justice agenda.

The woke mob needs enforcers to make the changes they demand happen. They get plenty of help from nervous TV and film executives. Corporations more generally have also gone woke, and it's hard to imagine any employee fighting the new rules without suffering the consequences. Including pink slips.

Big Tech joined the fray in recent years, providing perhaps the most frightening weapons in the social justice warrior's arsenal. President Donald Trump's 2020 electoral loss, combined with the George Floyd riots and the January 6, 2021 assault on the U.S. Capitol, pushed Big Tech censorship into overdrive. Right-leaning comics, or anyone eager to smite woke culture, found their work being banned or limited by massive platforms like TikTok and Facebook.

Ryan Long, a Canadian stand-up who moved to New York as the woke train barreled across his new home, found that out the hard way. Both Instagram and TikTok banned his comic video mocking news outlets that slammed white men as problematic. The comic's message was clear: judging a group of people by their skin color was racist.

These tech giants didn't like that message and banned the video.

For Long, being censored became part of his regular TikTok posting process, so he stopped sharing his sharply satirical snippets on that platform.

The Babylon Bee spotted this censorial trend long before other comic institutions for a simple reason. The right-leaning satire site found a target on its cyber back early in the woke revolution.

Absurdly, the *Bee* routinely has had its *satirical stories* "fact-checked" by *USA Today* and Snopes, two left-leaning entities that feed into Facebook's so-called Fake News filter. The social media giant works with these alleged fact-checking sources to reduce the amount of "fake news" on its platform. So, Facebook, in turn, has threatened to punish *The Babylon Bee* for spreading lies—even though its stories, like the site itself, are clearly intended as humorous exaggerations and lampoons.

One of the site's sharpest faux "news" articles generated a serious fact-check that threatened the site's survival. The article's farcical headline is a howler:

> CNN Purchases Industrial-Sized Washing Machine to
> Spin News Before Publication

To be fair, *The Bee* headline hit so close to home about CNN's biases that it had a whiff of authenticity. But that's what great satire does, right? It's also why the liberal media and Big Tech don't like *The Babylon Bee*.

Snopes then rushed to CNN's defense, helping apparently clueless readers understand the article was satire, not fact.

And since the *Bee's* CNN "article" failed the Snopes fact-check, Facebook told *The Bee* it could face dire consequences:

> "A page you admin (The Babylon Bee) recently posted the link (CNN Purchases Industrial-Sized Washing Machine To Spin News Before Publication) that contains info disputed by (Snopes.com), an independent fact checker," the Facebook notification told Ford. "Repeat offenders will see their distribution reduced and their ability to monetize and advertised[sic] removed."

USA Today also fact-checked not one but two *Bee* stories. Read the headlines for yourself and see if they were worth the investigation:

> With Moon Water Announcement, Trump Proposes
> Space Navy

> Ninth Circuit Court Overturns Death of Ruth Bader
> Ginsburg

It's worth noting that *The Onion*, an older and decidedly left-leaning satirical site, has avoided most, if not all, of the grief *The Bee* has endured.

Comedian Lee Hurst got suspended from Twitter after sharing the following wisecrack aimed at Greta Thunberg, the climate change activist:

> As soon as Greta discovers c***, she'll stop complain-
> ing about the single use plastic it's wrapped in.[238]

It's undeniably crude, but Thunberg turned eighteen at the dawn of 2021 and is a public figure whose commentary holds sway over a crucial issue.

Now, consider how many hard-left comics said far, far worse about President Donald Trump on social media over the past decade. Have any of those jokes been deemed beyond the pale and forced a suspension like this?

You don't need to fire up DuckDuckGo.com to find the answer.

CHAPTER 16:
Comedians Fight Back

THE WOKE REVOLUTION hit two institutions early and often: academia and Humor, Inc.

The 2019 movie *No Safe Spaces* addressed the former, a free speech assault by campus progressives with little resistance from the adults in charge. The movie proved frighteningly prescient, with woke insanity swiftly moving from universities to the "real world." We knew that would happen, but the speed at which it occurred took many by surprise.

Comedians endured the woke revolution long before it went mainstream, too.

The 2015 documentary *Can We Take a Joke?* gave us a frightening peek at the problem. Suddenly, the cultural mavens started treating stand-ups like politicians in training, weighing their laugh lines to see if they said the wrong things at the wrong time.

The film allowed button-pushing comics like Gilbert Gottfried, Adam Carolla, and Jim Norton to share why comedians need room to creatively roam, and why the emerging Thought Police threatens to upend their industry.

The film's director, Ted Balaker, told me Lenny Bruce wouldn't be welcome on today's college campus. Who would disagree at this point?

Another razor-sharp comedian, Mike Birbiglia, confessed during our 2016 chat why the mounting woke insurgency posed a threat to practitioners of his craft, or to any artist, for that matter.

"If we sanitize what we're doing, we're not gonna have great art any-more," Birbiglia said while promoting *Don't Think Twice*. Birbiglia is un-abashedly liberal, but like too many stars today, he now rarely leverages his social media accounts to speak against the woke mob.

Many comedians changed their acts, and social media messaging, once the woke mob took over. Some made the transition organically. Others seemed like they were protecting their posteriors, and their ca-reers, by doing so.

Comic masterminds like Judd Apatow have a body of work that hasn't aged well for the average Social Justice Warrior. Apatow's brand of white male dude bros who refuse to grow up are infinitely funny but problematic.

Is that why Apatow went woke?

A much smaller group of humorists have taken a stand. This deter-mined band of comedy misfits refuse to play by the new woke rules. They understand their jobs better than their critics. Be funny. Speak truth to power. Push us into places that make us uncomfortable. And stop wor-rying about which bit will "offend" which audience member. That comes with the territory.

The biggest names associated with this take no prisoners approach?

- Ricky Gervais

- John Cleese

- Adam Carolla

- Dave Chappelle

- Bill Burr

Other comics lack the industry clout of these truth-tellers, but that makes them even braver, considering the jokes they dare to share.

Many of them hunkered down at Compound Media. The service started in 2014 with *The Anthony Cumia Show*, hosted by half of the radio powerhouse Opie and Anthony. Compound Media offers a crush of video podcasts where the hosts are free to speak their minds. And boy, do they take full advantage of that freedom.

Timid listeners might want to sip some chamomile tea after a few episodes. Everyone else, especially those weaned on classic Howard Stern, will relish the no-holds-barred banter.

Sponsors are few, with the monthly fee providing the bulk of the revenue. That allows them to operate freely without worrying about a boycott from a major car manufacturer or fast-food franchise.

Aaron Berg, co-host with Geno Bisconte of Compound Media's *In Hot Water*, suggests the rise of woke comedy is a way for comedians to avoid spending years and years honing their craft. Woke comedians, for the most part, are "people who haven't been able to excel at the art form. It's an excuse for not being able to kill in the clubs," Berg says.

"The biggest killers, the funniest guys and girls, paid their dues. They were able to learn how to kill. These people don't want to put that work in…and they don't want to associate with those who want to put that work in."

Berg cites comedian Gary Gulman as an exception. Gulman, he says, shifted his material in recent years to reflect a more woke persona, but he retained the laughter.

"He's only good at it because he's been doing it for thirty years," he says. Otherwise, the woke comic operates on a different principle, he says, one that seems antithetical to the job description.

"Belly laughs shouldn't be a requirement," he says of their philosophy. "It should be right and proper and educational and progressive."

Some of these comics target folks like Berg directly. They may tag him, along with a comedy club, on social media to sway the latter from hiring him for a gig.

"He's a Nazi," Berg summarizes some attacks against him.

"These people are not good people," says Berg, who adds that many have their own skeletons in the closets that they're trying to hide. "I don't know if it's projection or deflection."

One thing is clear. They may be loud and riding the cultural wave, but he says they're in the minority.

Perhaps the funniest thing a woke comedian will do is insist an audience is wrong for not being offended as much as they are. He says the average New York comedy club is the picture of diversity, a room where a good comic can make every one of every nationality, creed, or color laugh. "You know what you're doing cannot be wrong," he says. Tell that to the woke observers, who fold their arms and wonder why the "stupid" audiences are laughing in the first place. "It's elitist," Berg says.

The surliest woke critique, he says, comes when his attackers insist he craves free speech to say something truly awful, like the "n-word."

"Nobody wants that. They just want to be able to say the things they're feeling, those things aren't always good," he says. "People would love to shut comedy down…. Comedy expresses freedom of thought, freedom of speech…they don't want people talking."

Chrissie Mayr also calls Compound Media home. She's fully aware it's one of the few "safe spaces" left for unexpurgated comedy. The *Wet Spot* hostess graduated college in 2005 and sounded like most of her peers, politically speaking.

"I would have been woke if I graduated college ten years later," Mayr says. Her political leanings, and sense of humor, evolved beyond graduation. She also developed a thicker skin and a propensity to find humor in virtually any situation. So, when a comedienne appeared, and abruptly walked off, the set of a Compound Media show, she and her colleagues had some fun with it.

The comic in question said she was being bullied by the show's fans, including one who noted she "could use a railroad spike in the keister," a comment that's both crude and in line with the Compound Media mythos.

Who could take such an insult seriously?

The battle progressed from there, including Mayr dressing up as an oversized railroad spike made from tinfoil.

"We're all comedians. We're all public figures. We leave ourselves out open to parody," she says, like the *Schtick or Treat* comedy show in New York where comedians impersonate other, more famous, comedians.

This particular comic, though, wasn't content slinging comebacks live or on social. "She turned a lot of comics against me," Mayr says, adding that a professional connection from NBC's *America's Got Talent* series called her personally to share what she was told about her. "It scared the s*** out of me," Mayr says. "And other comics rallied behind her."

Mayr's appearance at the January 6, 2021 D.C. protests also gave her professional grief. She wasn't near the violence that erupted that day, but she says one of her subsequent comedy gigs got calls asking if they were going to cancel her performance due to the connection.

"People will call the venues of shows…and say you're a white supremacist and a racist. How dare they hire you!" This led her to a position others like her have embraced. "Never apologize. It's about power and shutting down voices they don't like," she says.

All of this confirmed Mayr's decision to avoid a conventional comedy career. "I gave up the dream of [*Saturday Night Live*] so long ago…they expect a cookie-cutter performer."

Cancel Culture does two things to comedians like her, she says. It toughens you up and it makes someone more attractive to those seeking authentic comic voices.

"Society is wanting more raw, real comedians. Politicians are fake, our news is fake, it's pandering and bull****," she says.

The soft-spoken Lou Perez isn't as bombastic as Mayr or Berg, and he didn't set out to do political comedy. However, he couldn't help himself when he signed up with the *We the Internet TV* YouTube channel in 2015. The online outfit created comedy videos that dared to mock the Right and the Left. What made the troupe stand out, though, were videos that poked fun at the rising woke tide.

Killer sketches like "Social Justice Warrior Therapist," in which Perez's character is constantly challenged by his woke shrink, offered a fresh comic perspective from the mainstream.

"So you're a straight white cis male who feels alone…how could you ever feel alone, or unhappy?" the therapist scolds Perez's character.

In "ESL Students Learn New Gender Pronouns," a teacher explains to her befuddled students the new woke grammar rules.

Arguably the group's most dangerous sketch featured parents sharing how they let their three-year-old children decide more than their gender. *My son's an astronaut*, one proud papa beamed. The clip couldn't be found on YouTube at the time of this writing, alas.

The Libertarian Perez and his freewheeling colleagues couldn't help but target the on-campus hysterics when he first signed up.

"Trigger warnings, safe spaces…that seemed prime for mocking," Perez says. "We managed to make fun of 'safe spaces' before *South Park*. That's a fun thing."

He says the troupe's videos drew strong, positive reaction from college students aghast at the growing free speech attacks, along with right-leaning viewers. At times, Perez engaged with the channel's critics.

"We opened ourselves up to legitimate criticism and debate," he says. "The goals [of the woke crowd] seemed noble, to protect people who might be at risk," like sexual assault victims who tune out something following a trigger warning. Perez didn't mind fielding those conversations, but the cultural tone shifted in November 2016. The eighth of the month, to be exact.

He didn't notice "the woke stuff was an existential threat until [Donald] Trump came into office," he says. Or, as the woke crowd saw him, "the fascist dictator white supremacist who's now in office," Perez jokes, adding, suddenly half the country needed a safe space.

Comedian Steve McGrew knows all about woke culture. The openly conservative comic was being punished early and often by Facebook before it was cool (and darn near ubiquitous for people on the Right).

He lost an annual gig in Las Vegas after club owner Brad Garrett (yes, that Brad Garrett of *Everybody Loves Raymond* fame) learned McGrew supported Trump, and he found a new level of disdain in comedy circles for joining "The Deplorables" comedy tour.

The veteran stand-up saw the roots of P.C. culture flowering in the 1990s, long before terms like "safe spaces" became popular.

"When I was living in California and it was getting very P.C. out there, I was warning people then that this was not a good thing, that they were censoring you" McGrew says. "Don't do so many jokes about women, wives, and girlfriends, it's very misogynistic."

He says what came next has had a direct impact on how funny comics can be.

"Good comedy is almost dead. Everybody's afraid to make a joke about something because, 'Oh, that's mean and you don't want to get canceled,'" he says.

It isn't just offended audience members who want comics to steer clear of certain topics.

"Oh, yes, I've had agents tell me that I shouldn't do certain jokes, jokes that will kill everywhere in the world except in L.A. They would warn me that casting agents wouldn't find it funny and I could hurt my career. Obviously, it did," he says with a laugh. "But I'm still working and crowds still love me.... Besides, I have a massive amount of fun bashing the Left and their hysterical hypocrisy."

Other comics reach out to McGrew, wishing they could also be as open and brave, but fearing the fallout from taking that approach. They have a right to be afraid, he says.

"Until society changes and leans more to the Right, more comics are just gonna have to play the liberal lunacy game."

A select number of comics are tweaking their material, he says, to appease the Thought Police.

"I've seen several comics change their act to become more woke; they think it will make them more valuable and more wanted or in demand by the powers that be in Hollywood." Even black comics who rarely told race-related jokes are suddenly talking about racism and skin color, he says. "Nothing will get you a Netflix special quicker than being a woke urban comic."

Comedian Don Jamieson has to work the average room a little differently in the current environment. Stand-ups often will tweak their material for each new crowd, noting how a certain gag might hit harder in one city or club than the next.

The newer version of that approach has the host of *That Jamieson Show* on Compound Media assessing what material might rile what table or group. The comedy veteran knows most audiences in the forty-and-up bracket won't be "offended" by a certain punch line, but they may take their cues from younger patrons in the crowd, a demographic much quicker to offend.

"It creates a very strange vibe in the room," Jamieson says. "You unite the crowd as any great comic should do. You just have to figure out how to make it all work."

The dirty little secret about the offended audience members? Ninety-nine percent of them aren't actually offended. It's an act, part of the cultural conversation happening in the modern comedy era, he says.

"They're told they're supposed to be offended, by their peers," he adds.

Jamieson recorded his most recent comedy album, *Denim and Laughter*, from material he shared in every kind of venue, from rock halls to traditional comedy theaters. "I want the jokes to be battle-tested," he says. He hoped to grab, and entertain, as large a group as possible. That meant sneaking some anti-woke gags "in under their noses," he says. "It takes the piss out of them without them even knowing it. It adds another layer to [the comedy]."

He takes particular pleasure in making people laugh at jokes "they don't normally laugh at," he says, but he won't alter his approach to join the current climate. "I'm not gonna chase the trend…you lose all your integrity [if you do]. That's not my style," he says.

What's maddening to Jamieson is not knowing what joke or routine might "offend" a select group. Sure, politics is the ultimate hot button in modern times, followed closely by race and any "'fill-in-the-blank' shaming du jour." "Everything is 'triggering.' From joke to joke you have no idea where people are gonna get offended by."

He finds it amusing when fans buy some of his older comedy albums after a show and note that some of the material couldn't be told today. "What people call extreme comedy [today], fifteen years ago it was just called comedy," he says.

And don't get him started on comedians itching for "clapter" over laughs. For the uninitiated, that refers to jokes eliciting approving applause, not actual laughter. "I see it all the time, and it's pathetic," he says.

Canadian Mark Hughes became a comedian after battling drug addiction and serial stints in prison. Now, he uses his hardscrabble past as fodder for his personalized brand of stand-up comedy where nary a punch is pulled.

Hughes points to the 2012 incident involving Daniel Tosh's rape joke, and the subsequent apology, as the seed from which the woke movement grew.

"It was a watershed moment," Hughes says, as comics started to realize select topics were suddenly off limits. "By the time the general public knows about something like that culturally, it's been going on in the underground [for a while]." The conversation suddenly shifted to the "morality of jokes."

He could have played it safe, or at least safer, when he entered the business. "You have two choices—capitulate or double down." He chooses the latter.

What's maddening, Hughes says, is that the woke crowd doesn't reflect the average Joe or Jane who shows up to see a live comedian. Crowds understand some boundaries will be pushed over the next hour or so, and a few naughty words may be spoken along the way. That unwritten contract is clear for most customers, and they're happy to experience what happens next. They, Hughes insists, are the majority.

He's learned that fellow comedians are often the gatekeepers preventing a free flow of ideas in their field. "Comics turning on comics is new," he notes. Why? They fear being canceled, for starters. Hughes adds that this also helps winnow down the competition. Fewer comedians, more club dates to snag.

"There's more cachet in calling out someone, for being virtuous, rather than being funny…it's immediate gratification," he says. It doesn't help that the official comedy gatekeepers—talent agents, bookers, producers—are more woke than the general public.

Hughes sees an audience for his brand of humor, but getting it to their ears isn't as simple as it sounds. He sees a "distribution problem," where the Big Tech gatekeepers and streaming giants prefer to avoid comedians who could be "problematic."

Comedians like Ryan Long saw some of their less offensive material get memory-holed by Big Tech in 2021 after he zeroed in on the woke mob and its bylaws.

Others who felt a similar pinch include JP Sears, whose self-help hippie persona belies his true passion: freedom of expression.

If comedians rely on these distribution channels they could be in trouble, Hughes notes. Free-thinking comics need "a new distribution plan." "How does the general public find out about me? I can't get a Netflix deal or get on a major club roster, YouTube shadow bans my videos," he says.

Some comedians admit there's an upside to the current woke revolution.

Talents like Tim Dillon and Andrew Schulz are able to walk the oh, so fine line between poking the woke beast and staying on more conventional platforms like YouTube and Netflix, according to Berg. "There's a power to what Cumia formed," something *South Park* generated over the years by not bowing to any mob at any time. "The more pushback from these people, the bigger our audience gets," he says. "By not acknowledging their relevance, it's a very powerful thing."

Perez also sees a capitalistic boost for comics who are able to defy the new, unofficial comedy rules.

"A lot of people say, 'Oh, the woke stuff is gonna kill comedy,' but there's opportunity there, all this material that isn't being mined by the big boys," he says, noting the viral video success of rising star Ryan Long. "There's a huge hunger there, a lot of positive stuff that's happening in the midst of all this big unknown."

There's another side to Perez's optimism, one that leaves him unsure of his future at times. He wonders if being a comic constantly pushing back against the woke tide is worth it.

"I've had thoughts, even recently, that I'm putting independent stuff out there, trying to build up an audience," while wondering if he's "in the wrong game."

"Ultimately, this is what I do and have this need to do it," he says. "It would be a lot easier to just shut up and go along with it…but I feel I can't do it."

Becoming a father also forced him to question doing jokes that could trigger the Cancel Culture crowd.

"As a family guy and needing to provide for my family, perhaps the smart thing would be to shut up and just go with the flow or leave this industry entirely and just get a 'real job,'" he says. "I'm also looking at it as, I have the future of my children to look out for and the world I want to leave them…a world where their dad isn't afraid to speak up."

That description captures stand-up comedian and podcaster Jamie Kilstein, who wrote a powerful tribute to George Carlin upon the legend's passing in 2008. [239]

When Carlin and Bruce were playing dives, stand-up was still counter-culture. You could get arrested for speaking. They got arrested for speaking. George used to be a wacky-faced suit-and-tie observational stand-up until the day he saw Lenny Bruce—until he saw what stand-up could truly be: the art of pushing people's buttons. I know a lot of people felt the same way when they saw Carlin for the first time. That "oh s***" moment when you realize you're a fraud and everything you're doing is dogs***. Many comics ran home to their notebooks after hearing Carlin talk about drugs, censorship, or religion. Most, after that long night of soul-searching, got on stage two days later and talked about their girlfriends' periods, completely selling out last night's soul, instead opting for the easy road to Nowhere. How many comics still talk about what people already know, and what no one is afraid of because they figure there will always be guys like George? Well, now there aren't.

Anytime a club owner, an editor, a member of the audience, a reader, a blog commenter, a parent, an agent, a manager, or a TV executive tells you "You can't say that," say "F*** you. I just did. That means you're wrong." Then, think of George: hippy in handcuffs being dragged out of a club after knowingly breaking the law by saying what he wanted to say, smiling big, and thinking about how he would work this into the act.

No comic today faces a perp walk or handcuffs. The Woke Police, unarmed but determined, make sure it never gets that far.

Jamieson says a list circulated around the New York comedy scene in recent times warning club owners not to hire or work with a group of alleged white nationalist comics.

"Comics ratting out other comics. That's dangerous," Jamieson says. Except it's not just the millennial joke tellers snitching on their peers.

"I've seen big comics post on social media how happy they are that [President Donald] Trump was thrown off Twitter," he says, adding fellow free speech comic Tim Dillon had the best response to that sentiment: comics calling for any sort of free speech suppression aren't comics.

Jamieson always gravitated to the comedians who pushed the boundaries of what can and can't be said on stage. He quotes a classic line from Carlin, one that in and of itself could get the legend canceled today:

"I think it's the duty of the comedian to find out where the line is drawn and cross it deliberately."

"We need to keep our scene alive, keep comedy dangerous," Jamieson concludes.

CHAPTER 17:

Hope in the Age of Woke

THE CULTURAL FORCES LINED up against free expression, creativity, and all-American values look intimidating, if not downright invincible.

The Left conquered Hollywood, and now they're trying to silence their ideological foes. How many times did progressives attempt to remove Rush Limbaugh off the airwaves, much as they're attempting to do with Fox News superstar Tucker Carlson?

The biggest names in the culture bow to the mob, with few exceptions. No matter how much wealth, fame, or, yes, privilege a superstar has, it's often not enough to sufficiently stiffen their spine. The woke mob counts the media, academia, Hollywood, and Corporate U.S.A. as its foot soldiers (not counting the actual foot soldiers known as Antifa). Any one of those institutions alone would be formidable. Added together? They're nearly unstoppable.

I say "nearly" because the American DNA still matters, still rejects the speech-snuffing measures those institutions embrace. That spirit offers the last best hope that the woke war can be won, both in Hollywood and the culture at large.

The 2014 *Avengers* blockbuster gave us a killer line before the epic final battle.

> "I have an army," an arrogant Loki tells Tony Stark,
> a.k.a., Iron Man.

"We have a Hulk," Stark answers.

Freedom-loving Americans are still looking for their Hulk. They thought they had it in President Donald Trump, but his dizzying lack of discipline, combined with the most corrupt media in modern memory, took him down.

In the meantime, a small band of Happy Warriors in the grand Andrew Breitbart mold are ready to defend free speech on their terms. They're not mean and green, but their bravery matters. So does their rhetoric.

The unlikeliest Culture War soldier is Bill Maher.

Yes, that Bill Maher. He's an unabashed lefty who famously loathes religion of any kind. Still, he's one of the most consistent voices against the woke takeover we have.

His primary pulpit, the weekly HBO series *Real Time with Bill Maher*, allows him to weigh in on breaking news in ways his fellow late-night hosts refuse to do. Close your eyes and you can see Stephen Colbert lunging for the fainting couch after one of Maher's better diatribes.

The HBO star is constantly warning his fellow liberals about how the woke movement has gone too far and why free speech is in jeopardy.

Even more valuable? He preaches from his HBO pulpit, a place where most viewers are left of center…or they're masochists who like to see their views mocked on a weekly basis.

Either way, he's reaching people who would never dream of watching Fox News or perusing *The Daily Wire*.

What's more amazing is that Maher didn't slow his free speech roll as most of his colleagues did in our woke age. He doubled down, daring the powers that be to cancel him. Or, more importantly, to give his ideas a fair hearing. Nothing is quite as scary as that to a true Social Justice type.

It's why he's one of the most important voices in this fight. He's consistent, can point to a long history of free speech support, and is trusted by many of the Left who won't reflexively tune out his wisdom.

He was among the first major figures to be canceled, ironically enough, and, at the time, the Right played a large part in his silencing. Maher's infamous comments about the 9/11 hijackers, made just days after they killed roughly 3,000 Americans, proved tasteless and dumb.

We have been the cowards lobbing cruise missiles from
2,000 miles away. That's cowardly…staying in the airplane when it hits the building, say what you want
about it, it's not cowardly.[240]

His response, after both Sears and FedEx pulled their advertising from
Politically Incorrect with Bill Maher, was a snapshot of things to come.

"In no way was I intending to say, nor have I ever
thought, that the men and women who defend our
nation in uniform are anything but courageous and
valiant, and I offer my apologies to anyone who took
it wrong," Maher said in a statement.[241]

It wasn't a hostage-style apology, but a freewheeling comic shouldn't
have to apologize for a quip, even one as stupefying as his.

Even more amazing? ABC briefly had his back.

In a statement supporting Maher, ABC said his program is "a show that celebrates freedom of speech
and encourages the animated exchange of ideas and
opinions. While we remain sensitive to the current
climate following last week's tragedy…there needs
to remain a forum for the expression of our nation's
diverse opinions."[242]

Today? ABC would grovel for forgiveness…assuming the aggrieved
party was part of the Woke coalition.

ABC canceled Maher's series the following July, citing declining ratings and advertising struggles.

Perhaps that memory is partly why he refuses to back down today. No
matter. His voice, his ability to call out the woke mob, offers some hope.

Ricky Gervais could rob a bank and kick a puppy down a flight of
stairs during his escape, but conservatives would forgive him based on his
2020 Golden Globes appearance alone. *The Office* veteran burned Hollywood to the ground in that mesmerizing monologue shared in front of
their best and brightest.

That's true Hollywood bravery.

Gervais's routine angered all the right people, especially the hard-left reporters who cover Tinseltown. Here's a sample of that monologue, because any excuse is a good one to savor it anew:

> Apple roared into the TV game with *The Morning Show*, a superb drama about the importance of dignity and doing the right thing, made by a company that runs sweatshops in China. Well, you say you're woke but the companies you work for in China—unbelievable. Apple, Amazon, Disney. If ISIS started a streaming service you'd call your agent, wouldn't you?
>
> So if you do win an award tonight, don't use it as a platform to make a political speech. You're in no position to lecture the public about anything. You know nothing about the real world. Most of you spent less time in school than Greta Thunberg.
>
> So if you win, come up, accept your little award, thank your agent, and your God and f*** off, OK? It's already three hours long. Right, let's do the first award.[243]

That routine still leaves a mark. Gervais uses his various media appearances to stand up for free speech, explain why comedy needs to exist without a net, and he does so in ways that are both profound and profoundly funny.

> "I think offense is the collateral damage of free speech, and it's no reason not to have free speech," Gervais told the outlet. "That's what I'd say—it's the lesser of two evils. Having free speech and some people getting upset by it is the lesser of two evils because not having free speech is horrendous."[244]

Few causes have better spokespeople.

Many blame Twitter for providing rocket fuel to the woke mob, and it's hard to argue against it. Corporations see a few angry Tweets and they scurry for protection. Does it matter that the messages came from woke warriors with fewer than a hundred followers?

Nope. They see a few surly Tweets and they start penning their apologies.

One Twitter account almost makes being a part of the far-left cesspool worthwhile: Titania McGrath.

She's the fictional character created by British comic Andrew Doyle. This high priestess of woke sounds eerily like what a real SJW might say. And that's half the fun of it. Here's a quick sample of Titania's deep Twitter thoughts:

- All criminals are white, especially if they're not.

- So far today I've got a woman fired for claiming that sex is binary, shouted abuse at an old man collecting money for the British Legion, dog-piled people on Twitter for disagreeing with me and burned some books by Dr Seuss. It's SO exhausting being on the right side of history.

- Given that all white people are racist, whenever they are *not* being racist this simply means they are hiding behind a mask of non-racism, which is the most virulent form of racist behaviour. Therefore, there is nothing more racist than a white person who isn't racist.

Brilliant.

Doyle does more than skewer the wokesters on Twitter. He hosts a podcast, *Culture Wars with Andrew Doyle*, and appears regularly across the media landscape to share why woke spells doom for Western culture.

Sometimes the most powerful proponents of a cause are those who sided with "the enemy" and had a change of heart. It's akin to an addict turning his or her life around and become an addiction counselor.

It's why Keri Smith is such a valuable force for freedom in these murky times. Smith was a Woke True Believer for much of her life. The comedy manager helped introduce the woke revolution to the stand-up space, working with clients who embraced wokeism long before the culture did. She promoted woke jokes, knowing how influential comedy can be in changing hearts if not minds.

~~Yet something began to bug her about the woke movement, which~~ she now compares to a cult. She started to question elements of its belief system, a true no-no in any good cult. She also started educating herself about other philosophical movements, including the bootstrap ethos shared by Canadian professor Jordan Peterson.

Slowly she realized the folly of her belief system, and she eventually left the comedy world. She knew the connections she made as her formerly woke self would no longer function given her newly freed status.

Now, she co-hosts *Unsafe Space* with Carter Laren, a show where she scorches the latest woke headlines and tries to reach those who may be open to a new way of thinking. It isn't red-meat-driven like some conservative talk radio outlets. Instead, it's a mix of eye-rolls and entreaties to those who suspect their social justice views may be truly problematic.

The platform allows her to bring independent minded listeners into the freedom fold. She also champions the small but growing number of artists willing to take a stand against the Woke Police. It's one reason she cheers on Tom MacDonald, the white Canadian rapper who slams Social Justice Warriors in his thoughtful music.

She says,

> He explicitly challenges woke ideology in his lyrics, speaking truth and not worrying about what others think. You can tell he truly doesn't care about the opinions of others because he didn't even pick a cool rapper name! "Hello, I'm Tom MacDonald and I'm here to rap."

> He's evidence to me that young people are starving for authenticity and courage and something other than sanctimonious wrongheaded ideology in their entertainment. If you build it, they will come.

MacDonald's newest videos quickly rack up north of a million views shortly after posting.

Smith sees some of her fellow podcasters, particularly those covering the comic book realm, as leading the charge against the social justice groupthink. She cites Nerdrotic, Babyface Heel, Comix Division, Geeks and Gamers, and Eric July as 'casts that matter, culturally speaking. She says,

> These guys didn't start out looking to do any political or cultural commentary. They are hardcore fans of genres and entertainment mediums that are being decimated by woke ideology, and they've stepped up to the challenge of giving a voice to the silent majority in the middle. They prove to me that many people, maybe even most people, are not on board with woke ideology.

She also points to the wobbly nature of woke Hollywood executives as another glimmer of hope.

> Most of the suits…are not true believers in woke ideology. Most of them simply go along with trends. There was a time when I was pitching TV shows and everyone wanted something "like Anthony Bourdain's show but different." When they see something successful, they all try to replicate it and that is reflected in what is being sold and bought. If we can change the culture enough that woke ideology is rightfully mocked and shunned, these craven gatekeepers will change what they are looking for and what they are selling.

If that happens, the artists who glommed onto woke culture will suddenly shift gears, she predicts.

"If anti-woke material becomes popular, you will one day see all of these woke comics and singers and actors trying to walk back what they pushed on us and minimize their involvement with it," she predicts, akin to the Asch conformity experiments showing most people are followers. "Artists are no different from the masses on Facebook in this way. I'd say seventy-five percent of them speak the opinions that their social circle is speaking, even if that means they are living unconsciously and in dishonesty."

Smith focuses much of her energy on people like herself, souls who have good intentions but falsely think woke is the way to a better tomorrow. She offers a few tips for those who meet like-minded social justice types with the hope of "red-pilling" them. She says,

> First you have to discern if they are someone who is operating in good faith or not. If they are true believer, who is also operating in good faith, I would encourage you to listen to what they have to say. Ask them questions. Not only because people like to talk about their beliefs, but also so you can maybe help shake them out of their scripted answers and get them to think.

> Let them know you disagree with them, but do it in love. I once heard a reverend say, you have to meet people where they're at but treat them as though they were where they could be. Most of the people like myself who have left the cult of woke didn't do so after someone gave us a bunch of facts that didn't compute with our ideology. No. They'll disregard the facts if you don't appeal to their emotion first.

The non-woke have a distinct advantage over their Social Justice peers. Smith explains,

> I often call SJWs "joy eaters" because they ultimately seek to rob the world of joy and beauty, even if they are cognizant that they're being used for this purpose. Think of the shaming they engage in when one of their flock expresses joy or accomplishment at a "problematic" time or about a "problematic" subject like fitness. They're often piled on and told that their "privilege is showing" for daring to post success at the gym or

to share celebratory photos of graduation instead of a black square in support of BLM.

These people are miserable, and they want to make everyone else as miserable as they are. So one of the things you can do to push back is simply to be joyful. To try to add beauty to the world. To create. One of my favorite quotes is by Wendell Berry: "Be joyful, though you have considered all the facts."

You don't have to run out and start a podcast. You don't have to quit your job or confront Wokies at protests. You can push back in your own unique way, and in a way that brings you joy. Use humor. Start a garden. Take up knitting. Start a family. Homeschool your kids. Put your poetry out there. Put your music out there. Start a conversation with someone who disagrees with you, even if you are afraid. And do it with love.

Adam Carolla isn't a knitter, but he did start a podcast.

Now, he's far more than a one-man woke rebuttal. The carpenter-turned-podcasting-giant's own life offers a perfect, "Only in America" tale. He grew up poor, swatted aside the musings of his far-left parents, and learned a marketable trade despite his modest academic scores.

Carolla thought he could carve out a career in comedy, so he gently nudged his way into a radio station's good graces, later connecting with future chum and colleague Jimmy Kimmel. That, and a fortuitous pairing with future *Loveline* radio partner Dr. Drew Pinsky, set his entertainment career ablaze.

The most fascinating chapter came after his biggest failure. He landed, and later lost, a national radio gig meant to fill the gap left behind by radio titan Howard Stern.

Carolla could have looked for other radio gigs or reconnected with his TV ties. Or, he might have picked up his hammer and started his own construction company...Ace, Inc.

Instead, Carolla created a podcast all his own, the start of an amazing media empire.

The Adam Carolla Show became the most downloaded podcast of all time, according to Guinness, and he quickly branched out into documentary filmmaking, wine sales, related podcasts, and a bustling stand-up career.

Through it all, Carolla called every last shot. His self-made "pirate ship" made him the boss, which meant no one could cancel him no matter what joke he told. It's one reason he embraced the "no apology" template.

Because he could.

Last year conservative creators finally took Andrew Breitbart's message—"politics is downstream from culture"—to heart.

The Daily Wire announced a new slate of entertainment originals designed to buck the woke trends. The company already has some entertainment DNA, given former film producer Jeremy Boreing (*The Arroyo*) is the company's de facto "God King," but the presence of Andrew Klavan is even more inspiring.

Klavan's Hollywood screenwriting career includes work with Michael Caine (*A Shock to the System*) and Clint Eastwood (*True Crime*). He's also a first-rate novelist and someone who "gets" pop culture better than most conservatives.

Klavan also writes one mean foreword.

He's *The Daily Wire*'s not-so-secret weapon moving forward, a writer whose imagination is well-suited to the gargantuan challenge awaiting them.

And it *is* gargantuan.

The site's first volley couldn't have worked out better. *Run Hide Fight*, an existing title Team Daily Wire scooped up as its first feature film, did everything right. The plot—an empowered teen girl squares off against school shooters—is both dangerous and perfectly reasonable for unwoke storytellers. The film offered crisp pacing, solid acting, and action beats on par with many studio productions.

Naturally, film critics savaged it for reasons unassociated with the film's merits. That's how you can tell it was a direct hit. These same critics hailed Netflix's *Cuties*, a French film where the camera focuses in on sexualized, gyrating ten-year-olds.

The Daily Wire proved its own mission statement out of the gate with *Run Hide Fight*. The website isn't alone, though.

Newcomers like Creado, Loor TV, Angel Studios, and other proposed projects hope to join them sooner than later.

"The Hollywood border is now wide open and it's time for an invasion—an invasion of free-thinking people who want to see stories about what's good about America," says Nick Searcy, part of the Creado team, on the company's website. "Stories that transcend politics instead of being distorted by them." Creado promises a streaming service with content that extols America's virtues.

Loor TV, "unfiltered by Hollywood or church ladies," vows to smash through the woke wall separating audiences from the content they love most. The creative startup asks subscribers to steer their monthly fee toward the shows they want to see most.

Angel Studios, spun off in 2021 from the content filtering company VidAngel, promises to merge Christian storytelling with the power of crowdfunding. The company enjoyed sudden, shocking success when it raised $5 million in a week from consumers eager for more content like *The Chosen*, the studio's series based on the life of Jesus Christ. The studio also distributed the first season of the *Tuttle Twins*, based on the freedom-friendly children's books that promote capitalism, not socialism.

Imagine how the corporate media would react to, say, a Pixar film doing the same.

Chuck Konzelman and Cary Solomon of *Unplanned* fame are part of this budding, hope-filled revolution. Audiences, Konzelman says, crave entertainment product they feel comfortable watching, but getting access to those stories isn't as easy as it once was. It's why the duo is investigating a new distribution platform dedicated to family-friendly, right-leaning fare..

"I think we're gonna succeed," Konzelman says. "If conservatives would get serious, see the possibilities here are greater than they've ever been…there's a lot of us, and I think that the other side exaggerates how much there are of them."

Plus, Konzelman thinks the country's apolitical citizens may be drawn to this content. "They may not be conservative, but they're not these crazy, off-the-wall people. There's where the opportunity lies." It helps that woke rules limit the kinds of stories, and genres, available to progressive storytellers. "As the woke mania grows, and the tidal wave gets bigger and bigger, more genres that drop away with the value set that…that's what's creating a massive vacuum for entertainment product."

It took conservatives roughly forever to figure this all out. They still need to experience another cold blast of reality.

"As conservatives we do one thing that I don't think is a great idea," Konzelman says. "We go to the people who hate us most and say, 'Please distribute our product and treat us fairly.'"

"It's idiotic to expect your adversary to spread your point of view. It's naïve," his creative partner Cary Solomon adds. "We see this time as a very important time. It's now or never…we have to have a way to distribute material, and you have to have material that goes out into the ether. The time is now for us to wake up. You either give up all your values and become woke, or start fighting the good fight now."

Patrick Courrielche agrees.

"[The Left] view us as these infidels within their blue church. *Of course*, they're going to purge us," the "Red Pilled America" podcaster says. "That's why the onus is on us to create our own ecosystems and our own platforms. It's a very logical next step."

It won't be easy. Heck, it might just be impossible without your help, dear reader. You have the power to make this a reality, to give start-ups eager to defy the woke bylaws all the energy they need to succeed.

How?

Subscribe to their platforms.

Share their new content on social media.

Become unofficial PR agents for them, as much as possible.

Make their best shows and movies so absurdly successful that even Hollywood will take notice.

So far, conservatives have done a poor job on this front. Yes, we made 2019's *No Safe Spaces*, a modest hit for an indie docudrama ($1.3 million domestically). That number should have been five times bigger. Maybe ten. The movie couldn't have been more accurate in predicting our current sorry state of affairs. It was chilling and beautifully told, a smartly produced feature that didn't skimp on entertainment value.

Imagine if it had cracked the top five movies of the weekend upon its opening. Think of the message that would send, not just to the film's production team, but to entertainment journalists and the brave souls who co-starred in the film.

Conservatives traditionally eschew boycotts, and for some very good and obvious reasons. It's time to move to *buy*-cotts, to put our money toward content and companies that speak to our needs, our dreams, and our quest for a free speech future.

Make the rare, right-of-center movies runaway hits. Tell everyone you know about them. Supercharge their social media mentions in the very best ways possible. Kick in a few bucks for the next conservative crowdfunding feature.

You don't have to break your bank to do so. A dollar here, a social media share there, and suddenly there's a wave of cash and support flooding their coffers.

Can you imagine what might happen if an R-rated comedy came along that trashed the woke mindset…and it outgrossed every other mainstream comedy that month, or even that year?

That's power, cultural power. And, like Keri Smith said, it would convince a few studio executives that our woke moment could be yesterday's news.

Have hope. But help make that hope a reality.

Adam Carolla sees a sunnier tomorrow, too, and it's unwise to argue with a comic brimming with common sense. Carolla told podcaster Andrew Klavan why he thinks the cultural pendulum will soon swing to the free speech side, or at least nudge in that direction.

"Whenever you create a void, something will rush in and fill it," Carolla told Klavan. "Look at *Gutfeld!*," he said of Fox News's 2021 foray into the late-night wars. "There was never any kind of nighttime, late night thing that had any kind of conservative, right wing anything, and now there is."

Carolla drilled down deeper.

"All the cool kids are on the Left. The Right has Scott Baio and Ted Nugent," Carolla said with a chuckle. Once the laughter fades, though, capitalists might see the wisdom in reaching out to the so-called "uncool" types.

"I think media is starting to wake up to it, slowly…. There's a lot of people at that uncool kids' party. And they have credit cards and drive cars and they shop. How 'bout something for them? I think this is a trend you're gonna see."

Phelim McAleer didn't wait for his fellow conservatives to join the Culture Wars. He jumped the starter's pistol with projects like *FrackNation*, *Gosnell*, and *My Son Hunter*.

McAleer's team weaponizes crowdfunding platforms to fuel his craft, often relying on "verbatim theater" to power his storytelling. That's using existing documents (phone texts, court transcripts) to flesh out the screenplay or play. It's a brilliant way to head off critics eager to trash his work as more Fake News. They do it anyway, but they sound increasingly shrill in the process.

If Hollywood had a dozen Dallas Sonniers, the battle wouldn't look so intimidating.

Sonnier has a heady track record of knowing what the moviegoing public wants to see, and he envisions an American public rejecting the woke ideology. The *Brawl in Cell Block 99* producer points to the Oscar ratings plunge, and a similar shrinkage with the social justice-obsessed NBA ratings, as symptoms of a problem mainstream types refuse to admit.

"Hollywood has gone so far left. I'm delighted to see the rest of the world starting slowly to catch on and catch up," Sonnier says.

The Texas-based filmmaker is a critical part of a so-called "new" Hollywood, a system that allows for greater creative freedom with less woke shackles tying storytellers down. The irony is he isn't eager to make a conservative version of *La La Land*, even if his detractors are quick to label his efforts as such.

"Is art political? I say, 'Yes, it is.' That said, art and movies do not have to push an agenda. In fact, the more ambiguous they are in their own themes and stories, the more exciting it is to an audience member," he said.

It's why he predicts a growing conservative movie-making field, one where films that might have been made in the '70s, '80s, or '90s come alive again. Those pre-woke eras could make a lot of scratch, he figures, even if modern Hollywood is loath to return to that template.

"I plan to make movies with conservative companies without an agenda," he says. "All I'm doing is running away from an industry where my people, so to speak, are nearly tolerated, never encouraged, and sometimes even attacked."

Just don't be surprised if what flows from his company, Bonfire Legend, doesn't have an overt agenda…or even any political statements.

"Audiences don't want to be preached to…they don't wanna hear more sermons. That's what they have church for," he says. "They want to be entertained, to escape, to hear a good story. If you just distill it down to those basic core tenets…then you will have a rabid audience following you and watching your movies."

He envisions teaming with right-leaning talent as well as those "sick of the current system."

"Walk across the street and come make movies with us," he says, adding that exodus may have already begun. "Three recognizable actors reached out to us. 'Enough is enough. What's your next movie?'" he recalls them saying.

He still needs some help, though. "There's a massive responsibility for moderate and even center-Left folks to be more vocal and push back against the narratives in the press…the evils of conservatism and Christianity. If they would push back, this conversation would be over…we'd all get back to a more *United* States, a more united political environment."

Sonnier didn't want Hollywood to morph into its current, untenable shape, but he's hopeful for a brighter tomorrow, one brimming with better stories.

"There's lots of reasons for audiences to be hopeful," he says. "We can make some great movies and bring it directly to them."

John Nolte of Breitbart News takes a more measured approach to the current woke mania.

"This will come to an end when everyone grows tired of it, when the young fascists pushing it grow up and mature and face the regrets of youthful mistakes that come with growing up and maturing," Nolte says of an organic healing process that won't involve Hollywood's biggest, brightest stars.

He says,

They do not want to be booted from the Academy. They will never betray the Hollywood Club. Internally they might be having these discussions, but speaking out publicly would be seen as a betrayal of the clique and result in banishment.

There are plenty of people speaking about it quietly amongst themselves, and once they realize they are not alone and everyone's tired of it, artistic freedom will make a comeback," he believes.

Nolte compares the current mania to previous "moral panics," from the rush to ban alcohol in the 1920s, to 1950s-era Communist fears. He says,

These things pass. They always do. People grow and change. The reality of the commercial death of this junk hits home. It's going to take a while to shake out, but it will.... It always has. Remember, this is a moral panic, a terrible time where everyone's terrified not to be on the right side of an issue lest they be seen as one of "them."

Never in history have scolds and censors been remembered as anything but the villains they are. It will be the same this time.

If Nolte is correct, it'll be fascinating to see a future movie capturing this tragic chapter in pop culture history, one where Hollywood's biggest and brightest stars are the bad guys.

They just don't realize it. Yet.

ENDNOTES

1   Sam Amico, "Creator of 'All Rise' Fired After Complaints of Racial Insensitivity," *OutKick*, March 26, 2021, https://www.outkick.com/creator-of-all-rise-fired-after-complaints-of-racial-insensitivity/.

2   Kate Feldman, "'All Rise' Creator Greg Spotiswood Fired Over Allegations of Racism," *MSN*, March 26, 2021, https://www.msn.com/en-us/tv/news/all-rise-creator-greg-spotiswood-fired-over-allegations-of-racism/ar-BB1f08T2.

3   Lynn Elber, "PBS Chief Defends Filmmaker Ken Burns, Touts Diversity," *AP News*, February 3, 2021, https://apnews.com/article/ken-burns-pbs-diversity-d687d59a9c46584f0ed-6f3364ac0ed0f.

4   Jewel Wicker, "Film-makers Condemn PBS Over Lack of Diversity and Dependence on Ken Burns," *The Guardian*, March 31, 2021, https://www.theguardian.com/media/2021/mar/31/pbs-diversity-letter-ken-burns.

5   Tambay Obenson, "PBS Launches Major Initiatives in Continuous Commitment to Diversity, Equity, and Inclusion," IndieWire, August 10, 2021, https://www.indiewire.com/2021/08/pbs-tca-2021-diversity-1234656920/.

6   "Woke," *Merriam-Webster*, last accessed August 27, 2021, https://www.merriam-webster.com/dictionary/woke.

7   "Stay Woke," *Merriam-Webster*, last updated September 2017, https://www.merriam-webster.com/words-at-play/woke-meaning-origin.

8   Steve Rose, "How the Word 'Woke' Was Weaponised by the Right," *The Guardian*, January 21, 2020, https://www.theguardian.com/society/shortcuts/2020/jan/21/how-the-word-woke-was-weaponised-by-the-right.

9   Catherine E. Shoichet, "This Group Is Working Behind the Scenes to Change the Stories You See on TV," *CNN*, March 3, 2021, https://edition.cnn.com/2020/10/11/entertainment/immigration-tv-shows/index.html.

10 Alexa Moutevelis, "MacGyver Joins Black Lives Matter Protests Fighting 'Institutional Racism,'" *Media Research Center*, March 29, 2021, https://newsbusters.org/blogs/culture/alexa-moutevelis/2021/03/29/macgyver-joins-black-lives-matter-protests-fighting.

11 Tyler O'Neil, "Why Can't the Woke Trans Agenda Leave 'Star Wars' Alone?!," *PJ Media*, March 31, 2021, https://pjmedia.com/news-and-politics/tyler-o-neil/2021/03/31/why-cant-the-woke-trans-agenda-leave-star-wars-alone-n1436628.

12 Alex Zalben, "Marvel's Editor-in-Chief Explains Why 'X-Men' Character Iceman Came Out," *MTV News*, April 21, 2015, http://www.mtv.com/news/2139639/iceman-gay-all-new-x-men-axel-alonso-interview/.

13   Lucas Nolan, "Marvel's Latest Superhero Team Includes 'Safe Space' and 'Snowflake,'" *Breitbart*, March 19, 2020, https://www.breitbart.com/entertainment/2020/03/19/marvels-latest-superhero-team-includes-safe-space-and-snowflake/.

14   Bonnie Burton, "Star Wars Character Lando Calrissian Is Pansexual, and I Couldn't Be Happier," *CNET*, May 21, 2018, https://www.cnet.com/news/star-wars-solo-lando-calrissian-is-pan-sexual-and-i-couldnt-be-happier/.

15   Alana Mastrangelo, "Sia Apologizes, Deletes Twitter Account over Woke Backlash to Her Debut Feature Film," *Breitbart*, February 5, 2021, https://www.breitbart.com/entertainment/2021/02/05/sia-apologizes-deletes-twitter-account-over-woke-backlash-to-her-debut-feature-film/.

16   Alaina Demopoulos, "Lena Dunham's Plus-Size Fashion Line Is Another Missed Opportunity," *The Daily Beast*, April 9, 2021, https://www.thedailybeast.com/lena-dunhams-plus-size-fashion-line-is-another-missed-opportunity.

17   Mayra Mejia, "Why Lena Dunham's 11 Honoré Plus-Size Clothing Line Is So Disappointing," *NBC News*, April 8, 2021, https://www.nbcnews.com/think/opinion/why-lena-dunham-s-11-honor-plus-size-clothing-line-ncna1263469.

18   Lindsay Dodgson, "People Who Are Overweight Get Paid Less, According to a New Study," *Insider*, November 1, 2018, https://www.insider.com/overweight-people-earn-less-money-study-shows-2018-11.

19   Danielle Jennings, "Black Women Started the Body Positivity Movement, But White Women Corrupted It," *Hello Beautiful*, September 18, 2018, https://hellobeautiful.com/3009432/black-women-body-positivity-movement/.

20   Laura Emily Dunn, "Women in Business Q&A: Gwen DeVoe, Founder of Full Figured Fashion Week," *Huffpost*, June 16, 2015, https://www.huffpost.com/entry/women-in-business-qa-gwen_b_7592968.

21   Gianluca Russo, "Will Plus-Size Fashion Ever Pay Black Women Their Dues?," *Nylon*, February 26, 2021, https://www.nylon.com/beauty/will-plus-size-fashion-ever-pay-black-women-their-dues.

22   Juliet James, "The Problem with Lena Dunham's New Plus-Size Clothing Line Is Lena Dunham," *Huffpost*, April 8, 2021, https://www.huffpost.com/entry/lena-dunham-plus-size-clothing-line-honore_n_606e3bb8c5b6c70eccad7279.

23   Lauren Edmonds, "Stanley Tucci Says He Has 'Difficulty' with Argument That Gay Characters Should Only Be Played by LGBTQ Actors," *Insider*, January 31, 2021, https://www.insider.com/stanley-tucci-straight-actors-playing-gay-roles-2021-1.

24   Ryan Lattanzio, "Bo Burnham Wants 'Promising Young Woman' to Hold the Nice Guys' Feet to the Fire," *IndieWire*, January 28, 2021, https://www.indiewire.com/2021/01/bo-burnham-promising-young-woman-interview-spoilers-1234612517/amp/.

25   Kelly McCarthy, "Thousands of Twitter Replies Challenge Stephen King's Tweet on Diversity in Art," *ABC News*, January 16, 2020, https://abcnews.go.com/Entertainment/thousands-twitter-replies-challenge-stephen-kings-tweet-diversity/story?id=68326302.

26   Melissa Chen, "'Kung Fu Cavemen' Isn't Racist — Just the Victim of Moral Panic by a Self-Righteous Few," *New York Post*, March 31, 2021, https://nypost.com/2021/03/31/kung-fu-cavemen-isnt-racist-just-the-victim-of-moral-panic-by-a-self-righteous-few/.

27   Jack Shepherd, "The Simpsons: Matt Groening Defends Apu: 'The Conversation Is Tainted,'" *Independent*, July 19, 2018, https://www.independent.co.uk/arts-entertainment/tv/news/simpsons-matt-groening-apu-backlash-criticism-hank-azaria-a8454171.html.

28   Dave Itzkoff, "Why Hank Azaria Won't Play Apu on 'The Simpsons' Anymore," *New York Times*, February 25, 2020, https://www.nytimes.com/2020/02/25/arts/television/hank-azaria-simpsons-apu.html.

29   Amy Johnson, "'The Simpsons' Star Hank Azaria Reveals Why He Quit Apu Role: 'It Just Didn't Feel Right,'" *Yahoo! Entertainment*, February 25, 2020, https://www.yahoo.com/entertainment/the-simpsons-hank-azaria-apu-voice-143715139.html.

30   John Cleese (@JohnCleese), "Not wishing to be left behind by Hank Azaria, I would like to apologise on behalf on Monty Python for all the many sketches we did making fun of white English people…," Twitter, April 13, 2021, https://twitter.com/JohnCleese/status/1382035246875516928.

31   Tyler McCarthy, "John Cleese Mocks Hank Azaria for Apologizing about Voicing Apu on 'The Simpsons,'" *Fox News*, April 15, 2021, https://www.foxnews.com/entertainment/john-cleese-mocks-hank-azaria-apology-apu-simpsons.

32   Lou Perez, "The Problem with Apu's Critics," *Spiked*, November 6, 2018, https://www.spiked-online.com/2018/11/06/the-problem-with-apus-critics/.

33   Hari Kondabolu (@harikondabolu), "Agreed. There are so many ways to make Apu work without getting rid of him. If true, this sucks," Twitter, October 26, 2018, https://twitter.com/harikondabolu/status/1055904344980275200.

34   Erik Adams, "Hari Kondabolu on Loving *The Simpsons*, but Hating Apu (and Making a Movie About It)," *AV Club*, November 13, 2017, https://www.avclub.com/hari-kondabolu-on-loving-the-simpsons-but-hating-apu-1820344389.

35   Adam B. Vary, "Joe Biden on Gay Marriage: 'Will and Grace' Helped Educate America," *Entertainment Weekly*, updated May 6, 2012, https://ew.com/article/2012/05/06/joe-biden-will-and-grace-gay-marriage/.

36   Peggy Noonan, "Get Ready for the Struggle Session," last accessed August 27, 2021, https://peggynoonan.com/get-ready-for-the-struggle-session/.

37   "Identity Politics," *Dictionary*, last accessed August 27, 2021, https://www.dictionary.com/browse/identity-politics.

38   Chris Gardner, "Dana Walden Says ABC Passed on Pilots for Not Being Inclusive Enough," *The Hollywood Reporter*, April 14, 2021, https://www.hollywoodreporter.com/tv/tv-news/dana-walden-says-abc-passed-on-pilots-for-not-being-inclusive-enough-4165849/.

39   Cole Penz, "Matt Damon is Bringing Clean Water to the World's Poor," *Borgen Magazine*, August 15, 2020, https://www.borgenmagazine.com/matt-damon-is-bringing-clean-water/.

40   "Anavex Life Sciences Receives Michael J. Fox Foundation Grant for Clinical Study of ANAVEX®2-73 (blarcamesine) in People with Parkinson's Disease," Intrado Globe Newswire, January 11, 2021, https://www.globenewswire.com/en/news-release/2021/01/11/2156108/29248/en/Anavex-Life-Sciences-Receives-Michael-J-Fox-Foundation-Grant-for-Clinical-Study-of-ANAVEX-2-73-blarcamesine-in-People-with-Parkinson-s-Disease.html.

41   "REVEALED: Video Shows Mark Wahlberg Slamming Actors Who Compare Themselves to Soldiers…but Denies Remarks Were About Tom Cruise," *The Daily Mail*, November 14, 2013, https://www.dailymail.co.uk/tvshowbiz/article-2506908/Mark-Wahlberg-slams-actors-compare-soldiers.html.

42   Roisin O'Connor, "Mark Wahlberg's Hate Crimes History Resurfaces After Black Lives Matter Post," *Independent*, June 8, 2020, https://www.independent.co.uk/arts-entertainment/films/news/mark-wahlberg-racist-hate-crimes-wikipedia-george-floyd-protests-a9553911.html.

43   Connie Rusk, "Fans Accuse Harry Potter Actress Emma Watson of Prioritising Her Instagram 'Aesthetic' over Black Lives Matter Blackout Post by Putting a White Border Around It," *The Daily Mail*, June 2, 2020, https://www.dailymail.co.uk/tvshowbiz/article-8381735/Emma-Watson-accused-prioritising-Instagram-aesthetic-Black-Lives-Matter-post.html.

44   Rachel Handler, "Keira Knightley Agrees the *Atonement* Bookshelf Sex Scene Was Her Best Ever," *Vulture*, March 14, 2019, https://www.vulture.com/2019/03/keira-knightley-atonement-sex-scene.html.

45   Hannah Frishberg, "Keira Knightley Will No Longer Strip Down for Male-Directed Sex Scenes," *New York Post*, January 25, 2021, https://nypost.com/2021/01/25/keira-knightley-says-she-wont-do-male-directed-sex-scenes/.

46   Carly Johnson, "Ewan McGregor Finalises Divorce from Wife of 22-Years Eve Mavrakis… After Daughter Labelled Girlfriend Mary Elizabeth Winstead 'A Piece of Trash,'" *The Daily Mail*, June 11, 2020, https://www.dailymail.co.uk/tvshowbiz/article-8409003/Ewan-McGregor-finalizes-divorce-wife-Eve-Mavrakis-daughter-calls-girlfriend-trash.html.

47   Eugene Volokh, "'Hollywood Has the Best Moral Compass,' Said…," *Reason*, January 29, 2020, https://reason.com/volokh/2020/01/29/hollywood-has-the-best-moral-compass-says/.

48   John Lynch, "10 Actors Who Have Publicly Denounced Woody Allen or Donated Their Salaries to Charity After Working on His Movies," *Insider*, January 30, 2018, https://www.businessinsider.com/actors-who-have-spoken-out-against-woody-allen-or-donated-salaries-list-2018-10.

49   Kelly Coffey, "Kelly Marie Tran Says Her Disney Princess, Raya, Is Gay," *Inside the Magic*, March 7, 2021, https://insidethemagic.net/2021/03/raya-lgbtq-princess-kc1/.

50   Warner Todd Huston, "Natalie Portman Rewrites Classic Fairytales to Make Them 'Gender Neutral' So Children Can 'Defy Gender Stereotypes,'" *Breitbart*, March 15, 2021, https://www.breitbart.com/entertainment/2021/03/15/natalie-portman-rewrites-classic-fairytales-to-make-them-gender-neutral-so-children-can-defy-gender-stereotypes/; Christian Toto, "Celebs Who Embraced Defund the Police Cause Go Mum Amid Violent Crime Surge in Blue Cities," Just the News, last accessed July 14, 2021, https://justthenews.com/nation/culture/celebs-who-embraced-defund-police-cause-go-mum-amid-violent-crime-surge-blue-cities.

51   Yohana Desta, "Viola Davis Regrets Making The Help: 'It Wasn't the Voices of the Maids That Were Heard,'" Vanity Fair, September 12, 2018, https://www.vanityfair.com/hollywood/2018/09/viola-davis-the-help-regret.

52   Zack Sharf, "Bryce Dallas Howard: 'We Can All Go Further' Than Streaming 'The Help' Right Now," *IndieWire*, June 8, 2020, https://www.indiewire.com/2020/06/bryce-dallas-howard-calls-out-the-help-white-savior-1202236013/.

53   Christopher Vourlias, "Jonah Hill Wants to 'Challenge Traditional Masculinity,'" Variety, February 10, 2019, https://www.yahoo.com/entertainment/jonah-hill-wants-challenge-traditional-143446018.html.

54   Christian Toto, "Hill Apologizes for 'Superbad,' Toxic Masculinity," *Hollywood in Toto*, February 11, 2019, https://www.hollywoodintoto.com/jonah-hill-superbad-toxic-masculinity.

55   Megan Garber, "The Perma-Pump: *Jurassic World*'s Silliest Character," *The Atlantic*, June 15, 2015, https://www.theatlantic.com/entertainment/archive/2015/06/the-perma-pump-the-silliest-thing-in-jurassic-world/395834/.

56   Brian Truitt, "Review: 'Jurassic World: Fallen Kingdom' Is Big on Dino Power, Short on Substance," *USA Today*, June 20, 2018, https://eu.usatoday.com/story/life/movies/2018/06/20/review-jurassic-world-fallen-kingdom-big-dino-power-short-substance/716803002/.

57   Bryan Alexander, "Indoraptor Kills It as the Villainous New Dinosaur of 'Jurassic World: Fallen Kingdom,'" *USA Today*, June 19, 2018, https://eu.usatoday.com/story/life/movies/2018/06/19/new-dinosaur-indoraptor-kills-jurassic-world-fallen-kingdom/711576002/.

58   Bryan Alexander, "'Jurassic World: Fallen Kingdom' Star Bryce Dallas Howard Has No Apology for Those Heels," *USA Today*, June 20, 2018, https://eu.usatoday.com/story/life/movies/2018/06/20/bryce-dallas-howard-high-heel-controversy-jurassic-world-fallen-kingdom/716644002/.

59   Kelly Lawler, "Voices: 'Jurassic World' Has a Mother of a Problem," *USA Today*, June 16, 2015, https://eu.usatoday.com/story/life/movies/2015/06/16/jurassic-world-sexism-bryce-dallas-howard/28811873/.

60   Marlow Stern, "'Jurassic World': A Big, Dumb, Sexist Mess," *The Daily Beast*, June 10, 2015, https://www.thedailybeast.com/jurassic-world-a-big-dumb-sexist-mess.

61   Joyce Carol Oates (@JoyceCarolOates), "2017 the year it became embarrassing to be 'white'… especially if from a 'white, rural' region of US.," Twitter, November 10, 2017, https://twitter.com/JoyceCarolOates/status/929017428557877249.

62   Geoff Herbert, "SU Alum Joyce Carol Oates Says Dead Dinosaur Outrage Was a Jurassic Joke," *Syracuse*, June 11, 2015, https://www.syracuse.com/entertainment/2015/06/joyce_carol_oates_dinosaur_joke_jurassic_park.html.

63   NetflixFilm (@NetflixFilm), "Quick PSA: Can we stop calling films 'chick flicks' unless the films are literally about small baby chickens? Here's why this phrase should absolutely be retired (thread)…," Twitter, April 15, 2019, https://twitter.com/NetflixFilm/status/1117857893510832128.

64   Paul F. Tompkins (@PFTompkins), "If no characters smoked cigarettes in movies and TV made today you wouldn't miss it. You wouldn't be like 'Hey shouldn't that cop be smoking?'…," Twitter, February 13, 2020, https://twitter.com/PFTompkins/status/1227800654132867072.

65   Curtis M. Wong, "Charlize Theron Is Down to Star in Lesbian 'Die Hard' Reboot: 'Sign Me On'," *Huffpost*, February 24, 2021, https://www.huffpost.com/entry/charlize-theron-lesbian-die-hard-reboot_n_60366d15c5b6c0f82b49c47e.

66   Tyler Aquilina, "How Snubbing *I May Destroy You* Cracked the Golden Globes' Diversity Problem Wide Open," *Entertainment Weekly*, February 27, 2021, https://ew.com/awards/golden-globes/golden-globes-diversity-i-may-destroy-you-analysis/.

67   Aaron Couch, Tatiana Siegel, and Borys Kit, "Behind Disney's Firing of 'Mandalorian' Star Gina Carano," *The Hollywood Reporter*, February 16, 2021, https://www.hollywoodreporter.com/news/general-news/behind-disneys-firing-of-mandalorian-star-gina-carano-4133813/.

68   John Nolte, "Nolte: Hollywood PR Rep Admits Career Death If You Offend 'the Social Left' Online," *Breitbart*, February 17, 2021, https://www.breitbart.com/entertainment/2021/02/17/nolte-hollywood-pr-rep-admits-career-death-if-you-offend-the-social-left-online/.

69   Rachel Yang, "Karol G Apologizes for Using Black-and-White Dog to Promote Black Lives Matter in Tone-Deaf Tweet," *Entertainment Weekly*, June 1, 2020, https://ew.com/celebrity/karol-g-apologizes-black-white-dog-black-lives-matter-message/.

70   Giuliana (@giulivenu), "El discurso de que 'no hay razas' invalida las luchas que históricamente las minorías han tenido que enfrentar a causa del racismo...," Twitter, June 1, 2020, https://twitter.com/giulivenu/status/1267557212546834438?s=20.

71   Gabe (@highgab3), "love you karol g but saying we are all one race "human" is very ignorant. my people are losing there life BECAUSE of the color of their skin...," Twitter, May 30, 2020, https://twitter.com/highgab3/status/1266811701229506561?s=20.

72   Nate Nickolai, "Scarlett Johansson Claims Controversial Casting Comments Were 'Edited for Clickbait,'" *Variety*, July 14, 2019, https://variety.com/2019/film/news/scarlett-johansson-as-if-interview-1203267042/.

73   Caitlyn Becker, "'I Should Be Allowed to Play Any Person, or Any Tree, or Any Animal': Scarlett Johansson Opens Up About Politically Correct Casting as She Stuns in Retro Spread for *As If* Cover Story," *The Daily Mail*, July 12, 2019, https://www.dailymail.co.uk/tvshowbiz/article-7242081/Scarlett-Johansson-opens-politically-correct-casting-retro-spread-If.html.

74   Olivia Singh, "Scarlett Johansson Admits She 'Mishandled' the Backlash Over Her Casting as a Transgender Character," *Insider*, November 26, 2019, https://www.insider.com/scarlett-johansson-mishandled-backlash-over-casting-as-transgender-character-2019-11.

75   Chris Heath, "Best-Actress Contender Scarlett Johansson on Movies, Marriages, and Controversies," *Vanity Fair*, November 26, 2019, https://www.vanityfair.com/hollywood/2019/11/scarlett-johansson-oscars-issue-cover-story.

76   Variety, "Halle Berry Pulls Out of Playing Transgender Man After Backlash," NBC News, July 6, 2020, https://www.nbcnews.com/feature/nbc-out/halle-berry-pulls-out-playing-transgender-man-after-backlash-n1233040.

77   Gary Dinges, "'Extra' Host Mario Lopez Under Fire for Comments About Transgender Kids, #MeToo," Times-Gazette, July 31, 2019, https://www.times-gazette.com/news/20190731/extra-host-mario-lopez-under-fire-for-comments-about-transgender-kids-metoo?template=ampart.

78   Bang Showbiz NZ, "Florence Pugh Issues Apology for Cultural Appropriation," Yahoo! News, June 27, 2020, https://nz.news.yahoo.com/florence-pugh-issues-apology-cultural-093609149.html.

79   Judy Kurtz, "Anne Hathaway Apologizes Over 'Witches' Portrayal," The Hill, November 6, 2020, https://thehill.com/blogs/in-the-know/in-the-know/524815-anne-hathaway-apologizes-over-witches-portayal.

80   Mahita Gajanan, "Ryan Reynolds 'Unreservedly Sorry' for Getting Married at South Carolina Plantation," Time, August 5, 2020, https://time.com/5875919/ryan-reynolds-plantation-wedding-apology/.

81   Kyle Smith, "Celebrities' Gratuitous Apologies Make Black Lives Matter All About Them," *New York Post*, August 8, 2020, https://nypost.com/2020/08/08/celebrities-gratuitous-apologies-make-blm-all-about-them/.

82   Melinda Newman, "Morgan Wallen Tells Supporters 'Please Don't' Defend Me in New Apology Video," *Billboard*, February 10, 2021, https://www.billboard.com/articles/columns/country/9524724/morgan-wallen-apology-video-racial-slur.

83   Elise Brisco, "'I Know I Failed': Justin Timberlake Issues an Apology to Britney Spears and Janet Jackson," *USA Today*, February 12, 2021, https://www.usatoday.com/story/entertainment/celebrities/2021/02/12/justin-timberlake-apologizes-after-framing-britney-spears-backlash/6738766002/.

84   Justin Timberlake (@justintimberlake), "I've seen the messages, tags, comments, and concerns and I want to respond. I am deeply sorry for the times in my life where my actions contributed to the problem…," Instagram, February 12, 2021, https://www.instagram.com/p/CLMxYbGhTno/.

85   Daniella Scott, "'Lil Nas X Trolls Critics with Joke Apology for 'Satan Trainers,'" Cosmopolitan, March 29, 2021, https://www.cosmopolitan.com/uk/entertainment/a35962644/lil-nas-x-trolls-critics-apology-montero-satan-shoes/.

86   Jim Treacher, "Jay Leno Apologizes for Jokes About One Ethnic Group Out of Many," PJ Media, March 25, 2021, https://pjmedia.com/news-and-politics/jim-treacher/2021/03/25/jay-leno-apologizes-for-jokes-about-one-ethnic-group-out-of-many-n1434949.

87   Jim Treacher, "Obama Bites Dog," Daily Caller, April 17, 2012, https://dailycaller.com/2012/04/17/obama-bites-dog/.

88   Susan Wloszczyna, "Roseanne for President!," Roger Ebert, July 1, 2016, https://www.rogerebert.com/reviews/roseanne-for-president-2016.

89   Joe Rogan, Twitter Post, September 18, 2020, 1:14 PM, https://twitter.com/joerogan/status/1307020061215993856?lang=en.

90   Cameron Jenkins, "'The Bachelor' Host Apologizes for Controversial Comments Amid Petition to Remove Him from Show," The Hill, February 13, 2021, https://thehill.com/blogs/in-the-know/in-the-know/538755-the-bachelor-host-apologizes-for-controversial-comments-amid.

91   Moriba Cummings, "Tom Arnold Accused of Racist and Sexually Aggressive Comments Towards Trump Supporters Diamond and Silk," Bet, October 29, 2019, https://www.bet.com/celebrities/news/2019/10/29/tom-arnold-accused-racist-sexually-aggressive-comments-diamond-and-silk.html.

92   "Alec Baldwin: Fine, I DID Use a Homophobic Slur," TMZ, November 15, 2013, https://www.tmz.com/2013/11/15/alec-baldwin-homophobic-slur-twitter/.

93   Catherine Shoard, "Sarah Silverman: I Was Fired from Film after Blackface Photo Resurfaced," The Guardian, August 12, 2019, https://www.theguardian.com/film/2019/aug/12/sarah-silverman-fired-from-film-blackface-photo.

94   Anne Helen Peterson, Ira Madison III, and Alex Alvarez, "'Unbreakable Kimmy Schmidt' Has A Major Race Problem," BuzzFeed, March 17, 2015, https://www.buzzfeed.com/annehelenpetersen/the-unbreakable-kimmie-schmidt-has-a-major-race-problem.

95   "Tina Fey Will Not Apologize If You Are Offended by Her Jokes," Fox News, December 21, 2015, https://www.foxnews.com/entertainment/tina-fey-will-not-apologize-if-you-are-offended-by-her-jokes.

96   Christian Toto, "How Gil Birmingham Captures True Native Life," Hollywood in Toto, August 11, 2016, https://www.hollywoodintoto.com/gil-birmingham-interview-hell-high-water/.

97   "Tina Fey Will Not Apologize If You Are Offended by Her Jokes," Fox News, December 21, 2015, https://www.foxnews.com/entertainment/tina-fey-will-not-apologize-if-you-are-offended-by-her-jokes.

98   Tom Teodorczuk, "Will Ferrell Defends Racism in Get Hard: I Wanted to Portray an A**hole Who Is Ignorant about How the World Works," Independent, March 20, 2015, https://www.independent.co.uk/arts-entertainment/films/features/will-ferrell-defends-racism-get-hard-i-wanted-portray-hole-who-ignorant-about-how-world-works-10120336.html.

99   Christian Toto, "Gaffigan Veers to the Right, Slams Woke Film Critics," Hollywood in Toto, August 15, 2019, https://www.hollywoodintoto.com/jim-gaffigan-woke-film-critics/.

100   Daniel Nussbaum, "Amy Schumer's 'Snatched' Shredded by Critics: 'Lazy, Sloppy,' and Racist," Breitbart, May 10, 2017, https://www.breitbart.com/entertainment/2017/05/10/critics-savage-amy-schumer-movie-snatched-lazy-sloppy-witless/.

101   "Amy Schumer on 'I Feel Pretty' Backlash and Her Changing Comedy," CBS News, April 19, 2018, https://www.cbsnews.com/news/amy-schumer-on-i-feel-pretty-her-changing-comedic-voice/.

102   Christian Toto, "Critics Weaponize Whiteness Against Amy Schumer's 'Pretty' Pic," Hollywood in Toto, April 19, 2018, https://www.hollywoodintoto.com/i-feel-pretty-critics-schumer-white/.

103 Katie Walsh, "'I Feel Pretty' is Bold Take on Self-Love, but Premise Takes It On Superfi- cialy," Tribune News Service, April 18, 2018, https://www.yorkdispatch.com/story/entertain- ment/2018/04/18/feel-pretty-bold-take-self-love-but-premise-takes-superficially/526315002/.

104 Sara Stewart, "Amy Schumer's 'I Feel Pretty' is a Tone-Deaf Failure," New York Post, April 19, 2018, https://nypost.com/2018/04/19/amy-schumers-i-feel-pretty-is-a-tone-deaf-failure/.

105 Justin Chang, "Review: Amy Schumer Gives a Beaut of a Performance in the Uneven but Sweetly Amusing 'I Feel Pretty,'" Los Angeles Times, April 18, 2018, https://www.latimes.com/ entertainment/movies/la-et-mn-i-feel-pretty-review-20180418-story.html.

106 Christian Toto, "Critics Weaponize Whiteness Against Amy Schumer's 'Pretty' Pic," Hollywood in Toto, April 19, 2018, https://www.hollywoodintoto.com/i-feel-pretty-critics-schumer-white/.

107 P. Claire Dodson, "It's Time for Taylor Swift to Denounce the Nazi Nonsense," Fast Company, November 7, 2017, https://www.fastcompany.com/40492364/its-time-for-taylor-swift-to-de- nounce-the-nazi-nonsense.

108 Ryan Blocker, "Why I'm Afraid of White Women…and Taylor Swift," The Clyde Fitch Report, August 31, 2017, https://www.clydefitchreport.com/2017/08/taylor-swift-white- women-racism-music/.

109 Alanna Bennett, "Taylor Swift's Persona Is Not Built for 2017," BuzzFeed, November 10, 2017, https://www.buzzfeed.com/alannabennett/taylor-swift-persona-2017-reputation.

110 Tasneem Nashrulla, "Here Are 28 Reported Racist and Violent Incidents After Donald Trump's Victory," BuzzFeed News, November 10, 2016, https://www.buzzfeednews.com/arti- cle/tasneemnashrulla/racist-incidents-after-trumps-victory.

111 Jacob Shamsian, "There's No Reason Anyone Should Care About Taylor Swift's New Album," Insider, November 10, 2017, https://www.insider.com/taylor-swift-reputation-album-re- view-2017-11.

112 VICE Staff and Nathaniel Frank, "Why Silence Equals Death in the Age of Trump," Vice, December 23, 2016, https://www.vice.com/en/article/pgpmzz/why-silence-equals-death-in- the-age-of-trump.

113 Amy Zimmerman, "It's Time for Taylor Swift to Denounce Her Neo-Nazi Admirers," The Daily Beast, August 16, 2017, https://www.thedailybeast.com/its-time-for-taylor-swift-to-de- nounce-her-neo-nazi-admirers.

114 Maeve McDermott, "Taylor Swift Inspired 65,000 People to Register to Vote, Says Vote. org," USA Today, October 9, 2018, https://www.usatoday.com/story/life/music/2018/10/09/ taylor-swift-inspired-65-000-people-register-vote-says-vote-org-tennessee-phil-bredesen- trump/1574916002/.

115 Leslie Felperin, "'Miss Americana': Film Review | Sundance 2020," Hollywood Reporter, January 24, 2020, https://www.hollywoodreporter.com/movies/movie-reviews/miss-americana-film-re- view-1272591/.

116 Spencer Kornhaber, "The Queasy Double Message of Taylor Swift's 'You Need to Calm Down,'" The Atlantic, June 17, 2019, https://www.theatlantic.com/entertainment/archive/2019/06/tay- lor-swift-you-need-calm-down-hijacks-queerness/591829/.

117 Rebecca Jennings, "Taylor Swift's 'You Need to Calm Down' Wants to Be a Queer An- them. It Also Wants to Sell You Something," Vox, June 17, 2019, https://www.vox.com/the- goods/2019/6/17/18682588/taylor-swift-you-need-to-calm-down-gay-anthem.

118 Steven W Thrasher, "No, Jimmy Fallon, Donald Trump Isn't a Laughing Matter," The Guard- ian, September 16, 2016, https://www.theguardian.com/commentisfree/2016/sep/16/jimmy- fallon-donald-trump-hair-tonight-show.

119 "Jimmy Fallon Reveals Personal Pain Following Trump Fallout," AP News, June 20, 2018, https://apnews.com/article/d599adbc29d54df1b2a463d7ac3737f7.

120 Dave Itzkoff, "Chris Rock Tried to Warn Us," The New York Times, September 24, 2020, https://www.nytimes.com/2020/09/16/arts/television/chris-rock-fargo.html.

121 Lisa Respers France, "Jimmy Kimmel Apologizes for Performing in Blackface," CNN, June 23, 2020, https://www.cnn.com/2020/06/23/entertainment/jimmy-kimmel-blackface-apology/ index.html.

122   Nicole Sperling and Brooks Barnes, "The Oscars Are a Week Away, but How Many Will Watch?," *The New York Times*, April 18, 2021, https://www.nytimes.com/2021/04/18/business/media/academy-awards-tv-ratings-audience.html.

123   Dave McNary, "Hollywood Diversity Shows Some Gains, but Falls Short in Most Areas (Study)," *Variety*, February 27, 2018, https://variety.com/2018/film/news/hollywood-diversity-falls-short-ucla-report-1202711370/.

124   Sam Levin, "Hollywood Has Made 'No Progress' in On-Screen Diversity, Report Finds," *The Guardian*, July 31, 2018, https://www.theguardian.com/culture/2018/jul/31/hollywood-diversity-report-usc-no-progress-2017.

125   Will Thorne, "Oscars Viewership Sinks to New Low With 23.6 Million," *Variety*, February 10, 2020, https://variety.com/2020/tv/news/oscars-ratings-2020-1203499199/.

126   Nellie Andreeva, "UPDATE: Billy Crystal-Hosted Oscars Watched By 39.3 Million, Up From Last Year," *Deadline*, February 27, 2012, https://deadline.com/2012/02/oscars-up-from-last-year-in-early-ratings-236755/.

127   Hau Chu, "The Grammys Are the Latest Award Show to See a Drastic Drop in TV Ratings," *The Washington Post*, March 17, 2021, https://www.washingtonpost.com/arts-entertainment/2021/03/17/grammys-golden-globe-ratings-down/.

128   Kyle Smith, "The Problem Oscars," *National Review*, April 26, 2021, https://www.nationalreview.com/2021/04/the-problem-oscars/.

129   Clayton Davis, "The New Oscars Inclusion Rules Explained," *Yahoo! Entertainment*, September 10, 2020, https://www.yahoo.com/entertainment/oscars-inclusion-rules-explained-181124610.html.

130   Dexter Thomas, "Q&A: Meet the Woman Who Refused Marlon Brando's Oscar and Inspired Jada Pinkett Smith's Boycott," *Los Angeles Times*, February 5, 2016, https://www.latimes.com/entertainment/movies/moviesnow/la-et-mn-sacheen-littlefeather-oscars-20160204-htmlstory.html.

131   Stephen Battaglio, "Awards Shows Are Struggling to Draw TV Audiences. Should the Oscars Be Worried?," *Los Angeles Times*, April 13, 2021, https://www.latimes.com/entertainment-arts/business/story/2021-04-13/oscars-grammys-awards-shows-ratings-struggling.

132   Christian Toto, "Critics Weaponize Whiteness Against McKay, 'Vice,'" *Hollywood in Toto*, December 19, 2018, https://www.hollywoodintoto.com/critics-mckay-vice-white/.

133   Scott Mendelson, "'Vice' Review: Strong Performances Can't Save Useless Dick Cheney Biopic," *Forbes*, December 17, 2018, https://www.forbes.com/sites/scottmendelson/2018/12/17/vice-review-dick-cheney-christian-bale-amy-adams-adam-mckay-george-w-bush/.

134   Candice Frederick, "'Vice' Film Review: Adam McKay's Dick Cheney Biopic Shows the Triumph of Mediocrity," *The Wrap*, December 20, 2018, https://www.thewrap.com/vice-film-review-dick-cheney-christian-bale-amy-adams/.

135   Christy Lemire, "Terminator: Dark Fate," *Roger Ebert*, November 1, 2019, https://www.rogerebert.com/reviews/terminator-dark-fate-movie-review-2019.

136   "How We Grade," Mediaversity, last accessed August 29, 2021, https://www.mediaversityreviews.com/how-we-grade.

137   Ernest Owens, "Why You Shouldn't Celebrate Pixar's 'Soul' for Finally Having a Black Lead," *The Daily Beast*, December 27, 2020, https://www.thedailybeast.com/why-you-shouldnt-celebrate-pixars-soul-for-finally-having-a-black-lead.

138   Kirsten Acuna, "Pixar's 'Soul' is Getting Rave Reviews, But it Left Me Cringing Up Until the Very Last Minute," *Insider*, December 26, 2020, https://www.insider.com/pixar-soul-movie-review-2020-12.

139   Dani Di Placido, "The Warped Morality Of 'Wonder Woman 1984,'" *Forbes*, December 26, 2020, https://www.forbes.com/sites/danidiplacido/2020/12/26/the-warped-morality-of-wonder-woman-1984/.

140   Chris Nashawaty, "*Kin* is a Sci-Fi Coming-of-Age Thriller with a Big Gun Problem: EW Review," *Entertainment Weekly*, August 28, 2018, https://ew.com/movies/2018/08/28/kin-review/.

141   Joey Magidson, "Film Review: 'Roe v. Wade' is a One-Sided and Toxic Miscarriage of the Issue," *Awards Radar*, March 24, 2021, https://awardsradar.com/2021/03/24/film-review-roe-v-wade-is-a-one-sided-and-toxic-miscarriage-of-the-issue/.

142   David Ehrlich, "'Run Hide Fight' Review: Glib Cinestate Thriller Turns a School Shoot-
      ing into a Clichéd Action Movie," *IndieWire*, September 10, 2020, https://www.indiewire.
      com/2020/09/run-hide-fight-review-1234585582/.

143   David Rooney, "'Run Hide Fight': Film Review | Venice 2020," *Hollywood Reporter*, Septem-
      ber 10, 2020, https://www.hollywoodreporter.com/movies/movie-reviews/run-hide-fight-film-
      review-venice-2020-4056648/.

144   Joyce Slaton, *No Safe Spaces* Move Review, Common Sense Media, last accessed September 7,
      2021, https://www.commonsensemedia.org/movie-reviews/no-safe-spaces.

145   Vadim Rizov, "'Debate Me, You Coward,' Takes Movie Form in Adam Carolla's Abysmal *No
      Safe Spaces*," AV Club, October 23, 2019, https://www.avclub.com/debate-me-you-coward-
      takes-movie-form-in-adam-caroll-1839268667.

146   Caitlin Welsh, "VMAs Host Opens with Safe Space Jokes, and Bombs Hard," *Mashable*, August
      26, 2019, https://mashable.com/article/vmas-2019-host-sebastian-maniscalco-triggered-jokes/.

147   Alexa Valiente and Angela Williams, "Matt Damon Opens Up About Harvey Weinstein, Sex-
      ual Harassment and Confidentiality Agreements," *ABC News*, December 14, 2017, https://
      abcnews.go.com/Entertainment/matt-damon-opens-harvey-weinstein-sexual-harassment-con-
      fidentiality/story?id=51792548.

148   Kathleen Joyce, "Matt Damon: Weinstein and Franken 'Do Not Belong in the Same Catego-
      ry,'" *Fox News*, December 15, 2017, https://www.foxnews.com/entertainment/matt-damon-
      weinstein-and-franken-do-not-belong-in-the-same-category.

149   Jim Treacher, "Matt Damon Finally Shuts Up — and We Can Thank the #MeToo Crowd," *PJ
      Media*, January 16, 2018, https://pjmedia.com/news-and-politics/jim-treacher/2018/01/16/
      matt-damon-finally-shuts-can-thank-metoo-crowd-n55633.

150   Edward Helmore, "Minnie Driver: Men Like Matt Damon 'Cannot Understand What Abuse
      Is Like,'" *The Guardian*, December 17, 2017, https://www.theguardian.com/film/2017/dec/16/
      minnie-driver-matt-damon-men-cannot-understand-abuse.

151   Sara Nathan and Laura Italiano, "Tara Reade Says Biden Told Her 'I Want to F–k You' During
      Alleged Assault," *New York Post*, May 7, 2020, https://nypost.com/2020/05/07/tara-reade-
      says-biden-said-i-want-to-f-k-you-during-alleged-assault/.

152   Jon Levine, "Bill Maher, Charlamagne Tha God Spar Over Gov. Cuomo Sex Harassment
      Allegations," *New York Post*, March 6, 2021, https://nypost.com/2021/03/06/bill-maher-char-
      lamagne-tha-god-spar-over-gov-cuomo-allegations/.

153   Dominic Patten, "AMC Clears Chris Hardwick to Return to 'Talking Dead' After Sexual As-
      sault Claims," *Deadline*, July 25, 2018, https://deadline.com/2018/07/chris-hardwick-return-
      ing-talking-dead-amc-sexual-harassment-allegations-1202433461/.

154   Daniel Arkin, "Comedian Norm Macdonald Stirs Controversy with Comments on #MeToo,
      Roseanne," *NBC News*, September 12, 2018, https://www.nbcnews.com/pop-culture/celebri-
      ty/comedian-norm-macdonald-stirs-controversy-comments-metoo-roseanne-n908646.

155   Mollie Hemingway and Carrie Severino, "21 Reasons Not to Believe Christine Blasey
      Ford's Claims About Justice Kavanaugh," *The Federalist*, December 2, 2019, https://thefed-
      eralist.com/2019/12/02/21-reasons-not-to-believe-christine-blasey-fords-claims-about-justice-
      kavanaugh/.

156   L. Brent Bozell and Tim Graham, "Hollywood Balks at Brett Kavanaugh," *Investor's Business
      Daily*, July 13, 2018, https://www.investors.com/politics/columnists/brett-kavanaugh-holly-
      wood-liberal-media/.

157   TooFab Staff, "Hollywood Livid Over Brett Kavanaugh's Supreme Court Confirmation: 'Peo-
      ple Should Be F--king Terrified,'" *TooFab*, October 6, 2018, https://toofab.com/2018/10/06/
      brett-kavanaugh-supreme-court-confirmation-hollywood-livid/.

158   Janine Rubenstein, "Ava DuVernay: The Lack of Directors Who Are Women and People of
      Color Is 'Intentional,'" *People*, November 3, 2017, https://people.com/movies/ava-duver-
      nay-exclusion-of-women-minorities-in-hollywood-intentional/.

159   Robyn Merrett, "Rage and Tears: Celebrities React to Kavanaugh's Controversial Supreme
      Court Confirmation," *People*, October 6, 2018, https://people.com/politics/celebrities-re-
      act-brett-kavanaugh-confirmation-supreme-court/.

160 Alyssa Milano, "Alyssa Milano On Why She Still Supports Joe Biden & How She Would Advise Him About Tara Reade Allegations – Guest Column," *Deadline*, April 29, 2020, https://deadline.com/2020/04/alyssa-milano-joe-biden-tara-reade-allegations-guest-column-1202921826/.

161 Erin Coates, "Report: Nearly 100 Celebrities Who Were Outraged About Kavanaugh Have Gone Silent on Biden Allegations," *The Western Journal*, May 12, 2020, https://www.western-journal.com/report-nearly-100-celebrities-outraged-kavanaugh-gone-silent-biden-allegations/.

162 Emily Crane, "Entire Time's Up Board to Step Down Amid Andrew Cuomo Scandal," *New York Post*, September 6, 2021, https://nypost.com/2021/09/06/shonda-rhimes-eva-longoria-to-step-down-from-times-up-board/; Christian Toto, "Hollywood Group Born During #MeToo Faces Criticism It Didn't Live Up to Ideals," Just the News, August 20, 2021, https://justthenews.com/nation/culture/hollywood-group-born-during-metoo-faces-criticism-it-didnt-live-ideals.

163 Jessica Vacco-Bolanos, "Rose McGowan Calls the #MeToo Movement 'Bulls–t': 'I Just Think They're Losers,'" *US Weekly Magazine*, October 7, 2018, https://www.usmagazine.com/celebrity-news/news/rose-mcgowan-the-metoo-movement-is-bulls-t/.

164 All Posts by Nathalia Aryani, *San Diego Entertainer Magazine*, last accessed August 29, 2021, https://www.sdentertainer.com/author/naryani/.

165 Nathalia Aryani, "Movie Review: Haywire," *San Diego Entertainer Magazine*, January 25, 2012, https://www.sdentertainer.com/movies/haywire-movie-review/.

166 Rachel Leishman, "*The Mandalorian*'s Cara Dune Is a Fan Favorite and Gina Carano Is Why," *The Mary Sue*, May 22, 2020, https://www.themarysue.com/cara-dune-gina-carano/.

167 Evan Romano, "The Only Right Way to Watch the *Star Wars* Movies Is to Watch Them in Order," *Men's Health*, May 4, 2021, https://www.menshealth.com/entertainment/a30140997/star-wars-movies-in-order/; Evan Romano, "Here's When Each Episode of *The Mandalorian* Season 2 Will Be Released on Disney+," *Men's Health*, October 26, 2020, https://www.menshealth.com/entertainment/a34480743/the-mandalorian-season-2-how-many-episodes-release-schedule/.

168 Herb Scribner, "'The Mandalorian' Star Gina Carano Addresses Social Media Backlash," *Deseret News*, January 14, 2021, https://www.deseret.com/entertainment/2021/1/14/22231465/star-wars-mandalorian-gina-carano-scandal-political-beliefs.

169 Rebekah Barton, "'Mandalorian' Cast Speaks Out on Gina Carano and Her Future with Show," *Inside the Magic*, December 26, 2020, https://insidethemagic.net/2020/12/gina-carano-mandalorian-rwb1/.

170 Yohana Desta, "*The Mandalorian*'s Bill Burr on Gina Carano: 'She Was an Absolute Sweetheart,'" *Vanity Fair*, March 3, 2021, https://www.vanityfair.com/hollywood/2021/03/the-mandalorian-bill-burr-gina-carano.

171 Melissa Blake, "Casting Bryan Cranston as a Quadriplegic? Hollywood Could Do Better," *CNN* online, January 16, 2019, https://www.cnn.com/2019/01/16/opinions/bryan-cranston-wrong-actor-choice-upside-blake/index.html.

172 Jason Guerrasio, "Bill Burr Says Fired 'Mandalorian' Costar Gina Carano 'Was an Absolute Sweetheart,'" *Business Insider India*, March 3, 2021, https://www.businessinsider.in/Bill-Burr-says-fired-Mandalorian-costar-Gina-Carano-was-an-absolute-sweetheart/articleshow/81313423.cms.

173 Ross A. Lincoln, "Jimmy Kimmel Called Out for Gay Jokes About Sean Hannity and Trump," *Yahoo! Entertainment*, April 7, 2018, https://www.yahoo.com/entertainment/jimmy-kimmel-called-gay-jokes-sean-hannity-trump-020431777.html.

174 Free Enterprise Project, last accessed August 29, 2021, http://freeenterpriseproject.org/.

175 Gabrielle Bruney, "Disney and Netflix Are Threatening to Boycott Georgia Over Its Draconian Abortion Ban," *Yahoo! Entertainment*, May 30, 2019, https://www.yahoo.com/entertainment/disney-netflix-threatening-boycott-georgia-134000177.html.

176 Jessica Napoli, "Gina Carano Slams Former Sen. Heidi Heitkamp for Calling Her a 'Nazi,'" *Fox News*, March 30, 2021, https://www.foxnews.com/entertainment/gina-carano-fires-back-heidi-heitkamp-nazi-comment.

177 Tristin Hopper, "Dunkirk is Racist, Sexist, Anti-French Propaganda: All the Worst Dunkirk Takes (So Far)" *National Post*, August 02, 2017, https://nationalpost.com/entertainment/movies/dunkirk-is-racist-sexist-anti-french-propaganda-all-the-worst-dunkirk-takes-so-far.

178 Nickelodeon, "Nick News: Kids and the Impact of Climate Change | Full 1-Hour Special," YouTube, video, April 22, 2021, https://www.youtube.com/watch?v=WU4NngYwrVA.

179 Paul Sacca, "Nickelodeon Teaches Children about 'Environmental Racism,' Disables Comments After Getting Smashed for 'Indoctrinating Our Kids,'" *Blaze Media*, April 25, 2021, https://www.theblaze.com/news/nickelodeon-environmental-racism-reactions.

180 Benjamin Lee, "Paul Feig Turned Down Ghostbusters 3 to Focus on All-Female Reboot," *The Guardian*, June 1, 2015, https://www.theguardian.com/film/2015/jun/01/paul-feig-turned-down-ghostbusters-3-to-focus-on-all-female-reboot.

181 Laurel Raymond, "With Ghostbusters, Women in Science Are Finally Given the Spotlight," *Think Progress*, July 20, 2016, https://archive.thinkprogress.org/with-ghostbusters-women-in-science-are-finally-given-the-spotlight-b5e499edf0cd/.

182 Stephanie Merry, "People Hate the 'Ghostbusters' Trailer, and Yes, It's Because It Stars Women," *The Washington Post*, March 4, 2016, https://www.washingtonpost.com/news/arts-and-entertainment/wp/2016/03/04/people-are-hating-the-ghostbusters-trailer-guess-why/.

183 Adam Howard, "Sexist 'Ghostbusters' Backlash Coincides With 2016 Gender Divide," *NBC News*, May 26, 2016, https://www.nbcnews.com/news/nbcblk/sexist-ghostbusters-backlash-coincides-2016-gender-divide-n580921.

184 Sam Adams, "Why the 'Ghostbusters' Backlash Is a Sexist Control Issue," *IndieWire*, July 14, 2016, https://www.indiewire.com/2016/07/ghostbusters-reboot-backlash-1201705555/.

185 Alan Zilberman, "The Real Reason Men of a Certain Age Hate the 'Ghostbusters' Remake," *Roger Ebert*, June 16, 2016, https://www.rogerebert.com/features/the-real-reason-men-of-a-certain-age-hate-the-ghostbusters-remake.

186 Anthony D'Alessandro, "'Ghostbusters': How Its $46M Opening Creates a Quandary – Weekend Box Office Postmortem," *Deadline*, July 18, 2016, https://deadline.com/2016/07/ghostbusters-weekend-box-office-1201787149/.

187 Christian Toto, "Roeper: Critics Graded 'Ghostbusters' on a Curve," Hollywood in Toto, August 23, 2016, https://www.hollywoodintoto.com/roeper-critics-ghostbusters-biased/.

188 Manohla Dargis, Wesley Morris, and A.O. Scott, "So That's Who You Call: The Politics of the New 'Ghostbusters,'" *The New York Times*, July 18, 2016, https://www.nytimes.com/2016/07/19/movies/so-thats-who-you-call-the-politics-of-the-new-ghostbusters.html.

189 June Eric Udorie, "Ghostbusters Needed to Show That Black Women Can Be Scientists Too," *The Guardian*, July 26, 2016, https://www.theguardian.com/commentisfree/2016/jul/26/ghostbusters-black-women-scientists-leslie-jones.

190 Pamela McClintock, "'Ghostbusters' Heading for $70M-Plus Loss, Sequel Unlikely," *Hollywood Reporter*, August 10, 2016, https://www.hollywoodreporter.com/news/ghostbusters-box-office-loss-sequel-unlikely-918515.

191 Hilary Lewis, "Paul Feig 'Didn't Realize' Original 'Ghostbusters' Was a 'No Girls Allowed' Clubhouse," *Hollywood Reporter*, October 13, 2016, https://www.hollywoodreporter.com/news/paul-feig-ghostbusters-backlash-fights-938225.

192 Robyn Bahr, "'American Pie Presents: Girls' Rules': Film Review," *Hollywood Reporter*, October 12, 2020, https://www.hollywoodreporter.com/news/american-pie-presents-girls-rules-film-review.

193 Justin Kroll, "Andy Garcia to Star in Latinx 'Father Of The Bride' Pic for Warner Bros. and Plan B," *Deadline*, March 18, 2021, https://deadline.com/2021/03/andy-garcia-latinx-father-of-the-bride-warner-bros-plan-b-1234717553/.

194 Rick Porter, "'National Treasure' Series a Go at Disney+," *Hollywood Reporter*, March 24, 2021, https://www.hollywoodreporter.com/live-feed/national-treasure-series-disney-plus.

195 Rebecca Jones, "Mel Brooks: Blazing Saddles Would Never Be Made Today," *BBC News*, September 21, 2017, https://www.bbc.com/news/entertainment-arts-41337151.

196 Ryan Lattanzio, "Mariel Hemingway Says Woody Allen's 'Manhattan' '100 Percent' Couldn't Come Out Today," *IndieWire*, April 18, 2021, https://www.indiewire.com/2021/04/woody-allen-manhattan-mariel-hemingway-1234631164/.

197 Hannah Yasharoff, "In the Era of #MeToo, Is It Still OK to Laugh at 'Animal House'?," *USA Today*, July 27, 2018, https://www.usatoday.com/story/life/movies/2018/07/27/animal-house-turns-40-can-we-still-laugh/822642002/.

198 "Exclusive Survey Reveals Shocking Statistic of Sexual Misconduct in Hollywood," *USA Today*, February 21, 2018, https://eu.usatoday.com/story/news/pr/2018/02/21/usa-today-exclusive-survey-reveals-shocking-statistic-sexual-misconduct-hollywood/359543002/.

199 Kevin Fallon, "Why Molly Ringwald Spoke Out About John Hughes and #MeToo: 'Things Have to Change'," *The Daily Beast*, April 28, 2018, https://www.thedailybeast.com/why-molly-ringwald-spoke-out-about-john-hughes-and-metoo-things-have-to-change.

200 David Ng, "Cancel Hitchcock: 'Psycho,' 'Guess Who's Coming to Dinner,' Among the Iconic Films Turner Classic Movies Deems Problematic," *Breitbart*, March 5, 2021, https://www.breitbart.com/entertainment/2021/03/05/cancel-hitchcock-psycho-guess-whos-coming-to-dinner-among-the-iconic-films-turner-classic-movies-deems-problematic/.

201 Armond White, "Why *GWTW* Lives Matter," *National Review*, June 12, 2020, https://www.nationalreview.com/2020/06/gone-with-the-wind-art-worth-saving/.

202 John Loftus, "John Wayne's Heroes and Anti-Heroes," *National Review*, July 25, 2020, https://www.nationalreview.com/2020/07/john-wayne-heroes-and-anti-heroes/.

203 Armond White, "Turner Classic Movies: Enemy of Film-Watchers," *National Review*, March 31, 2021, https://www.nationalreview.com/2021/03/turner-classic-movies-enemy-of-film-watchers/.

204 Nick Givas, "'Kindergarten Cop' Screening Canceled in Oregon, Compared to 'Gone with the Wind'," *Fox News*, August 4, 2020, https://www.foxnews.com/us/kindergarten-cop-screening-canceled-police-brutality.

205 Tim Gray, "10 Problematic Films That Could Use Warning Labels," *Variety*, June 17, 2020, https://variety.com/2020/film/news/gone-with-the-wind-problem-films-forrest-gump-1234640666/.

206 Tim Gray, "10 Problematic Films That Could Use Warning Labels," *Variety*, June 17, 2020, https://variety.com/2020/film/news/gone-with-the-wind-problem-films-forrest-gump-1234640666/.

207 Jonty Bloom, "How Product Placements May Soon Be Added to Classic Films," *BBC News*, April 19, 2021, https://www.bbc.com/news/business-56758376.

208 Andrew Magnotta, "The Beatles Are the Best-Selling Rock Band of 2020," *iHeart*, July 15, 2020, https://www.iheart.com/content/2020-07-15-the-beatles-are-the-best-selling-rock-band-of-2020/.

209 "Playlist: Woke," Spotify, last accessed August 28, 2021, https://open.spotify.com/playlist/37i9dQZF1DWVBevLcUtH0o.

210 Will Richards, "Big Thief Apologise for T-Shirt Design with 'Reckless, Offensive Imagery'," *NME*, April 3, 2021, https://www.nme.com/news/music/big-thief-apologise-for-t-shirt-design-with-reckless-offensive-imagery-2913270.

211 Charu Sinha, "Mumford & Sons Banjoist Winston Marshall 'Taking Time Away From the Band'," *Vulture*, March 10, 2021, https://www.vulture.com/2021/03/mumford-and-sons-banjoist-taking-time-away-from-the-band.html.

212 CBS News, "Mumford & Sons Member Apologizes for Supporting Controversial Writer," *WTOP News*, March 11, 2021, https://wtop.com/music/2021/03/mumford-sons-member-apologizes-for-supporting-controversial-writer/.

213 Brian Mansfield, "Ozzy Osbourne Bit the Head Off a Bat 33 Years Ago Tonight," *USA Today*, January 20, 2015, https://www.usatoday.com/story/life/entertainthis/2015/01/20/ozzy-osbourne-bit-the-head-off-a-bat-33-years-ago-tonight/77604434/.

214 Miranda Sawyer, "Michael Stipe: 'The Male Idea of Power Is So Dumb'," *The Guardian*, April 24, 2021, https://www.theguardian.com/music/2021/apr/24/michael-stipe-the-male-idea-of-power-is-so-dumb.

215 Julia Carrie Wong and Kari Paul, "Twitter Permanently Suspends Trump's Account to Prevent 'Further Incitement of Violence'," *The Guardian*, January 9, 2021, https://www.theguardian.com/us-news/2021/jan/08/donald-trump-twitter-ban-suspended.

216 Craig Jenkins, "The Trouble with Woke Pop Stars," *Vulture*, May 17, 2017, https://www.vulture.com/2017/05/katy-perry-miley-cyrus-and-the-woke-pop-problem.html.

217 "Katy Perry Under Fire for Obama Joke," *CNN* online, video, May 1, 2017, https://www.cnn.com/videos/entertainment/2017/05/01/katy-perry-black-hair-obama-joke-instagram-origvstan-aa.cnn.

218 Roisin O'Connor, "Met Gala: Katy Perry Attracts Criticism for John Galliano Dress at New York Event," *Independent*, May 2, 2017, https://www.independent.co.uk/arts-entertainment/music/news/met-gala-katy-perry-john-galliano-dress-criticism-2017-designer-red-veil-antisemitism-a7712831.html.

219 Craig Bro Dude (@CraigSJ), "Katy Perry Cultural Appropriation World Tour Coming To A City Near You," Twitter, July 31, 2014, https://twitter.com/CraigSJ/status/494927747773632512.

220 Hunter Harris, "The Most Uncomfortable Moments from Katy Perry's Ultraliteral 'Bon Appétit' Video, in GIFs," *Vulture*, May 12, 2017, https://www.vulture.com/2017/05/katy-perry-bon-appetit-music-video.html.

221 Dodai Stewart, "On Miley Cyrus, Ratchet Culture and Accessorizing With Black People," *Jezebel*, June 20, 2013, https://jezebel.com/on-miley-cyrus-ratchet-culture-and-accessorizing-with-514381016.

222 Trace William Cowen, "Miley Cyrus Receives Backlash for 'Appropriating' Hip-Hop Culture," *Complex*, May 4, 2017, https://www.complex.com/music/2017/05/miley-cyrus-receives-backlash-appropriating-hip-hop-culture.

223 Tobi Thomas, "'Woke' Culture Is Threat to Protest Songs, Says Don Letts," *The Guardian*, March 16, 2021, https://www.theguardian.com/music/2021/mar/16/woke-culture-is-threat-to-protest-songs-says-don-letts.

224 Claire Shaffer, "Van Morrison to Release Protest Songs Against Covid-19 Lockdown," *Rolling Stone*, September 18, 2020, https://www.rollingstone.com/music/music-news/van-morrison-covid-19-protest-songs-1062169/.

225 Chad Childers, "Sex Pistols' Johnny Rotten Calls Out 'Spoilt Children' for Woke Culture," *Loudwire*, April 27, 2021, https://loudwire.com/sex-pistols-johnny-rotten-calls-out-spoilt-children-woke-culture/.

226 "ALICE COOPER: 'When Musicians Are Telling People Who to Vote For, I Think That's an Abuse of Power,'" Blabbermouth.net, December 29, 2018, https://www.blabbermouth.net/news/alice-cooper-when-musicians-are-telling-people-who-to-vote-for-i-think-thats-an-abuse-of-power/.

227 David Marcus, "Watch: Morrissey to Protester: 'Go, Goodbye, We Don't Need You,'" *The Federalist*, October 2, 2019, https://thefederalist.com/2019/10/02/watch-morrissey-to-protester-go-goodbye-we-dont-need-you/.

228 Rick Roddam, "The Greatest Hotel Room Trashers in Rock History," 103.7 The Hawk, April 23, 2014, https://kmhk.com/the-greatest-hotel-room-trashers-in-rock-history/.

229 Dana Rose Falcone, "Jerry Seinfeld: College Students Don't Know What the Hell They're Talking About," *Entertainment Weekly*, June 8, 2015, https://ew.com/article/2015/06/08/jerry-seinfeld-politically-correct-college-campuses/.

230 Dean Obeidallah, "Jerry Seinfeld Doesn't Get Political Correctness," *CNN* online, June 11, 2015, https://www.cnn.com/2015/06/10/opinions/obeidallah-jerry-seinfeld.

231 "Amy Schumer Apologizes for 'Racist' Rape Joke About Hispanics: 'I Am Taking Responsibility,'" *Yahoo! Entertainment*, July 7, 2015, https://www.yahoo.com/entertainment/s/amy-schumer-apologizes-racist-rape-joke-hispanics-am-040050364.html.

232 Ron Dicker, "Pete Davidson Basically Rescinds Apology to Dan Crenshaw in Netflix Special," *Huffpost*, February 26, 2020, https://www.huffpost.com/entry/pete-davidson-rescinds-apology-dan-crenshaw-netflix-special_n_5e564641c5b62e9dc7da85c8.

233 Alasdair Duncan, "Comedian Nikki Glaser Apologises After Body Shaming Taylor Swift In Netflix Doco," February 1, 2020, https://www.pedestrian.tv/entertainment/nikki-glaser-taylor-swift-apology/.

234   Dalia Mortada, "Comedian Trevor Noah Apologizes for Joke About War Between India and Pakistan," NPR, March 4, 2019, https://www.npr.org/2019/03/04/700009264/comedian-trevor-noah-apologizes-for-joke-about-war-between-india-and-pakistan.

235   Scaachi Koul, "Why Punching Down Will Never Be Funny," *BuzzFeed News*, October 6, 2016, https://www.buzzfeednews.com/article/scaachikoul/why-punching-down-will-never-be-funny.

236   Christian Toto, "WaPo, USA Today Play Dumb as Comics Avoid Biden Jokes," *Hollywood in Toto*, March 9, 2021, https://www.hollywoodintoto.com/media-biden-jokes-snl/.

237   Sarah Polus, "Caitlyn Jenner Slams Jimmy Kimmel for Calling Her 'Trump in a wig,'" *The Hill*, June 12, 2021, https://thehill.com/blogs/in-the-know/in-the-know/558166-caitlyn-jenner-slams-jimmy-kimmel-for-calling-her-trump-in-a.

238   Katie Storey, "Comedian Lee Hurst 'Doesn't Regret' Vile Greta Thunberg Tweet That Saw Him Suspended from Twitter," *Metro*, March 21, 2021, https://metro.co.uk/2021/03/21/comedian-lee-hurst-suspended-from-twitter-over-greta-thunberg-joke-14279339/.

239   Jamie Kilstein, "George Carlin: Crossing the Line," *HuffPost*, June 23, 2008, https://www.huffpost.com/entry/george-carlin-crossing-th_b_108626.

240   "White House Reprimands Maher," Associated Press, September 26, 2001, https://apnews.com/article/3252060d30bef9a1cc01fd20b9eeb85d.

241   ABC News, "Maher Apologizes for 'Cowards' Remark," ABC News, January 6, 2006, https://abcnews.go.com/Entertainment/story?id=102318&page=1.

242   "Maher Apologizes for 'Cowards' Remark," *ABC News*, January 6, 2006, https://abcnews.go.com/Entertainment/story?id=102318&page=1.

243   Milly Vincent, "'Accept Your Little Award, Thank Your Agent, and Your God and F*** Off, OK?': The Full Transcript of Ricky Gervais' Outrageous Golden Globes Monologue," *The Daily Mail*, January 6, 2020, https://www.dailymail.co.uk/news/article-7856311/Accept-award-f-OK-transcript-Ricky-Gervais-Golden-Globes-monologue.html.

244   Joseph Wulfsohn, "Ricky Gervais Defends Free Speech: People Being Offended Is 'the Lesser of Two Evils,'" *Fox News*, January 2, 2020, https://www.foxnews.com/entertainment/ricky-gervais-free-speech-golden-globes.

ACKNOWLEDGMENTS

'D LIKE TO THANK the following people who directly, or indirectly but with the best of intentions, made *Virtue Bombs* possible.

That list begins with my wife, who disagrees with 98.54 percent of my political opinions (no, I will not round up…) but supports my career with zero hesitation. She allowed me to go rogue and pursue my journalism dreams on my terms, swallowing hard during the early, money-lite years en route to this book.

I'd also like to thank Joseph Granda, a wise sounding board and constant source of professional and personal support.

Bombardier Books editor David Bernstein had the gall to suggest I had a book in me, and that faith mattered when I realized a chapter had to be quite a bit longer than your average blog post.

Veteran editor Danny Wattenberg also helped guide me over the years, always cautioning to keep any biases at bay when dissecting Hollywood.

And a hearty thank you to this book's foreword contributor, Andrew Klavan. No one "gets" pop culture on the Right quite like him, and if I've written with a fraction of his clarity and insight I'll be lucky.

ABOUT THE AUTHOR

CHRISTIAN TOTO is an award-winning journalist and film critic who runs HollywoodinToto.com. He regularly contributes to The Daily Wire, RealClearInvestigations, TheHill.com, and JustTheNews.com. He belongs to the Critics Choice Association.